Essential Reiki

A Complete Guide to an Ancient Healing Art

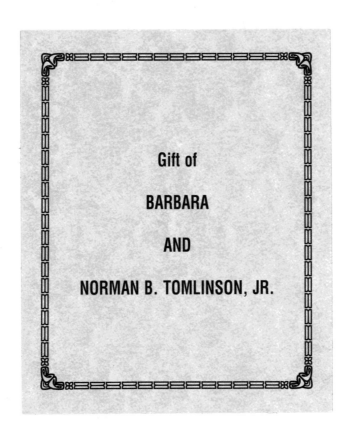

Other books by Diane Stein

The Natural Remedy Book for Women

All Women Are Healers: A Comprehensive Guide to Natural Healing

The Goddess Celebrates: An Anthology of Women's Rituals

Casting the Circle: A Women's Book of Rituals

Dreaming the Past, Dreaming the Future: A Herstory of the Earth

Lady Sun, Lady Moon

Natural Healing for Dogs and Cats

The Kwan Yin Book of Changes

The Women's Spirituality Book

The Women's Book of Healing

Stroking the Python: Women's Psychic Lives

ESSENTIAL REIKI

A COMPLETE GUIDE TO AN ANCIENT HEALING ART

Diane Stein

The Crossing Press Inc., Freedom, CA

ACKNOWLEDGMENTS

Many people have helped to make this book possible. First of all I thank Elaine Goldman Gill and John Gill, co-owners of The Crossing Press for their encouragement and willingness to publish what may be a controversial book. Teaching Elaine Reiki I, II and III at the Mystical Dragon Bookstore in Carlsbad, California (Lammas, 1993), was one of my high points of this lifetime. I thank Richard Donovan for legal advice, Diana Acuna for alternate teaching techniques and symbol information, and Sasha Daucus for help in locating rare books and for her constant encouragement. Jane Brown and Linda Page read and critiqued the manuscript, and Jane Brown and Carol Hunner provided important material on the Ki Exercises. Patty Callahan of Brigit Books, St. Petersburg, Florida and Joy Weaver of Treasures Bookstore, Tampa, Florida were also instrumental in book searches.

Laurel Steinhice and Suzanne Wagner were among the women who shared channeling sessions on Reiki with me over several years. Detong Cho Yin patiently explained Buddhism to me when I knew nothing about it and offered other information that proved vital to this book. I also thank the several people who gave me my own Reiki training, knowing that I would share everything I learned and would eventually write about it. They gave me training in traditional and modern ways at a time in my life when paying for it was impossible. Some gave me information by phone and mail, some gave me traditional teaching to supplement my nontraditional methods, and others offered insight and even attunements at first meetings. Though they are unnamed I thank them all deeply.

I also wish to thank my many teaching Reiki III's, the students who are continuing to carry Reiki to as many people as wish to learn it at affordable prices. A few of the many include Jill Elizabeth Turner, Anastasia Marie Zepp, Jane Brown, Sasha Daucus, Diana Acuna, Tom Oakley, Carolyn Taylor, Lisa Severn and Liz Tarr. I thank them for their friendship and their work.

Healing and medicine are two very different disciplines and the law requires the following disclaimer: The information in this book is not medicine but healing, and does not constitute medical advice. In case of serious illness consult the practitioner of your choice.

© Copyright 1995, Diane Stein

Cover and book design by Victoria May

Illustrations by Ian Everard

Calligraphy by Carl Rohrs

Printed in the U.S.A.

Cataloging in Publication Data

Stein, Diane, 1948–

    Essential Reiki : a complete guide to an ancient healing art / Diane Stein.

       p. cm.

    Includes bibliographical references.

    ISBN 0-89594-736-6

    1. Reiki (Healing system) I. Title.

RZ403-R45S74 1995

615.8'52--dc20   95-2643

                                                        CIP

For Elaine Goldman Gill

CONTENTS

ILLUSTRATIONS

That which is a mystery shall no longer be so, and that which has been veiled will be revealed; that which has been withdrawn will emerge into the light, and all women shall see and together they shall rejoice.

Alice Bailey [1]

When you heal yourself and assist others with their self-healing, you heal the Earth.

*You **do** make a difference.*

Laurel Steinhice
Channeling the Earth Mother [2]

I believe there exists One Supreme Being—the Absolute Infinite—a Dynamic Force that governs the world and universe. It is an unseen spiritual power that vibrates and all other powers fade into insignificance beside it. So, therefore, it is Absolute!...

I shall call it "Reiki"....

Being a universal force from the Great Divine Spirit, it belongs to all who seek and desire to learn the art of healing.

Hawayo Takata [3]

1   Alice Bailey, *The Rays and the Initiations, Vol. V.* (New York, NY, Lucius Publishing Co., 1972), p. 332. As quoted in Rosalyn L. Bruyere and Jeanne Farrens (Ed.), *Wheels of Light: A Study of the Chakras, Vol. I* (Sierra Madre, CA, Bon Productions, 1989), p. 17.

2   Laurel Steinhice in Diane Stein, *Dreaming the Past, Dreaming the Future: A Herstory of the Earth* (Freedom, CA, The Crossing Press, 1991), front page.

3   Hawayo Takata in Paul David Mitchell, *Reiki: The Usui System of Natural Healing* (Coeur d'Alene, Idaho, The Reiki Alliance, 1985), pp. 5–6.

FOREWORD: IMPORTANT

To become a Reiki I, II or III practitioner requires receiving the attunements in person from a teacher who has also received the attunements and training. This book cannot be a substitute for that direct initiation process. After receiving the attunements, this book is a Reiki practitioner's and teacher's guide. It is the first book to put the full Reiki teaching into print for Western healers in a modern format, and possibly the first to do so anywhere since the ancient world.

In this time of change and crisis for people and the planet, healing is too desperately needed for it to be kept secret or exclusive any longer. Always have respect for the sacredness of the information that follows and for the Goddess's gift of Reiki. Use it only for the highest good of all, and use it freely for any who may choose to benefit by it. What you send out returns to you multiplied manyfold. Reiki is Universal Love.

Full Moon in Virgo
March 26, 1994

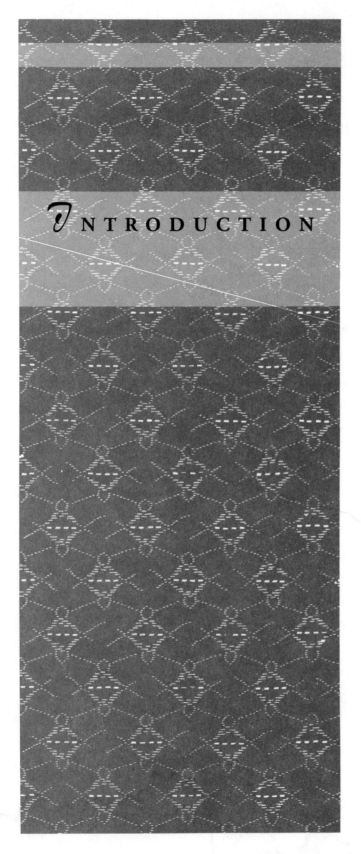

INTRODUCTION

I first experienced hands-on healing at the 1983 Michigan Women's Music Festival, along with several other healing techniques. From that point on I knew I wanted to devote my life to healing. I wished that I were "psychic" and could learn to do the things other women seemed to do so easily. For the next five years I read every book I could find on the subject—there weren't many of them then—and experimented (mostly on myself) with what I had learned. I felt I was just beginning, but I was still working very hard at it and still wishing I could learn more and grow stronger. My healing did not seem powerful to me. I was also teaching others healing techniques, primarily crystals and gemstones and laying-on-of-hands, and seeking ways to make the learning easier and more powerful for others. I somehow felt that there was a piece of information missing, something that would increase the effectiveness of hands-on healing plus make it as easy and simple as I suspected it could and should be.

In August, 1987, (just before the Harmonic Convergence) I found the key but it seemed totally out of reach. At a metaphysical dinner and gathering I met two beautiful gay men. They watched me do a brief hands-on healing then asked me, "Who taught you Reiki?" I replied that I hadn't had Reiki training and didn't even know what it was. The men insisted that what I was doing was Reiki and asked to feel my hands. They both declared that my hands were hot and that was the mark of a Reiki healer. I wanted to know more.

Later when the two men gave me a full body Reiki healing session in my home, I knew that this was the simple healing system I'd been looking for. I asked where I could find Reiki training and what it cost, and was appalled to learn that the initial Reiki training, Reiki I, cost at that time $150 and that there was only one woman in the city who could teach it. Reiki II cost $600, and Reiki III/Master–Teacher's training, at $10,000 was seldom given, even if affordable to the seeker. No scholarships were possible. I was waitressing for a living at that time, and barely paying my rent. Reiki would have to wait.

Soon after, one of the men received his Reiki II training. We began to talk for long hours about healing, and the high cost of this training was a frequent subject. One of the men felt that the high cost was necessary, that it signified a commitment, while the other saw things more my way—that healing and healer's training should be available to anyone who will use the experience to benefit themselves or others. I felt that my job as a writer and healer was (and is) to teach any method and give any information on healing that I had available to me. Cost or compensation is not primary, and to me any cost that puts the information out of reach is immoral. The men knew that any information on healing I could receive from them would probably one day turn up in my books.

When my friend with Reiki II training began trying to pass Reiki attunements, though he was still a Reiki II and had not had the teacher's training of Reiki III, I asked him to try it on me. For several months he refused. In January of 1988 the three of us decided to begin doing healing together on the AIDS floor of a local hospital, and he changed his mind. I received my Reiki I attunement at Candlemas, February 2, 1988 and it was very evident that the attunement process had worked for me, despite the Reiki II status of the man who gave it.

I felt filled with an energy I had never before experienced or dreamed existed. I was filled with light and with love for all Be-ings. My healing ability immediately strengthened, more than I had believed possible, and the ease of using Reiki confirmed that this was the healing method I had been seeking. If my hands had been hot in doing healings before, they were far hotter now. I knew at that time that I wanted to teach Reiki, but had no idea how that could happen.

We began our hospital healing work, a period of time that I feel changed me from a beginner to a healer, and when my friend completed his Reiki III training that summer I participated in his first teaching class. Because I was still earning less than $300 a month and could not pay the class fee of $150, I was allowed to attend and to receive the Traditional attunements, but was not given a certificate of having taken the class. My friend supervised the chapter on Reiki that appears in my book *All Women Are Healers* (The Crossing Press, 1990), but would not teach me further. I began to teach the Reiki I hand positions in my workshops and to talk frequently about one day going further with Reiki training and learning how to teach it.

In November, 1989, I made a workshop trip to the Midwest, sponsored by two women I had met at the 1988 Michigan Women's Music Festival, and had developed a meaningful friendship with. One of the women had recently received her Reiki III training from a teacher who also felt that the healing method needed to become more available. She did not have the $10,000 Traditionally required for a Reiki III fee but had received the training for much less. Her teacher was experimenting with modern teaching methods and had also been Traditionally trained. Completely by surprise during the weekend, she gave several of the workshop group Reiki I training and gave me Reiki II, with a certificate for both degrees. She promised to give me Reiki III at our next meeting, saying, "I almost did it now, but couldn't find the symbol handouts."

Though we met twice in the following year, the woman found excuses not to continue the teaching and I was becoming very frustrated. Since I had received my initial Reiki I attunements from a Reiki II practitioner, I resolved to figure out how to do it. I reasoned that placing the Reiki II symbols in the receiver's Crown chakra and Heart chakra, as well as their hands, was the basis of the process, and this was in fact close. Having only Reiki II, however, I was missing symbol keys and had no way of discovering what those missing symbols were.

After a phone conversation with a woman I had never met in which I mentioned my efforts, I received in the mail on a torn piece of notebook paper the Traditional Reiki III Master's symbol. With that, my experiments became more effective and some of my attempts resulted in the receiver opening to the energy. I continued to teach in my workshops as much of the information as I had, explaining that as a Reiki II I was experimenting.

In another phone conversation in 1990, I mentioned to my Midwestern Reiki II teacher that I had been trying to pass attunements. Her anger was immediate and intense, and we had a very strong argument about it. "You promised me the full information," I reminded her, "but you didn't keep your promise." The woman phoned me back about an hour later, saying, "If you're going to do it anyway, you might as well do it right." She then gave me the process for passing Reiki attunements over the phone.

I used her method, which was a modern one, and now my receivers began to open to the Reiki I energy in an undeniable way. They did not open strongly, however, and not everyone developed the hot hands and inner sensations that mark a Reiki opening. My Reiki II teacher continued to instruct me by telephone, with bits and pieces of information I had to fit together myself. I grew more and more frustrated but I had no other source for the teaching.

In June, 1990, at Summer Solstice I taught a workshop weekend near Denver. In the workshops I offered Reiki I attunements on an experimental basis to anyone who wished to try it. Six women agreed and all opened to the Reiki energy. After the weekend in Denver, the partner of my Reiki II teacher, who was also travelling in the area, came to spend a day with me. A friend of hers whom I hadn't met before drove her to the house I was staying at and remained for dinner. During dinner I talked about the workshops and how I wished for the Reiki III attunement, "so I could do it right." The friend said, "I don't have time for any teaching, but if all you need is the attunement I can do that right now." Sitting at the dining room table over dessert, she gave me my Reiki III initiation. I have never heard from her again, but I thank her deeply. My attunements after that became immensely more powerful, and fully reliable—everyone opened to the energy. I was now a Reiki Master (teacher), ready to teach.

In February, 1991, at Candlemas again, I did a workshop weekend in another city. I taught Reiki I and II together and watched a woman in the class scowl and frown through the whole day's session. When it was over she said she was a Traditional Reiki Master/Teacher and wanted to speak to me. She thoroughly scolded me for several aspects of my teaching. One thing she protested was my allowing my students to watch me pass the sacred attunements—something I continue to do. She protested my method of passing the attunements as not the Traditional method, insisting that any change in the Traditional way makes the system no longer Reiki. I disagreed.

The woman housing me intervened at this point with the suggestion that the woman teach me the "right" way and then certify me, or otherwise stop wasting my time. The woman agreed to do so and spent a hour or so the next day instructing me in Traditional attunement and teaching methods. She repeated my Reiki III attunement in the Traditional format as well. The woman promised me a certificate which she never issued, saying that she would not do so unless I adopted her strictly Traditional methods. What I was using by that time was a combination of my Reiki II teacher's methods and my own, and as they were highly effective I was not willing to change them.

In May, 1991, at Beltane—I am noticing as I write this how most of my Reiki landmarks have happened on the Wiccan Sabbats— my earlier Reiki II teacher sent me a copy of a "new" Reiki III symbol, urging me to try it. I did so reluctantly, but continue to use that new symbol as its increased power is undeniable. It moved my teaching still further away from the Traditional methods of teaching Reiki healing. At the end of that month I attended the Southern Women's Music and Comedy Festival and reached another milestone in my journey to become a Reiki Master.

At that Festival, I did not teach Reiki as the workshop attendance numbers were too high, much higher than the limited number of attunements I can pass in a day. I taught instead a Natural Remedy workshop, and in the workshop two women revealed to me that they were dying. I offered them Reiki attunements if they wanted them and told them where to meet me at the end of the workshop. I borrowed two folding chairs and initiated the women, hoping to ease their process and give them a healing tool. When I looked up after doing so, there was a line of women waiting who also wanted the attunement. A Reiki II present in the group helped me by teaching hand positions, as I gave Reiki attunements for at least the next two hours! I was worried about giving these attunements without the benefits of a full workshop but my spirit guides urged me on with "Keep going, keep going" every time I asked.

The next day I did a booksigning in the craftswomen's area and the line formed again, and I continued to pass Reiki I attunements. Later I was told that word was going around the festival to "Get in line, Diane Stein's giving women the spiritual experience of their lives." Most had no idea why they were in line, and yet my spirit guides continued to tell me, "Keep going." All in all, I probably passed 150 attunements in the two days, entirely without charge. It was too much for me physically, and I was ill for some three weeks after—twenty-five attunements in a day are enough. If nothing else, the experience showed me how much Reiki is needed and by how many.

After that festival I felt I had been shown my work, to teach Reiki to as many woman (and men) who want it as possible. This magnificent healing system must be made available to everyone, regardless of whether they can afford the cost of the teaching or not. I have continued on this path to this day, though at times I have had difficulty in explaining to workshop and festival producers why this healing method is so important. Upon hearing about my Southern Festival adventures, my Reiki II teacher, who until that time had still been dangling her Reiki III teaching and certification before me, refused to continue teaching me. She said I was abusing Reiki by giving it away and cancelled our again made plans to complete the teaching.

Though I have now been a Reiki Master for four years and have taught many hundreds of students, I have no official Traditional certification. I no longer feel it to be important. I offer my own certification under the title of nontraditional Reiki to my students, fully convinced that I am missing nothing in my ability to teach and be effective. For my birthday at Fall Equinox, 1992, one of my students presented me with a certificate. "You trained me," she said, "so I'll certify you!" It was a joke we both enjoyed. I have by this time trained several hundred Reiki III students, many of whom are now teaching. I have asked them to carry on my ethics of low prices and scholarships where needed, and to continue my demystification of a healing system that needs to be universal. Many women and a few men are following in the path.

THE FIRST DEGREE

CHAPTER ONE

THE REIKI STORY

Reiki is a laying on of hands touch healing system of incomparable ease and power. What it can do and how it works is the subject of this book, but to fully appreciate Reiki it is first necessary to know where it came from and how it reached the West. The story spans almost all of the written records of humanity, and the healing system itself is certainly older than any written account. I have done my best to discover Reiki's origins through research and reading, but many gaps remain. Much pertinent information has never been translated into English and even more information has never been placed into print in any language. The Traditional Reiki story begins in the 1800s, but Reiki was ancient even then.

Information before written records can be obtained only through channeling, and though material received in this way must be considered speculative, it is nonetheless interesting and thought-provoking. While unverifiable, the material is too fascinating to overlook and I believe it to be highly valuable. In 1990, for my book *Dreaming the Past, Dreaming the Future* (The Crossing Press, 1991), psychic Laurel Steinhice described the twelve source planets that were the original colonizers of the Earth. Most of these are located in the Pleiadian star system, with a few in the star systems of Sirius and Orion.[1] People did not evolve on Earth, we were brought here from a variety of planetary cultures, and a number of channelers are now also describing them in their writings. A few scholarly translators of ancient documents are beginning to verify this as well, though at this time it still requires courage to do so.

In 1991 I asked Laurel for channeling about the origins of Reiki. She described Reiki as having originated with the planet that also brought the many-armed gods and goddesses to Earth, the root culture of what became pre-patriarchal India. The Indian god we know today as Shiva, female at that time, was responsible for bringing Reiki here, and s/he wants to be remembered for the gift. When the human body for this planet was designed, Reiki was incorporated into the genetic coding as a birthright of all people.[2]

Reiki is a part of every one of us. It was once universal and was never meant to be lost. Children of early Earth, in the civilization we call Mu today, received Reiki I training at the beginning of grade school. They received Reiki II at what we would define as junior high school age. Reiki III, the Teacher/Master's training, was required for educators and was available to any who wanted it. When the people of its root culture left the mainland of Mu to colonize what is now India and Tibet, Reiki continued with them, though Mu was eventually lost. The Earth changes that destroyed first Mu and then Atlantis resulted in severe cultural disorganization, causing the healing system to remain the knowledge of only a select few. When in the nineteenth century a Japanese man sought the origins of Jesus' and the Buddha's method of healing, he found them in the ancient remnants of Shiva's early culture, in the esoteric teachings of India.

The Traditional Reiki story[10] begins in the mid-1800's with Mikao Usui, who was principal of the Doshisha University in Kyoto, Japan, and also a Christian minister. Asked by his students to be shown the method by which Jesus did healing, Usui began a ten-year quest to find and learn the skill. When Christian authorities in Japan told him that this healing was not talked about, much less known, Usui sought the information through Buddhism. There are striking resemblances between the life of Buddha in India (Gautama Siddhartha, 620–543 BCE) and the life of the historical Jesus. Usui was told by Buddhist monks that the ancient spiritual healing methods had been lost, and that the only way to approach them was by entering the Buddhist teachings, the Path to Enlightenment.

Mikao Usui then travelled to the United States, where he lived for seven years. When he received no further answers from Christians here, he entered the University of Chicago Divinity School. He is said to have received his Doctor of Theology degree there, where he studied comparative religions and philosophies. He also learned to read Sanskrit, the ancient scholarly language of India and Tibet. Usui still found no answers to his quest to learn the methods of this healing. There is no further mention of Mikao Usui as a Christian or a minister, but only as a Buddhist who after his return to Japan resided in a Zen monastery .

It is interesting to note that in a search for records, Reiki Master William Rand found that Mikao Usui had never been to Doshisha University, as principal, teacher or student. Further, there are no records of his attendance at the University of Chicago, nor of his receiving a degree.[11] It would be easy to speculate that the Christian aspects of the story were added in the West, to make the startling power of the Reiki healing system acceptable to Americans. The parallels between Buddhism and the early teachings of the historical Jesus (rather than religious Christianity or Church doctrine), however, require another look. I divert from the Reiki story to examine them briefly.

Buddha, the great savior of India, was born in the year 620 BCE near the Nepal border. He was the son of a king, and his birth name was Gautama Siddhartha. The prince was kept entirely innocent of suffering in the world, living in an enclosed palace and not permitted to go outside of it. Upon reaching adulthood he desired to see the real world so strongly that he disobeyed his father's wishes and escaped from his golden prison. For the first time he saw old age, illness, death, poverty and suffering, and it awakened in him his karmic heritage to relieve all people of pain.

Forsaking his wealth and his much beloved young wife, Gautama Siddhartha chose the path of a homeless wanderer. He lived under trees, begged for his food, and meditated on how to prevent suffering. Seated under a fig tree in meditation one day he was shown the way to heal all people, and this revelation under the Bodhi tree was the first Enlightenment. The Sakyamuni Buddha discovered that attachment to worldly things and even to people, with the greed and negativity that such attachments inevitably cause, are the source of human suffering. Actions based upon these attachments produce karma, both positive and negative, that hold the person's spirit to the Earthplane. Karma causes people to be reborn again and again, for the purpose of resolving the situations. Rebirth and living on the Earth are the source of human suffering, and yet karma cannot be cleared except by reincarnation in a human body.

The answer to this paradox, how to resolve karma and end the cycle of reincarnation and rebirth, is the essence of Buddhist teachings. This philosophy, which accepts the gods and Goddesses of whatever culture it is practiced in, has had profound impact on every major religion including Christianity. Buddhist teaching is based upon the principle of compassion for all living things, nonaggression towards people and animals and no killing of people or animals, and loving nonattachment while helping others. To the Buddhist, healing means much more than healing the body, as the mind and emotions must also be healed, and healing must first of all be spiritual. The world is seen as illusion, a creation of Mind derived from the Void. Many of the parables and stories found in later Christianity are taken directly from Buddhism, including the Parable of the Mustard Seed, the story of the Prodigal Son, the Sermon on the Mount and the Temptation in the Desert by evil.

The Buddha's discovery of the Path to Enlightenment made possible the Enlightenment of others. A number of Buddhas followed Gautama Siddhartha, and a number of Be-ings known as Bodhisattvas. A Bodhisattva (savior) is a person who has attained Enlightenment and therefore is no longer required to reincarnate. Yet s/he returns to Earth in body for the purpose of bringing others out of suffering and pain and into Enlightenment with her. Two of the most familiar female Bodhisattvas, though Buddhism lists few women in this light, are Kwan Yin in China (called Kannon in Japan) and Tara in Tibet. I believe that Mary and Jesus are examples of Bodhisattvas, also.

Buddha and several of the Buddhas who followed him were called The Great Physicians (as Jesus was later called). So much emphasis was placed on healing, both physical and spiritual, in early Buddhist practice that it became the norm later to discourage it as a distraction from the Enlightenment Path. What is today called Reiki was known in India from the time of Gautama Siddhartha. It was partly described in the Buddhist *Sutras* (holy books), but more likely it was transmitted through oral teaching. Several of the early Buddhist scriptures describe the effects of spiritual healing—freedom from suffering and reincarnation in a "Pure Land" where Enlightenment can be gained—rather than the actual healing methods. Rituals and prayers for calling upon the Buddha of Healing are described in several texts.

Concepts, more familiar to the West, of psychic technique, visualization, initiation/attunement, meditative states, and spiritual healing involving mind, emotions and body indicate a form of Buddhism called Tantra or Vajrayana. Tantra is a highly esoteric form of Mahayana Buddhism that was developed in Tibet. It requires complete dedication and many years of psychic meditative training. Tantra is known in the West mistakenly as sexual practice; instead its goal is union and oneness with all Be–ing. This union is personified by the visualized—not in flesh—sexual partner. Two outgrowths of Tantric practice are the development of psychic abilities and healing skills. The adept is taught to use these only when

necessary, as they are distractions from the Enlightenment process.[12]

Tibetan Buddhism also involves the concept of Tulkas, the reincarnation with retained previous-life memory of certain high level adepts. Today's Dalai Lama is an example of a Tulka. Some time after the death of a Dalai Lama, the monks of the order begin to seek his reincarnation, whom they identify by numerous signs and tests. The new Lama, still a young child, is then taken to the monastery for training to resume the role he left in his past lifetime. This is an important connection between mystical Buddhism and Jesus, and I will describe it further.[13]

Written material on Tantric Buddhism does not offer clear step-by-step descriptions of how to achieve the Path. The material is meant only for adepts, and is taught orally. The manuscripts are carefully protected for fear of profanation and therefore are written to be deliberately obscure. A teacher is required to unravel the mystical language, and the teacher does so only to students deemed qualified and ready.[14] Teachings are sometimes lost if the Teacher/Master does not accept students to pass them on to; lost practices are occasionally regained by psychic rediscovery. The Tibetan *Tantra Lotus Sutra*, a text written in the second or first century BCE, offers the symbol formula for the technique of Reiki.

How did this technique of Reiki healing—though as Reiki is a Japanese word it would not have been given that name—reach Jesus in the Middle East? According to German writer and researcher Holger Kersten in his fascinating book *Jesus Lived in India* (Element Books, Ltd., 1991), Jesus was a reincarnated Bodhisattva, as described above—a Tulka. His birth was awaited by members of a Buddhist order, and the "Three Wise Men" followed the unusual astrological conjunction of 5 BCE to find him. Buddhism had spread throughout the East by that time, and there were Buddhist centers in most Middle Eastern countries.

The child would have been two years of age at the time and in danger from Herod who had received prophecies of an Essene leader newborn who would challenge Roman rule. An Essene Buddhist-type monastery existed at Qumran near the caves that later housed the Dead Sea Scrolls. As a mystical order and possibly even a Buddhist order, the Essenes were aware of these prophecies. Essene

CHRONOLOGY

India

620 BCE	Birth of Gautama Siddhartha, Sakyamuni Buddha, on the India-Nepal border.
543 BCE	Death of Gautama Siddhartha at Kusingara, India.
2nd to 1st Century BCE	Tantra Lotus Sutra written,[3] other healing texts extant.
7 BCE	Historical birth of Jesus.[4]
5 BCE	The "Three Wise Men" come from the East (India) to seek the reincarnation of an Enlightened One. They take Jesus and family to Egypt and India.
27 or 30 CE to 30 or 33 CE	Jesus returns to Jerusalem for 2–3 years.[5]
30 or 33 CE	The Crucifixion. Evidence that Jesus survived it.[6]
46 or 49 CE	Jesus returns to India 16 years after the Crucifixion.[7]
110 CE	Death of Jesus in Srinagar, India. Legends say he lived to 120 years of age, not unusual for his time.[8]

Japan

Late 1800's	Mikao Usui's quest for Reiki.
1925	Chujiro Hayashi receives the Reiki Master's degree (Reiki III) at age 47.
1930	Death of Mikao Usui. He made 16–18 Reiki Masters, sources vary.
May 10, 1941	Death of Chujiro Hayashi. He made 13–16 Reiki Masters including the first women, his wife Chie Hayashi and Hawayo Takata.

Hawaii

December 24, 1900	Birth of Hawayo Kawamuru (Takata).
March 10, 1917	Marries Saichi Takata.
October, 1930	Death of Saichi Takata.
1935	Takata goes to Japan for healing at Maeda Hospital in Akasaka, then to Hayashi's Reiki clinic, Shina No Machi, Tokyo. She is healed in 4 months.
Spring, 1936	Takata receives Reiki I from Chujiro Hayashi.
1937	Takata receives Reiki II from Hayashi then returns to Hawaii. She opens her first healing clinic in Kapaa.
Winter, 1938	Takata receives Reiki III from Hayashi in Hawaii. On February 22, 1938, Chujiro Hayashi announces Hawayo Takata as Reiki Master and his successor.
December 11, 1980	Death of Hawayo Takata. She made 22 Reiki Masters from 1970–1980. Some sources give death date as December 12.[9]

teachings included concepts of reincarnation and karma, the immortality of the soul, compassionate peacefulness and simple living.[15] Recognizing the Tulka they sought in the child Jesus, or perhaps summoned by the Essenes who recognized him, the "Wise Men" took the boy and his family East with them. The child was raised and trained first in Egypt and then in India. With access to Buddhist Mahayana and Vajrayana training, he returned to Jerusalem as an adult, a Buddhist adept, and a Reiki healer. He was also a Bodhisattva.

Holger Kersten goes on to trace the remainder of Jesus' life, providing logical argument for his survival of the Crucifixion. There are numerous mentions of him as Issa or Yuz Asaf in the Buddhist *Sutras* and as Ibn Yusf in Islamic writings. Most sources describe his past or note the crucifixion scars, making the identification unmistakable. Jesus survived and lived a very long and well-respected life as a holy man in India.[16] The graves of Mary, Mary Magdalene and Yuz Asaf (Jesus) are known and considered places of worship in Mari, Pakistan (Mary), Kashgar, India (Mary Magdalene), and Srinagar, India (Jesus). The sites are clearly labeled.[17] Kersten cites twenty-one documents that describe Jesus' residence in Kashmir, India, after the crucifixion plus numerous indicative place-names.

Much of this scholarly information has been suppressed by the Christian church, which reflects more the teachings of Paul than the Buddhist-influenced Jesus. The historical Jesus is a fascinating figure, and his presence in the Reiki story is vindicated. If he also trained others in the healing method—and the New Testament states that at the least he trained his disciples—then Reiki reached a larger portion of the ancient world outside of India than may have been previously known. It was probably lost from Christian doctrine through the intervention of Paul, who seems to have reinterpreted Christ's teachings. By the Fifth Century, the crucial concepts of rebirth and karma were dropped from Church canon, and Jesus' healing method—which could have helped so many—was also lost to the developing West. The healing remained active only with the Buddhist adepts, who used it but did not publicize its existence.

Mikao Usui returned to Japan and took residence in a Zen Buddhist monastery where he found the texts describing the healing formula, which he now could read in their original Sanskrit. The material did not include, however, information on how to activate the energy and make it work. As has been stated, such obscuring of information in the *Sutras* was intentional, done to keep the often powerful material from hands not ready to know and use it properly. Hawayo Takata describes this:

> He went into studying the Sanskrit, and when he later studied very hard to master it, he found a formula. Just as plain as day. Nothing hard, but very simple. Like two and two equals four… And so he said, "Very well, I've found it. But now, I have to interpret this, because it was written 2500 years ago—ancient. But I have to go through the test."[18]

The test was a three-week period of meditation, fasting and prayer on Mt. Koriyama in Japan. He chose his meditation site and piled twenty-one small stones in front of him to mark the time, throwing away one stone at the end of each day. On the final morning of his quest, in the darkest hour just before dawn, Usui saw a projectile of light coming toward him. His first response was to run from it, but then he thought again. He decided to accept what was coming and the answer to his meditation, even if it resulted in his death. The light struck his third eye and he lost consciousness for a time. Then he saw "millions and millions of rainbow bubbles"[19] and finally the Reiki symbols as if on a screen. As he saw each of the symbols, he was given the information about each of them to activate the healing energy. It was the first Reiki attunement, the psychic rediscovery of an ancient method.

Mikao Usui left Mt. Koriyama knowing how to heal as Buddha and Jesus had healed. Walking down the mountain he experienced what is traditionally known as the four miracles. First, he stubbed his toe walking, and instinctively sat and put his hands on it. His hands became hot and the torn toe was healed. Next, he reached a house that served pilgrims at the bottom of the mountain. He asked for a full meal, not wise after twenty-one days fasting on water, but ate it without discomfort. Third, the woman serving the meal was afflicted with toothache, and placing his hands on the sides of her face, he healed her pain. When he returned to his monastery, and was told that the director was in bed with an arthritis attack, he also healed the monk.

Usui named the healing energy Reiki, which means universal life force energy, and next took the method into the slums of Kyoto. There he lived for several years doing healing in the town's beggars' quarter. In the culture and ethic of his time, people with deformities, missing limbs or with apparent dis-eases were supported by the community as beggars. After healing each of these people, he asked that the person start a new life, but he found the same faces returning. Seeing people that he thought healed still begging instead of making an honest living, he became discouraged and left the slums. The people themselves were angry because with their dis-eases healed, they could no longer make their way as beggars and would now have to work.

Usui's experience in the slums is used to justify the high price of Reiki training today, the premise being that people would not appreciate the healing because they did not pay for it. Usui's failures may be due, not to the fact that the beggars did not pay, but to the fact that he healed only their bodies, not their mind and spirits. Buddhist doctrine de-emphasizes healing the body, stating that the only healing is spiritual and depends upon entering the Path to Enlightenment. Once a person has reached Enlightenment, she no longer needs to reincarnate, and this is the way to end suffering. Buddhists describe the Path to Enlightenment as the only true and valid healing method.

Mikao Usui became a pilgrim, taking Reiki on foot through Japan, carrying a torch and lecturing. In this way he met Chujiro Hayashi, a retired naval officer still on reserve status. Hayashi received his Reiki Master's training from Usui in 1925, at the age of forty–seven and became Mikao Usui's successor. Usui died in 1930, having made sixteen or eighteen Reiki Masters (the major sources vary), though none but Hayashi is mentioned by any Reiki source. Chujiro Hayashi trained teams of Reiki practitioners, both men and women, including sixteen Masters in his lifetime. He opened a healing clinic in Tokyo, where healers worked in groups on people who lived at the clinic during the time of their healing. Reiki healers also went to the homes of people unable to come to the clinic. It was to Chujiro Hayashi's Shina No Machi clinic that Hawayo Takata came for healing in 1935.

Hawayo Kawamuru was born on December 24, 1900, to a pineapple cutter's family on the island of Kauai, Hawaii, at Hanamaulu.[20] Too small and frail for plantation work, she took jobs while still in public school, helping to teach younger children, and worked as a soda fountain clerk. Once out of school, she was offered a servant's job at the large and wealthy plantation owner's house. She lived at the plantation for the next twenty-four years becoming housekeeper and bookkeeper, a position of great responsibility. She met and married the plantation's accountant, Saichi Takata, in 1917, and they had a happy marriage and two daughters together.

Saichi Takata died of a heart attack at the age of thirty-two in October, 1930. Over the next five years Hawayo Takata, widowed and with two small children to raise, developed nervous exhaustion and severe physical problems. She was diagnosed with gall bladder dis-ease that required surgery, but had a respiratory condition with breathing difficulties that made the use of anesthetic dangerous for her. Her health deteriorated, and she was told that without surgery she would not live, but that surgery might kill her. After a sister died in 1935, Takata took the news to her parents who had returned to live in Tokyo, and afterwards entered the Maeda Medical Hospital in Akasaka.

For several weeks, she rested in the hospital and then was scheduled for surgery. By this time she was also diagnosed with appendicitis and a tumor, as well as gallstones. The night before the surgery she heard a voice saying, "The operation is not necessary." She heard it again on the operating table while being prepared for the anesthetic, and getting up from it asked the surgeon if there was another way for her to heal. The doctor told her, "Yes, if she could stay in Japan long enough for it," and told her about Chujiro Hayashi's Reiki clinic. The surgeon's sister, who had been healed by Hayashi's healers and had taken Reiki training, took her there that day.

Takata lived at the clinic and was completely healed in body, mind and spirit in four months. She asked to be trained in Reiki but at first she was refused, not because she was a woman but because she was a foreigner. Hayashi did not want the practice of Reiki healing to leave Japan at that time. Eventually, he relented because of the intervention of the Maeda Hospital surgeon. Hawayo Takata received her Reiki I training in Spring, 1936. She joined the teams of healers that worked at the clinic, and in 1937 Takata received Reiki II and returned to Hawaii. She had lived in Japan for two years.

Her first Reiki clinic was in Kapaa, and she was successful in her work. She obtained a massage therapist's license to protect her legally from the harassing authorities.

In the winter of 1938, Chujiro Hayashi visited Takata in Hawaii and they did a lecture tour together. She received her Reiki III training from him at this time, and on February 22, 1938, Hayashi announced Hawayo Takata as a Master/Teacher and as his successor. He insisted that she not give the training away without charge. He also told her that when he summoned her, she was to come to him in Japan immediately. In 1939 she opened her second healing center in Hilo. In 1941, Takata awoke one morning to psychically see Hayashi standing at the foot of her bed. She knew this was the summons and took the next available boat to Tokyo.

When Takata arrived at the Reiki clinic, Chujiro Hayashi, his wife Chie Hayashi, and the other Japanese Reiki Masters were present. He told her that a great war was coming and that all involved with Reiki would perish and the clinic would be closed. He had feared earlier that Reiki would be totally lost to the world and therefore had made Takata—a foreigner—his successor. Chujiro Hayashi said further that as a naval reserve officer he had been drafted, and that as a healer and medic he would not take life. He determined to accept his own death instead, and therefore he had summoned Takata.

On May 10, 1941, in the presence of his students, Chujiro Hayashi stopped his own heart by psychic means and died. The great war he predicted was World War II, and Reiki was indeed no longer available in Japan. Chie Hayashi survived, but their house and clinic were taken over by the Occupation, and she was not able to operate it as a healing center.

Takata was the means by which Reiki continued. She had brought it first to Hawaii, then she brought it to mainland United States, and finally to Canada and Europe. She lived to be eighty years of age, but she always looked decades younger. She trained hundreds of people in the Reiki healing system. In the last ten years of her life, from 1970–1980, she initiated twenty-two Reiki Masters, both women and men. Hawayo Takata died on December 11, 1980.

In her healing clinics, if a client was seriously ill and needed many healings, she trained someone in the family in Reiki to do the treatments. When the client was strong enough, they took the training as well. Takata taught by telling stories and by example. She did not allow her students to take notes, and she did not teach in the same way with every class. Sometimes she started the healing positions at the head, and other times at the middle of the body or even at the feet. In her teaching of Reiki Masters, the Reiki III degree, her work varied as well. The Master/Teachers she trained were not all taught in exactly the same ways.

Mrs. Takata always charged her students, even her own family members. She came to feel that it was indeed necessary, that people who didn't pay for the learning didn't value it or use it. She felt that those who did not pay for the teaching would not be a success in business or in life.[21] The teachers she trained continue to charge high prices, high enough to make Reiki financially exclusive, out of reach for most people.

In my opinion, the high price of any healing system is morally wrong in today's distressed world, though there is also merit in Takata's understanding and experience with this. Some students indeed devalue what they haven't paid dearly for. The American culture fosters this concept of respect based upon prices paid, rather than upon intrinsic worth. I have found, however, that while a few students do not understand the value of what they have received, Reiki always still benefits them in some important way.

Since Hawayo Takata's death Reiki has gone through many changes in the West. Phyllis Furumoto, Takata's successor and granddaughter, has been named the Grand Master of Usui Traditional Reiki. Teaching techniques and methods have undergone changes, and several branches of Reiki have evolved. Each of these branches claims to possess the only correct way, but the fact is that all the methods work and all of them were derived from Hawayo Takata's teachings.

Usui Traditional Reiki, also called Usui Reiki Ryoho, is probably the closest to what Hawayo Takata originally brought from Japan. It teaches Reiki in three degrees with Reiki III as the Master/Teacher's training. Very few people are accepted for Traditional Reiki Master's training; even those who can afford the $10,000 have to be invited. Some teachers of Reiki now divide the third degree into two levels, Reiki III Practitioner and the Reiki III teaching degree. Some call the Reiki III Practitioner's degree an advanced Reiki II. One system, Radiance, divides Reiki training into eleven degrees, declaring the higher levels to go beyond and extend Takata's teaching. An increased number of degrees also means increased cost.

Teaching methods within the degrees also vary. Most teachers teach Reiki I in the same way, with some changes and additions in the second degree. The greatest variations come with Reiki III, however, with differences in the method of passing attunements. The Traditional attunement/initiation method requires four attunements each for Reiki I and some teachers use four for Reiki II, while some modern methods use only one combined attunement for each degree. In my own teaching and in this book, I divide Reiki into three degrees only, and my Reiki III degree includes the full teaching information. Though trained in both attunement methods, I prefer to use the modern way that passes the degrees in one attunement for each. This to me is more powerful, besides being significantly simpler. The material of this book reflects these methods and includes all three degrees in detail. My methods are more modern than Traditional Reiki—they have been refined by the criteria of what works best and most easily.

Reiki is changing and evolving since the time of Mikao Usui, Chujiro Hayashi and Hawayo Takata. It is reaching more people, particularly where some nontraditional teachers are now no longer charging high fees. How the Buddha taught laying on of hands healing, and how Jesus learned and taught it are no longer known. The origins of Reiki need to be honored, while at the same time respecting the changing world and the changing needs of people and the Earth. It is my hope that this book will carry on the teaching of Reiki, preserving effective methods so that they can no longer be lost, and at the same time putting Reiki within reach of any who want to learn it. Reiki is love, and in this time of planetary crisis, we all need all the love we can get.

"Reiki" written in Japanese in different styles of writing

1   Laurel Steinhice, in Diane Stein, *Dreaming the Past, Dreaming the Future: A Herstory of the Earth,* pp. 196–199, June 3, 1990.

2   Laurel Steinhice, Personal Communication, February, 1991.

3   Dated in Raoul Birnbaum, *The Healing Buddha* (Boulder, CO, Shambala Publications, Inc., 1979), p. 26–27.

4   Holger Kersten, *Jesus Lived in India: His Unknown Life Before and After the Crucifixion* (Dorset, England, Element Books, Ltd., 1991), p. 86. Dates on the life of Jesus are from this source. Their importance to Reiki will become apparent.

5   *Ibid.,* pp. 124–125.

6   *Ibid.,* p. 127 ff.

7   *Ibid.,* p. 174, date p. 183.

8   *Ibid.,* pp. 205–206.

9   Dates from 1800 to 1900 are duplicated in several Reiki sources. A primary reference is Fran Brown, *Living Reiki: Takata's Teachings* (Mendocino, CA, LifeRhythm, 1992).

10   The Traditional Reiki story is available in virtually every book about the Reiki system of healing. My primary source for it here is Hawayo Takata, *The History of Reiki as Told by Mrs. Takata* (Southfield, MI, The Center for Reiki Training, 1979), audiotape and transcript.

11   William L. Rand, *Reiki: The Healing Touch, First and Second Degree Manual* (Southfield, MI, Vision Publications, 1991), p. 2.

12   John Blofeld, *The Tantric Mysticism of Tibet: A Practical Guide to the Theory, Purpose and Techniques of Tantric Meditation* (New York, NY, Arkana Books, 1970), pp. 36–40.

13   Holger Kersten, *Jesus Lived in India,* pp. 86–91.

14   John Blofeld, *The Tantric Mysticism of Tibet* pp. 198–199. Much of my understanding of Buddhism comes from this excellent book.

15   Holger Kersten, *Jesus Lived in India,* pp. 106–108.

16   *Ibid.,* p. 150 ff.

17   *Ibid.,* pp. 186–187, 196–197, 203–206.

18   Hawayo Takata, *The History of Reiki as Told by Mrs. Takata,* transcript p. 4.

19   *Ibid.,* p. 6.

20   Virtually every book on Reiki describes Hawayo Takata's life. The main sources used here are: Fran Brown, *Living Reiki: Takata's Teachings,* and Helen J. Haberly, Reiki: *Hawayo Takata's Story,* (Olney, MD, Archedigm Publications, 1990), pp. 11–44. Both books are highly recommended.

21   Hawayo Takata, *The History of Reiki as told by Mrs. Takata,* transcript pp. 14–15.

CHAPTER TWO

WHAT IS REIKI?

The act of laying hands on the human or animal body to comfort and relieve pain is as old as instinct. When experiencing pain, the first thing most people do is to put their hands on it. When a child falls and scrapes her knee, she wants her mother to touch it (or kiss it) and make it better. A mother's instinct when a child is feverish or ill directs her to place her hands on the baby's forehead. Human touch conveys warmth, serenity, and healing. It also conveys caring and love. When an animal is in pain, a dog or cat's first instinct is to lick the pain area—for the same reasons that a person applies touch with her hands. An animal mother will also lick her young in distress. This simple act is the basis for all touch healing techniques.

The living body, human or animal, radiates warmth and energy. This energy is the life force itself, and has as many names as there are human civilizations. Mary Coddington, in her book *In Search of the Healing Energy* (Destiny Books, 1978), fills an entire volume discussing the history of this energy in various cultures. The Polynesian Hunas call this healing force *Mana,* and the Native American Iroquois people call it *Orenda.* It is known as *Prana* in India, *Ruach* in Hebrew, *Barraka* in the Islamic countries, and *Ch'i* in China. Some individual healers have termed it *Orgone Energy* (Wilhelm Reich), *Animal Magnetism* (F.A. Mesmer), and *Archaeus* (Paracelsus). In Japan the energy is termed *Ki* and it is from this word that Reiki is named.

Ch'i Kung instructor Mantak Chia defines Ch'i (the Chinese equivalent of Ki) as: "energy, air, breath, wind, vital breath, vital essence…the activating energy of the universe."[1] Ch'i Kung is an ancient Asian healing discipline. It works to enhance and conserve Ch'i by directing energy movement within the body. Ch'i or Ki is an electrical type of energy that creates the body, and determines the state of health. When Ki departs the living organism, life has departed. Ch'i or Ki is also the essential life force of the Earth, the planets, the stars, and the heavens, and these sources of the energy affect the living body's Ki. Everything alive contains Ki and radiates it—it is the biomagnetic energy of the aura.

In the life force energy of Reiki, the person who is attuned as a Reiki healer has had her body's energy channels opened and cleared of obstructions by the Reiki attunements. She now not only receives an increase in this life energy or Ki for her own healing, but becomes connected to the source of all universal Ch'i or Ki. This source can be described in any way the healer chooses to name it. I call it Goddess. Other terms might be God, the Higher Self, the First Source, the Universe, or whatever can be termed primary creation or life energy. Reiki is not a religion or affiliated with any religion. This life force energy is the source of life itself and far older in concept and fact than any religious philosophy.

While everything that has life has Ki, a Reiki attunement connects the receiver in an increased way to its limitless source. Upon receiving the first attunement in Reiki I, the receiver becomes a channel for this universal healing energy. From the time of the attunement and through the rest of her life, all she needs to do to connect with healing Ki is to place her hands upon herself or someone else and it will flow through her automatically. The attunement, by placing the person in direct contact with the source of Ki, also increases the life force energy of the person who has received it. She experiences an energy that first heals her, and then also heals others without depleting her. In the few short minutes of the attunement process, the receiver of Reiki energy is given a gift that forever changes her life in every positive way.

The process of attunement or initiation is what sets Reiki apart from every other form of laying on of hands or touch healing. The attunement is not a healing session, it creates the healer. In Reiki I, the student receives the first combined attunement (four attunements, if she takes the class from a Traditional Reiki Master). She receives an additional attunement in Reiki II, and one more attunement in Reiki III. Each degree's attunements increase the positive power of her ability to channel Ki. It is the attunements themselves that are Reiki, and without this process—which must be passed directly from Teacher/Master to student—the healing system is not Reiki but something else.

Attunements are given one-on-one and may be made into a beautiful ritual or done quickly and without ceremony. Either way, receiving an attunement is a magickal gift. In the process, the teacher begins by standing behind the receiver drawing the symbols. She then repeats the process at the front and returns again to stand behind the student to complete it. Receivers experience as many different things as there are students. Some perceive colors, others see pictures, some reexperience past lives—especially past lives in which they have had Reiki before.

Some are filled with light or a feeling of total peace, wonder or love. Some students may perceive more than others do. The sensations are definite but very gentle. When asked to place her hands upon someone else to bring the energy through, the new Reiki healer may experience for the first time the Reiki characteristic of heat radiating through her hands.

From this point on, the person who has received the attunement is a Reiki practitioner, with abilities opened in her that she did not know were there. The attunement does not give the receiver anything new; it opens and aligns what was already a part of her. The process is much like plugging in a lamp in a house already wired for electricity; when the healer puts her hands down with the intent to heal, she has turned on the light. Traditional teachers say that if you receive Reiki in this lifetime, it is because you have had it before in other incarnations. They say that Reiki is a remembering, and I believe it goes further than that. We have all had Reiki in past lifetimes; it is a part of our genetic heritage and part of all of us.

Reiki is divided into three degrees. In Reiki I, the attunement itself heals physical level dis-eases in the person who receives it. Her physical health often changes for the better in the months following the initiation. Reiki I healing sessions are primarily for self-healing. The Reiki I healer can also do healing for someone else who is physically present. Such healing is known as direct healing—the healer must directly place her hands upon herself or the other person. (The Reiki I hand positions are discussed in the next chapter.)

It takes three or four weeks to adjust to the Reiki I attunement. During that time the Reiki energy may turn on at odd non-healing moments. The person may feel spacey or tingly, have intense dreams including past life dreams, or experience detoxification symptoms. These can include diarrhea, running nose, or increased urination. The person will still feel well. What is happening is that the energy is adjusting and increasing the new healer's capacity to channel it. More Ki energy is entering her aura and body than she has experienced before, and her aura and chakras are clearing. If the process becomes uncomfortable, doing a healing on oneself or another rebalances the energy and decreases the sensations. After receiving Reiki I, it is best to do as many healing sessions as possible for at least the first month, including a daily self-healing.

The Reiki II attunement measurably increases the amount of healing energy, and the attunement focuses upon emotional, mental and karmic healing in the person who receives it. After the attunement, old emotions, unhealed former situations, past lives, and negative mental patterns resurface to be fully healed at last. This can take as long as six months to complete, and though not always comfortable the process is positive and necessary.

Healing with Reiki II adds considerable power to direct sessions. It also adds the methods and tools for doing healing with someone not physically present—distance healing. In Reiki II, three of the Reiki symbols are introduced and used consciously for the first time. With Reiki I, the symbols are already in the healer's aura and they emerge unconsciously through her hands when she heals. Reiki II begins directing their energies. It also offers preliminary information on channeling the energy required to pass attunements as a Reiki III.

Reiki III is the Master/Teacher's degree. A Master is simply a teacher, one who has mastered a discipline. No ego or ownership is otherwise involved in the term. The attunement involves spiritual level energy and achieves spiritual healing in the person receiving it. This energy is pure joy, oneness with all life, and connection with Goddess/Source. After the hard work that follows the Reiki II attunement, Reiki III is a joyous gift. In doing healing sessions, the Reiki III practitioner experiences a further increase in her ability to channel healing energy, and her healing ability also reaches a higher level. Reiki III includes two more symbol keys, more esoteric information on the symbols, and the method of passing attunements. This degree is only recommended for the serious healer, and especially for those who wish to teach Reiki and make Reiki a major part of their lives.

The learning process begins with Reiki I. Once receiving the initial attunement, the person has only to place her two hands down to heal, either on a pain area or using the Reiki full-body hand-positions. The Ki energy does the rest, without any direction, flowing through the healer's hands. The healer may or may not know what needs healing, but the energy has an intelligence far beyond human and will go where it is needed. It is not drawn from the healer or from her aura, but from the Goddess/life source. The healer places her hands on the series of positions that constitute a session, and Reiki does the rest. The energy also heals on all of the body's levels—physical, emotional, mental and spiritual.

Reiki energy heals the whole person. In healing a headache, for example, Reiki may also heal other organs and levels. Though the healer's hands are on the person's pain area, her head, many headaches have their source in the digestive system. If the headache is caused by intestinal disturbance, the energy goes to the intestines, as well as to the head pain. These are both physical-level areas. If the headache has emotional causes, stress for example, Reiki also heals on that level. Likewise if the source of pain is at the mental or spiritual body levels. If the person receiving the healing also has another dis-ease, perhaps allergies, Reiki will act there too, whether she has mentioned it to the healer or not.

People and animals are more than physical Be-ings. We have a dense physical body that is immediately perceptible by sight and touch, but we also have three other bodies. These nonvisible, nonphysical bodies are energy levels comprised of Ki that direct the state of the physical body. Healing cannot be physical alone, but must include the vibrational energy bodies. Where medicine treats only the physical body, healing—and particularly Reiki healing—treats all four bodies. Healing, therefore, goes much further than medicine, and is far more complete in its results. In the example of the headache, taking an aspirin may relieve the head pain but it does nothing to heal the source. Reiki deals not only with the evident pain, but with the cause of the pain. With an aspirin the headache is likely to return after three hours; with Reiki the headache is permanently gone.

This is especially true for more serious dis-eases. The source of any physical dis-ease is probably more than physical, and the nonphysical causes must be healed to heal the body pain. Most metaphysical healers believe that all physical pain has nonphysical roots in emotional trauma, negative mental patterns, or spiritual despair. To heal the dis-ease, these roots must be discovered and treated. This has been the major work of two women, Louise Hay (*Heal Your Body* and *You Can Heal Your Life,* Hay House, 1982 and 1984), and the earlier Alice Steadman (*Who's the Matter With Me?,* ESPress, Inc., 1966). Both women present a listing of body parts or dis-eases with their definitions of where the illnesses originated.

These definitions can be highly accurate for some people, less so for others. Neither author has a current

Problem	Source	Problem	Source
Accidents	Expressions of anger, frustration, rebellion.	Head	Us, what we show the world, something radically wrong.
Anorexia/ Bulimia	Self-hate, denial of life nourishment, "not good enough."	Headaches	Invalidating the self.
Arms	Ability to embrace, old emotions held in joints.	Heart	Heart is love and blood is joy. Heart attacks are a denial and squeezing out of love and joy.
Arthritis	Pattern of criticism of self and others, perfectionism.	Knees	Inflexibility, unable to bend, pride, ego, stubbornness, fear of change, self-righteousness.
Asthma	Smother-love, guilt complex, inferiority complex.	Legs	Fear or reluctance of moving forward, not wanting to move. Varicose veins: standing where we hate.
Back	Upper = not feeling supported emotionally, needing support. Middle = guilt. Lower = burnout, worrying about money.	Lungs	Inability to take in and give out life, denial of life. Emphysema or too much smoking = denial of life, inferiority.
Breasts	Mothering, over-mothering a person/thing/place/experience. Breast cancer: deep resentment attached to over-mothering.	Migraines	Anger and perfectionism, frustration. Masturbate to stop.
		Neck	Flexibility issues.
Burns, Boils, Fevers, Itis, Sores, Swellings Anger.		Overweight	Needing protection, insecurity
Cancer	Deep resentment, distrust, self-pity, hopelessness, helplessness.	Pain	Guilt seeking punishment, notice where it manifests.
Colon	Constipation is inability to let go, diarrhea is fear of holding; constipation = lack of trust of having enough, hoarding.	Sinus	Irritated by someone.
		Skin	Threatened individuality, others have power over you. Thin-skinned, feeling skinned alive, need self-nurturing.
Ears	Too hard to accept what is said. Earaches = anger, deafness = refusal to listen.	Stiffness	Stiff body = stiff mind, inflexibility, fear, "only one way," resistance to change. Where manifests = where pattern is.
Feet	Self-understanding, moving forward.	Stomach	Inability to digest ideas and experiences. Who or what can you stomach? Fear.
Fingers	Index = ego, anger and fear. Thumb = worry. Middle = anger, right: a man; left: a woman. Hold with other hand to release. Ring = unions and grief. Little = family and pretending.	Strokes	Negative thinking, stopping of joy, forcing change of direction.
		Swelling	Stagnated thinking, bottled-up tears, feeling trapped.
Genitals	Femininity or masculinity issues, rejecting sexuality, "sex is dirty," "women's bodies are unclean." Bladder infections: being pissed off, holding in hurts. Vaginitis: romantically hurt by a partner. Prostate: self-worth and sexual prowess. Impotence: fear or spite against mate. Frigidity: fear, sexual guilt, self-disgust. PMS: denial of female cycles or female worth. VD: sexual guilt.	Throat	Fear of change, inability to speak up, anger, frustrated creativity. Laryngitis = too angry to speak; sore throat = anger; tonsillitis or thyroid = stifled creativity, deeply stifled creativity in leukemia.
		Tumors	False growth, tormenting an old hurt, not allowing healing. Uterine tumors: nursing slights to femininity, misogyny.
Hands	Holding on too tightly to money or relationships. Arthritis = self-criticism, internalizing criticism, criticizing others.	Ulcers	Fear, not being good enough, lack of self-worth.

political awareness, and their definitions reflect this. For example, Louise Hay lists menstrual problems as a "rejection of one's femininity,"[3] rather than a rejection of women's second-class status in society. Adding-in this awareness makes the definitions more valid. Some metaphysical healers also misuse these definitions, and the concept of karma (the carryover of situations from past lives), by blaming people for their pain. Their attitude is, "Here's why you have this, you did it yourself, now go and fix it." Their justification for this is that illness is karmic and a punishment, that people choose their dis-eases and their pain, and they can also choose not to have them.

Karma is not that simple. The laws of karma posit that each lifetime has a pre-life agreed-upon series of things to learn, and having a dis-ease or condition may be a way of setting up that learning. Karma, in definition, simply means action, and every action has a reaction. Another way of stating this is the Wiccan adage, "What you send out comes back to you." Errors in life require redress, understanding, or a change of attitude to heal them. They may simply require experiencing the emotions fully to resolve them. If this does not happen in the lifetime where the situation occurs, it may happen in a succeeding one. It is not to be considered as punishment.

A person may develop a dis-ease as a way of facilitating a needed learning. A very impatient person in one lifetime, for example, may agree to become bedridden or confined to a wheelchair in her next life to be forced to learn patience. The situations are seldom that clear or simple, however. It is also too easy to say that if you break your leg in this lifetime, it is because you caused someone else to break theirs in a past life. It is a misunderstanding of karma to believe that someone has chosen her dis-ease, when such choices and agreements are made in the pre-life state without in-body consciousness or awareness.

Buddhists feel that karma is generated by emotional attachments which are carried from one lifetime to the next. This is the force that requires people to return to Earth again and again, to resolve the situations and emotions. They feel that the Path to Enlightenment heals all karma and frees people from the cycle of rebirths, but that karma can be resolved only while incarnated in a body. Some healers ask if using Reiki to heal dis-ease interferes with a person's karma, or requires the healer to be karmically responsible for that person. My understanding of this is that if someone is healed by Reiki or

any other means it is a *fulfilling* of their karma or it would not have happened. The healer is not responsible, she is only the channel for the energy. Such healings are between the person receiving the healing, her own spirit guides, and the Goddess. There is more discussion of karma under Reiki II.

With that in mind, how are emotional sources and karma used in Reiki healing? Gently, compassionately, and with respect. In using a Louise Hay or Alice Steadman this-life definition in a healing, first make it a question rather than a statement: "Is it possible that you are experiencing skin rashes because someone is 'getting under your skin'?" If the receiver of the healing says "No," ask her what the cause is, as she perceives it. In the relaxed state of the healing, she may be able to access the cause, though before the session she didn't know. She may access a past-life memory, where seeing the situation usually resolves it. Use her answer not to judge her, but to increase her self-awareness. If she says it's because she feels threatened in her living situation, ask her what she needs to do to change it. And ask her how you as the healer can help her.

That may mean listening to her talk about her difficulty, or making the healing a safe place for her to express her anger or to cry. In about one out of four Reiki healings, usually when the healer has her hands on either the throat or heart position, the person receiving the treatment will experience an emotional release. This means that she will express emotions regarding her dis-ease or situation, frequently the held-in emotions that are the direct source of her dis-ease. The person may cry, get very angry, start to talk about what happened to her, giggle, or get very restless. The healer's role in this is supportive. She stays with the person experiencing the release and lets it take its course, while continuing the Reiki hand positions and the healing.

The healer needs to be totally nonjudgmental. She may hear things that are horrifying, but cannot react. Her job is to make the person expressing the emotions feel totally safe and to listen. If the receiver is crying, tell her, "It's okay to cry, it's safe to do that here. Get it all out, it's fine." If the person describes a this-life trauma—having been incested as a child, for example—support her in her pain. Say things like "Look how strong you were to survive it. It's over now and will never happen again. You are wonderful and good." If she is angry, tell her, "You have a right to be angry. Get it all out now." If she reaches a past-life trauma, she may be opening the source of a this-life pattern. By supporting the release, the emotions that caused her dis-ease are expressed. This is a major healing; the woman will heal now, whereas she could not have done so before.

If the woman gets very restless or seems to be trying to speak and cannot, encourage her to say what she needs to. People in this culture, particularly women, have been so fully trained not to express their feelings that opening up a strong emotion can be very frightening. By making the healing session a space safe enough to express anything she needs to in, these emotions come out. Start them by asking her, "Can you tell me what's happening?" or "Can you describe what you are seeing?" If she isn't ready to talk yet, don't force her. Once the receiver of the healing starts talking, however, tears or anger may come next. Again, the release of these withheld emotions is an important healing in itself.

The first time a new healer experiences the emotional release of someone she is healing, she will probably be frightened by it. These releases generally last only for a few minutes; they are resolved by the time the healer reaches the leg positions. Though sometimes intense and scary for the healer, they do great good for the person receiving the Reiki session. The Universe seems to protect inexperienced healers, too—the healer will only be given situations she can handle. The more serious and intensive sessions come when the healer is ready for them. Once a person has begun to use Reiki, her healing also becomes more and more guided. By connecting with spirit guides consciously or not, the healer knows what to say, and when and how to say it. In an emotional release, or in any other situation, the healer knows what to do. She may wonder later how she thought of it.

After the healing, the person who experienced the release feels immeasurably lighter and better, and the healer has grown as well. This is the time to talk of other actions, such as seeking a support group for an incest survivor, or understanding a past life pattern. Because of the protective nature of Reiki energy, the healer is far less likely to absorb others' pain or emotional states than in most forms of healing. If she has done so, all she need do is acknowledge it to herself and release it. After a Reiki session, both healer and receiver are energized and filled with balanced energy. The healer who has brought the Reiki energy through her hands to the other person has also received a healing.

Because of these complexities, and because Reiki energy heals whatever needs healing, what happens in a session cannot be predicted. It is literally out of the healer's hands, though the healer's hands are doing the Reiki. The healer can only promise that Reiki benefits everyone that experiences it. She cannot promise that a Reiki session will cure a particular dis-ease, or promise any other specific result. Reiki relieves pain, speeds the healing process, stops bleeding, relaxes the receiver, and balances the person's chakras and aura energy. Respiration slows during a Reiki session, and blood pressure lowers; emotional calming occurs. Whatever else may happen is up to the Goddess or Source energy, and it is not predictable.

This does not mean that miracles can't happen—they frequently do. Everyone who has worked with Reiki energy has stories about the results. In one instance I worked with the two gay men to do healing for a young AIDS patient near death in the hospital. He had a fever of 107.8 degrees Fahrenheit and was not expected to live longer than that night. He was unconscious and hallucinating, and very restless. When we did the healing, one of the men did the head positions, and the other held the patient's feet, while I did the Reiki positions on the torso. During the healing I somehow knew that his fever had dropped three degrees, though there was no way I could have known that. After the session, we turned on the temperature monitor again (we had shut it off to be able to reach the man in his bed), and sure enough his fever had dropped three degrees.

We waited half an hour and did a second session and this time the fever broke. We watched the digital numbers on the monitor actually shift while we were working. The young man regained consciousness while we were still in the room, and he talked with his mother for the rest of that night. There was unfinished business to resolve, and the healing gave them both time to resolve it. The man died the next morning, in a calm, deep sleep. His mother called me then, and thanked me for the time together that the healing had given them and for her son's calm death. If someone is terminal, Reiki will not prevent their passing over or hold them back, but it eases the process.

In another instance, a woman friend fell at work and injured her back. She was diagnosed with four herniated spinal discs and a ruptured one. Because of her overweight condition, age, and poor health (heart dis-ease, diabetes, post-polio), it was decided that she could not have surgery. Instead she was told she would spend six months in a nursing home, and then be taught to use a wheelchair. I visited her in the hospital. She showed me a large lump above her knee that the doctors had biopsied for a suspected tumor. I put my hands on it, felt that it was a muscle spasm, and the lump resolved to normal under my hands. After that brief healing, the daily blood tests suddenly showed that she no longer needed injection insulin—she had been on 75 units per day for thirteen years. The nurses monitored her blood levels several times a day, but she never returned to insulin use.

When she entered the nursing home, I went to see her with two of my students and we did a full-body healing session. When we came again a week later, she was on the patio and had walked there herself. We did another session. The woman remained in the nursing home for two and a half weeks instead of six months, and she left walking. The nurses and doctors had no idea how it happened. The same evening we sat on the patio, I also did healing for another visitor's small dog, who kept coming to me for the energy. The dog asked for it, though his owner was none the wiser, and my friend, who was aware of my Reiki work, just smiled. A few weeks later she told me that Ralph the dog had just had his blood tests, and the liver dis-ease that threatened his life seemed to have disappeared. The dog's blood work was normal, his owner had no idea why, and when I touched the dog on the patio that day, I had no idea that the dog had a liver problem.

In another instance, a woman came to me with three large lumps in her breast, ranging from walnut to lemon sized. I tried to convince her to go to a doctor, but she had made the clear decision not to allow the medical system to operate on her and amputate her breast. I felt at first that the lumps were too far advanced for successful holistic healing, but with two other Reiki III healers we began doing weekly healing sessions. She also began to use herbs—poke root internally and in compresses, castor oil compresses, chaparral and shark cartilage.

After a month, a dark circular area developed on her breast that we felt would abscess. We told her not to stop the process if that happened. At almost three months, with the help of a drawing salve from Mexico, the breast finally developed the largest abscess I have ever seen, about two inches across. It drained for several weeks and

by the end of that time all three lumps were gone. I asked her to get an antibiotic for the infection from a doctor she knew, and she did so. Though the process was painful and frightening to her, an abscess is not life-threatening in the way that cancer is.

One of my students offered the following story. Her daughter had her first child, a boy who was born with only ten percent of normal hearing. The grandmother did frequent healings on the child, and he and his grandmother developed a deep rapport. When the baby was five months old, her daughter called the grandmother for help. The child was screaming in a way she had never heard before and his mother didn't know what to do. My student went and calmed the baby with Reiki, and then said, "Just for the heck of it, get his ears tested." At the next pediatric visit, she learned that the baby's hearing is now normal.

Such experiences are genuinely awesome. Reiki does not come from the healer, but from the Universe through her. The healer cannot take credit for what happens in the healings. In fact sometimes nothing happens. Or nothing perceptible at the time. Likewise, the healer is not responsible if no healing takes place. There may be a very good reason for this. It may be the woman's karma to experience the dis-ease fully, even if it leads to her death. Death is a healing, too.

The person receiving the healing may also, consciously or not, refuse the energy, deciding to retain her dis-ease or to die. There may be reason for someone to keep a dis-ease; it may be giving her something she has no other way to obtain. She may want to be taken care of for a while. When I perceive that happening, I try to make the receiver aware of it, not in a judgmental way—she has a right to her free choice—but to make the process conscious. With it conscious, the person can fully look at the situation and she may make a different choice. If she chooses to die, however, she will do so.

I feel it is never ethical to say, "I healed this person." The only person who can heal someone is herself. Healing can only happen in her own body. A healer's role is simply to channel the energy, which the receiver can use in any way that is best for her needs. I fully believe healing to be a three-way agreement, between the healer, the receiver, and the Goddess/Source. A healer also does not do a healing *to* someone, but only *with* them. Without the receiver's agreement and participation in the process, no healing can take place. The only rule in Reiki I is the receiver must give the healer permission to do the healing. With that agreement, whatever happens in the session is what was meant to occur.

Reiki is totally positive and can never cause harm to any living thing, whatever their condition or status. It is valid for use on anyone, no matter how young, old or frail. Elders, infants, and children respond well to Reiki healing, as do pets and plants. If anyone is ill, in pain or in emotional distress, Reiki helps. For the person or pet that is healthy, Reiki relaxes and rejuvenates. The positions balance the left and right hemispheres of the brain and balance all the chakras and the energy field. They clear and increase the animal or human body's flow of life force Ki. When someone is dying, Reiki eases the process but will not prevent the person or animal from passing over at the designated time. For the grieving loved-ones, Reiki is a comfort and a help as well.

While Reiki will not heal most congenital birth defects, it can bring about clear improvements in even seemingly hopeless conditions. For the person living with a permanent disability, the Reiki energy may not be able to correct her condition, but helps to make living with it as comfortable as possible. The energy eases pain, relaxes tense muscles, and calms the emotions. Where a limb or body part has been amputated, Reiki cannot replace it, but it will help the person adjust to the loss and to new ways of functioning.

Yet I have experienced some "impossible" healings in these cases too. In one instance of a brain-damaged infant, daily Reiki sessions led to more rapid development, beyond what doctors had predicted. Another instance involved a three-week-old baby with a hole in the heart wall. My student's Reiki sessions in the week before corrective surgery resulted in a simpler process and easier recovery than expected. The defect proved smaller than the X-rays had shown before the healings, and the baby was stronger. I have seen this happen in other surgeries when Reiki is done beforehand—faster recovery and the problem becoming less serious than had been previously predicted.

Once on a workshop trip, a woman brought to me a six- or seven-month-old baby. "This baby is brain dead," said the woman, "Or so the doctors told me." The baby was perfectly normal, and I said so. The woman told me her story. "About six months into the pregnancy the doc-

tors started doing a lot of tests and taking a lot of pictures, but wouldn't tell me why. Finally, they said that my baby was anencephalic; she would be born without a skull or brain function and would die a few days after birth. I was horrified. I belonged to a women's ritual group, and three of the women were Reiki I's. Twice a month at our meetings they put me in the center of the circle and did healing for me. My baby was born normal, and the doctors still don't know why. They have all sorts of pictures of a baby without a skull. She was also the easiest delivery of three children."

Sometimes after a healing or during a series of healings, the person or pet receiving Reiki treatment begins to detoxify. This is similar to what may happen after the healer's first Reiki attunement. She may develop diarrhea, odorous or discolored stool, increased urination, body odor, temporary skin rash, a running nose and cold symptoms, or excessive perspiration. This is a release from the body of dis-ease-causing toxins, and should be supported rather than stopped. The healer needs to be aware that this may happen and that it does no harm. She should tell her client not to suppress these symptoms with medications, but to let the poisons leave the body in their own way.

A detox generally lasts a few days. What distinguishes a cleansing reaction from a dis-ease process is that during the cleansing, despite the symptoms, the person still feels well. Advise her to drink frequent glasses of pure water, and to eat lightly or do a liquid fast for a few days. After what is termed a "healing crisis" of this sort, the person feels better than she has in a long time, and her healing is well under way. From this point, the healing of her dis-ease proceeds rapidly.

Occasionally a healer learns that the person receiving a healing does not believe in it. If that person gives permission for the healing, and if she is open to it, the healing happens with or without belief. Someone who is not open to it, however, or refuses it inwardly, can block the process. For some people, though they give permission for the session, the idea of nonmedical healing is more than their belief system can adapt to. They may say yes, but still refuse to admit the energy. If that happens, the healer can usually sense that she is being blocked. She can gently tell the receiver what she perceives, but it is still up to the receiver to choose.

Reiki will not violate anyone's free will. If the person refuses the energy, the healer can do no more. When this situation occurs for a new or inexperienced healer, it can shake her confidence, especially when the receiver insists she is accepting the energy—but she isn't. The problem is with the receiver, not the healer. Be aware that this refusal can happen and that you have done your best. It happened to me with one of the first healing sessions I ever did, and I did not realize for years what had happened.

The receiver may also say she feels nothing—or sometimes in a Reiki session the *healer* thinks that nothing has happened. Sometimes the healer feels nothing, while the receiver feels a great deal. In these cases, trust in the Reiki energy. The healing is happening, whether anyone perceives it or not. Occasionally in a session, the receiver suddenly feels an increase in her pain. This lasts for a few moments, and I tell people to "breathe into it" while it lasts. Reiki can condense several days of a headache or other dis-ease into a few moments this way, and it is worth waiting it out. When it ends and the additional pain is gone, *all* of the pain is gone. I ask my healing guides to make this pain as quick and easy as possible, but sometimes it has to be. It never lasts long and never causes harm.

When we did Reiki for the woman with the breast lumps, several times she experienced tremendous burning sensations in the tumor areas. This was very painful, more so than usually happens, and the episodes frightened the woman and worried me. I repeatedly asked my spirit guides to be gentler. They replied that they couldn't, but it wouldn't last long. It occurred for about ten minutes in each session. The effect of the healings was that of burning out the tumors, and the lumps healed completely.

Reiki can be used alone or in conjunction with medical (or veterinary) treatment. It will not interfere with medications or other procedures, other than to make them more effective and the patient more comfortable. The energy speeds healing, sometimes in spite of medical system methods. For a woman on chemotherapy, for example—a treatment holistic healers feel does more harm than good—Reiki supports the positive effects while helping to decrease the negative ones. It works more happily and effectively with holistic methods that are more positive for the body's healing. Reiki and herbs or homeopathy work beautifully together. Charging medications or holistic remedies with Reiki before taking them also increases their effectiveness. Where medications like insulin or high blood pressure drugs are involved, check the blood levels frequently as the need for them may decrease.

Reiki can help a broken bone heal more rapidly, but it is best to wait until after the bone is set to do healing directly over the break. Sometimes the Ki energy heals very quickly, and if the break has not been set yet, this healing may not be positive. Before the setting, do Reiki on other parts of the body, but not over the break. Never place your hands directly on top of a wound or broken skin. Put your hands nearby and the energy will go to where it is needed, without causing more pain or risking infection. Once the bone is set, Reiki works very well through the cast.

Despite the warnings I was taught not to do Reiki over a broken bone until it's set, I have another story. A friend fell from the side of her porch, and it was very obvious that a bone in her ankle was broken. I told her she needed to have it X-rayed, but she refused and asked me to heal it. This woman would not go to a doctor, not even for a broken bone. I was uncomfortable with this, but agreed to try the healing. I put my hands on her ankle and again received the message that the bone was broken. I said silently to my guides, "This is the only healing for this broken leg she's going to get. Let's do it right the first time." I felt the bone move into place under my hands. The woman wore tight high-topped boots for several weeks to support her leg. She took vitamin C and comfrey for the inflammation, and though black and blue initially, it healed well. She was lucky, but I don't recommend doing it that way.

There is one other example when it is best to wait to use Reiki. A man had cut his finger off accidentally with a woodworking saw. He placed the amputated part in a glass of water and went to the emergency room immediately. Along the way he did Reiki on his hand. When he got to the hospital, he was asked why he had waited so long to come—the wound had healed too much to make reattachment of the finger possible. The accident had happened just twenty minutes before, but Reiki energy can speed healing that drastically.[4]

I have mentioned charging medicines and remedies with Reiki. To do so, hold the bottle between your hands and let the energy flow. There are many other ways to use this, too. Holding your hands palm down over food may have been the original way of blessing a meal. Charging a glass of water with Reiki makes the water itself into a healing remedy. You can also charge the bandaging material this way. Crystals can be charged with this energy, too, though more effectively once you have the Reiki II and III symbols. I have even used Reiki on my car, when I lived in a cold climate and needed to make sure it would start in the morning.

As a healing system of great power, it is also important to know that there is very little you can do wrong in this healing. The Reiki energy has an intelligence far beyond human knowledge, and all it takes to activate it is to place your hands on the positions or where there is pain. The energy will do the healing and do it well. The healer needs no advanced psychic ability or even awareness of the process. One benefit and outgrowth, however, of receiving Reiki training is that the healer's psychic ability begins to grow, almost from the time of her first attunement, and it grows in every way.

One of the first things that happened for me upon receiving Reiki I was that I developed a psychic ability to diagnose. When I put my hands on a pain area, I often know what is wrong, and the skill can be highly accurate. Please note, however, that diagnosis by a nonmedical person is considered illegal in America—use this type of ability carefully. Before telling someone in a healing session what you see, use caution and think first. If a situation seems serious, suggest a doctor. It is usually unwise to diagnose cancer (for example). I believe in honesty when doing healing, but only with responsibility. It is also usually inappropriate to tell someone that they may be dying. Psychic information can be wrong, and the disease can change along the course of the healing process. Remember to use compassion at all times.

Healing is needed by most of us at the end of this planetary age. There isn't time in this crisis to wait years for the mastery of a skill. With Reiki, all it takes is the attunement, and the student is immediately a healer. We need all the healers we can get now, and then some. The potential for self-empowerment with Reiki is tremendous, especially for women. Remember that empowerment means validation of a genuine skill and ability, not ego. For the person receiving Reiki treatment, great benefits can come immediately, even with only one healing. Reiki allows people to take more control of their health, and to often avoid the high cost, inhumanity and invasive methods of the medical system. Reiki cannot replace medicine, but in many cases it can do things that medicine can't and do them much more gently and positively.

For an acute, self-limiting dis-ease (like the flu, colds, headache or a sprained ankle) one Reiki healing session may be enough to help. When conditions are serious or chronic, however, more sessions may be required. I compare Reiki to charging a battery; if a person is in relatively good health, she may need only a little charging. If she is more seriously ill, she may need a lot. At Chujiro Hayashi's Reiki clinic, people received team healings daily or more often until they were well. For someone with cancer or AIDS, daily healings may give better results than weekly ones, and it may take some time to start changes. When someone is chronically ill, I suggest she receive Reiki attunements, both as a self-healing tool and for the benefit of the attunement itself. If you have received Reiki attunements, do self-healing daily, whether you are ill or not. As the person's battery charges, the frequency of the healings can decrease.

There are several differences between Reiki and other laying on of hands or touch healing methods. The most important difference for me with Reiki I was that I stopped taking on other people's symptoms. When I did healing previously, the woman with menstrual cramps would leave feeling fine, but I had her cramps. I learned to ground the energy and release it, but it often took as long as doing the healing took. I was sometimes very sick after healing sessions. From the time of my first Reiki I attunement, this situation changed completely. I no longer take on others' pain, though occasionally in a healing I will feel sensations in my body that give me information. As soon as I acknowledge what I'm being told, the sensations go away.

I could never have begun AIDS healing in hospitals if I were still absorbing symptoms in that way. Nor could I have done such intensive healing work if I finished healings feeling as drained as I did before Reiki. With Reiki, I finish healings feeling clear, balanced, grounded, energized, and otherwise feeling good. If I need healing myself at the time I'm doing a session for someone else, I receive Reiki automatically as I work. This in no way detracts from giving the receiver what she needs. (Avoid doing Reiki, or any healing work, if you are very ill or angry.) With Reiki also, I found the strong increase in power and effectiveness I was looking for. The more the healer uses this Reiki energy, the stronger her healing ability becomes.

There is one more thing unique to Reiki, and I have purposely left it for last. This is the Reiki Principles. While Reiki is not a religion, but older than all religions, it remains true to Eastern philosophy. Reiki comes from a culture that has given the West virtually all of our metaphysical techniques and probably all of our ethics. Mahayana Buddhism and its Vajrayana outgrowth developed in very ancient times the skills of meditation, visualization, ritual, spiritual and herbal healing, dreamwork, conscious dying, sexual healing with respect for women, past life regression, every sort of psychic development and ability, and more. In studying Tantric Buddhism (Vajrayana) for this book, I was startled to find there the roots of every religion, including my own Wicca.[5] How different the world might have been if Jesus' *true* teachings, from this source, had become Christianity.

I have seen a number of variations of the five simple Reiki principles, something different in almost every book on Reiki. They are said to have been written by Mikao Usui. The list as given by Hawayo Takata on her audiotape, *The History of Reiki as Told by Mrs. Takata* (Vision Publications, transcript page 11) is probably the closest to the original:

> Just for today, do not anger.
> Just for today, do not worry.
> We shall count our blessings and honor our fathers and mothers, our teachers and neighbors and honor our food.
> Make an honest living.
> Be kind to everything that has life.

Another version of the Reiki Principles, from Larry Arnold and Sandy Nevius' *The Reiki Handbook,* reads:

> Just for today I will give thanks for my many blessings.
> Just for today I will not worry.
> Just for today I will not be angry.
> Just for today I will do my work honestly.
> Just for today I will be kind to my neighbor and every living thing.[6]

A further version reads:

> Just for today do not worry.
> Just for today do not anger.
> Honor your parents, teachers and elders.
> Earn your living honestly.
> Show gratitude to everything.[7]

My own choice uses the list directly above, but adds to it a sixth principle: "Respect the Oneness of All Life." It therefore becomes basically Mrs. Takata's version (which I had not seen until recently). These principles bear careful thought, and using them daily makes Reiki a way of life. They violate no one's religion or religious ethics.

How these compassionate commandments are interpreted can vary according to the individual. Often someone asks, "I was incested, how can I honor my parent?" I ask that person if she can honor her *other* parent, or some other person who may have acted as a *true* parent for her. Others ask about anger. I advise them not to nurse rage and resentment, not to hold on to it until it explodes. Expressing honest feeling and clearing the air without letting the anger smoulder unresolved seems to me the essence of this Principle.

Receiving Reiki I is a milestone in a person's life, and from the time of the attunement one's life is forever changed. While these changes are fully positive, the new healer may need something to hold on to as her life becomes very different from what she has previously known. The Reiki Principles can help in this process of accelerated growth and new beginnings. Meditating upon them is calming and strengthening, and a very good thing to do during self-healing sessions. I ask my students to look at them and consider them, before setting them aside. The one that reads "Show Gratitude" may be the most important Principle of all.

Most learning about Reiki comes from doing healings and letting the energy teach the healer. I ask my new Reiki I's to do a self-healing session daily after receiving the attunement, and at least three full-body healings a week for others for the first month. The more the student uses Reiki, the more it teaches her, and the stronger her healing ability gets. The more it is used, the more Reiki also works in the healer's life to accelerate her personal growth and self-healing.

My dedication in this lifetime is to teach healing to as many people as can benefit from it. I learn every healing method I can access, looking for effective techniques that I can pass on to others who need them. Reiki gives me something no other system can: in the space of an afternoon I can take people who have no concept of healing or energy and send them home as competent Reiki practitioners. Any other healing discipline requires years of study to gain competence. When those new Reiki I's leave my classes, I am fully sure of their abilities and have a clear knowing that all of their work will be positive. Reiki can never do harm and no one can make a mistake. This is perhaps the most important reason of many that I hold Reiki in such high regard. On this, I have never had a student disagree.

THE REIKI PRINCIPLES [8]

Just for today I will give thanks for my many blessings.

Just for today I will not worry.

Just for today I will not be angry.

Just for today I will do my work honestly.

Just for today I will be kind to my neighbor and every living thing.

---

1 Mantak and Maneewan Chia, *Awaken Healing Light of the Tao,* (Huntington, NY, Healing Tao Books, 1993), p. 31.

2 Louise L. Hay, *You Can Heal Your Life* (Santa Monica, CA, Hay House, 1984), Chapter 14.

3 Louise L. Hay, *Heal Your Body: The Mental Causes for Physical Illness and the Metaphysical Way to Overcome Them* (Santa Monica, CA, Hay House, 1982), p. 25.

4 I do not know the source of this story, but some people have told me that a few Reiki teachers have given such warnings. The same people warn against doing healing on unset broken bones.

5 For more on this, read John Blofeld, *The Tantric Mysticism of Tibet* (Arkana Books, 1970).

6 Larry Arnold and Sandy Nevius, *The Reiki Handbook* (Harrisburg, PA, PSI Press, 1982), p. 27.

7 Bodo Baginski and Shalila Sharamon, *Reiki: Universal Life Energy* (Mendocino, CA, LifeRhythm Press, 1988), p. 29.

8 Larry Arnold and Sandy Nevius, *The Reiki Handbook* (Harrisburg, PA, PSI Press, 1982), p. 27.

Chapter Three

The Reiki Healing Session

Once you've received the Reiki I attunement, this chapter teaches you how to apply the energy. It includes information and hand positions for self-healing, direct healing with others and pets, and group healing teams. Once you begin to do healings, the full miracle of Reiki starts to manifest. I have told some of my Reiki healing stories, and every healer tells me her own. The true magick of Reiki is in the doing.

The first thing a healer needs to know is how to hold her hands. Both hands, held palms down, are always used in Reiki. Fingers and thumbs are extended and held together (as if they had socks over them, not mittens, says my favorite six-year-old Reiki I). They are placed on the Reiki positions, and rested gently there, completely relaxed and with no exerted pressure. The life force energy, or Ki, that produces the healing flows through the chakras in the centers of the palms and the tips of each finger. If for some reason both hands cannot be placed on a position, place one hand on the position and the other somewhere else on the body. Both hands must be on the receiver's body, or held just above it, for the energy to activate and come through.

Though the hands are always used in Reiki healing, they are not the only place Reiki energy flows from. Once you have had the Reiki I attunement, it is a surprise to find that the energy can flow through any part of your body. If the soles of your bare feet are resting against your dog and you have the intent to use Reiki, the energy flows through the soles of your feet and the dog receives the benefit. Resting your feet in bed on your mate's leg or back also brings forth the energy in this way, if you intend to do healing. Shiatsu therapists may find the energy flowing as they use their elbows to create massage pressure.

Energy through the hands can happen at other times than in healing, too. My artist friends with Reiki tell me that the energy turns on when they are doing their art. New Reiki I's often report their hands growing hot at odd times, and this may happen for the first few weeks. If you are sitting close to someone who needs the energy, your hands may heat up, also. This can be somewhat embarrassing in movie theaters, but unless you tell them, they never know. If it happens with friends, ask if they'd like a healing—they will swear that you are psychic. Reiki can activate when your hands are resting on your own body. Take advantage of the suggestion.

How to hold the hands to do Reiki

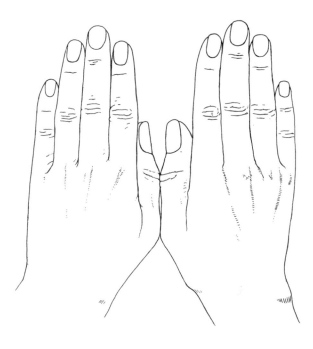

When both hands are rested on oneself or another with the intent to heal, Reiki automatically starts flowing. As soon as the hands are lifted, it stops. No request or other method is needed to turn Reiki on and off. Once the energy begins, the healer or receiver usually notices heat sensations, and this is an identifying characteristic of Reiki. After receiving the Reiki I attunement and bringing the energy through for the first time in the classroom, hot hands happen in most healings. If what the person receiving the healing needs is cold, however, the healer's hands will give her cold. Sometimes the healer feels her hands are very hot, while the receiver of the energy feels coolness, and vice versa. Every healing and healing position can be different.

With her hands placed on a Reiki position, the healer feels a cycle of sensations. Initially, she feels the expected warmth of body heat, but as her hands remain in place other feelings begin. There may be sensations of heat, cold, water flowing, vibrating, trembling, magnetism, static electricity, tingling, color, sound, or (extremely rarely) pain moving through the healer's hands. The healer may feel as if her hands have gone to sleep, with a pins-and-needles sensation. The person receiving the healing may feel the same things or different ones, or she may feel nothing. The sensations change from position to position, and healing to healing. They are unpredictable, but there is almost always a sensation of some kind.

These continue for what at first seems like a long time, generally as long as five minutes. Then the sensations end and quiet body warmth returns. This completes the position, and signals the healer to move to the next one. As Callie, my six-year-old Reiki I friend put it: "It goes up, and then it comes down, and then you can move." I can't think of a better way to describe what happens. If you *don't* move, the cycle simply begins again: body warmth, several minutes of sensations, and body warmth again. Often, a position takes less than the expected five minutes, and this is fine; go by the feeling in your hands. Unless the receiver of the healing has back trouble, the positions on her back will probably take less time.

Occasionally, the sensations seem to go on forever, and the healer's hands feel glued in place. Continue as long as you need to be there. If your hands feel free to move and the sensations go on and on, however, stay a reasonable time and then move to the next position. More healing needs to be done here, but the pain didn't develop overnight and one session may not be enough to heal it. This is usually an area or position where much Reiki is needed, but since the full treatment session takes as long as an hour and a half, spending too much time in one place is not beneficial. After she has completed a few healings, the healer develops a sense of when it is time to move. Honor your intuition, and remember there is no right and wrong. The sensations may be less distinct in self-healing than in healing others.

Very little conscious focusing is required when using Reiki. Put your hands down with the intent to heal and the energy flows—no matter what else you may be doing or thinking about at the time. (When doing any other form of hands-on work, the energy also turns on, as for massage therapists). I have often taught a workshop while my hands are doing Reiki as I talk. The person receiving the healing is not deprived, the energy needs no directing. Your hands will tell you when to change positions. There are many occasions when your full attention is necessary, however. If the receiver is experiencing an emotional release or past life memory, needs guidance through a visualization process, or wants to talk about what is happening to her, the healer is required to be fully with her. Psychic knowing gained in Reiki sessions can be important—these are only received in silence. In doing self-healing as well, notice the thoughts that arise while your hands are on your body; they may give important information.

When using Reiki with dogs, cats or young children, the healing session is different than with human adults. Most animals and children do not have the patience to stay still for the length of time a full Reiki session requires. Both also have the ability of absorbing energy far more easily and quickly than adult humans can. A position may be as short as thirty seconds. When a pet is feeling well, she may reject the energy completely—she'll just walk away. When an animal is ill, however, she usually accepts it. A pet that is ready to pass over will often reject it. Pets can also reject it for other reasons. Reiki on babies puts them to sleep and they usually like it anytime.

To give Reiki in these cases, place your hands on the child's or pet's body wherever they comfortably fit or over the pain area. Hold them in place and the Reiki will go where the energy is needed. Do the positions if the body is large enough. A very tiny animal, like a lizard, gerbil or bird, can be held in your two hands between your palms. When the pet has had enough, she will tell you so—she gets very restless or leaves. If she needs more, she comes back in a few minutes and may come back again and again. Repeat the process for as long as the animal asks for it. In children, your hands will tell you when the position or healing is done, or the child may tell you directly by getting restless. An older child may ask you to stop the healing.

Cats are particularly aware of Reiki energy, but they have an attitude about it. They feel that cats invented it, and they want to keep it. They may not be pleased to share it with a human. If they need healing, however, they will accept it and probably criticize your technique. One new Reiki III practiced passing attunements with her classmates, and her cat was in the room. The cat's psychic comment when the visitors left was, "I knew that!" They can be wonderful healers themselves and are usually an asset in any Reiki session, as long as the healing's receiver likes cats.

Dogs are more laid back; Reiki energy tickles them. Of my two Siberian Huskies, Copper loves it and will take as much as I can or want to give him. Kali will not accept it from me at all, but is glad to accept it from my

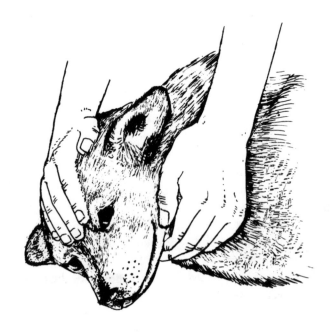

friends. Like cats, when dogs need healing they usually accept it. When I give Reiki sessions for people, Copper sends rainbows through his paws and is often a help, but Kali gets too excited. She is extremely sensitive to psychic energy and doesn't like it. Be careful of the pet that becomes a Reiki junkie or hogs the massage table; they can get to be a pest.

With children, the situation is similar. Your hands may cover several body positions on a child at once. Like animals, children absorb the energy extremely quickly, and they will indicate when they've had enough. When they say so, move your hands or stop the healing. Babies and toddlers are very attracted to Reiki energy. A young child free to roam in a room where her mother is receiving or doing a healing can become a distraction. The child may try to climb up onto the massage table and join the session (along with the cats or the sixty-pound dogs). It is better to keep them in another room until it is their turn. Children trained as Reiki I's tend also to complete the healing positions extremely quickly, in a minute or less. Yet, they feel the standard energy cycle and are aware of when to move.

Since a complete Reiki session can take a long time, at least an hour and often longer, it is important to consider where and when to do them for oneself and others. If you are putting your hands only on a pain area or one position, this is less an issue than if you are doing a full treatment. Self-healing sessions are very nicely done in bed the last thing at night or first thing in the morning. If it is not comfortable to do all of the positions, do what positions are in reach. Self-healing also works very well when you are sitting relaxed in a chair, perhaps watching television.

When doing Reiki for others, it is important for both receiver and healer to be very comfortable. The receiver has to lie still, first on her back and then on her stomach, for at least an hour. Put a pillow under her knees if she has back problems, and under her hips or head if she needs them. If working on a floor, put a pad or blanket under both of you, and the healer may sit more easily on a pillow. The healer spends a long time at each position and may do several positions before physically moving. It is a shame to have to stop or move because of a foot falling asleep or back cramps. The easiest arrangement for all concerned is a massage table; I use mine with a rolling office chair and sit to do Reiki. When doing healing on a floor or bed, the healer must learn to relax her own body and to find what physically works best for her.

If someone receiving Reiki is in the hospital or ill, they may not be able to turn over. Do the positions on the front of the body only in this case. There may be positions hard to reach, and again if they can't be reached, skip them. It is always best to do the full Reiki session, but where this is not possible do what you can, or put your hands only over or near the pain area. While it is best to do a session with the receiver lying down, doing it with her sitting in a chair is also possible. In doing healing for someone in a public place, I often place my hands only on her shoulders and let the energy flow through. Any Reiki is better than none.

Most healing sessions are done quietly, and I recommend silence at least while doing the head positions. After that, the receiver may begin an emotional release that should not be stopped or distracted. Focus fully on the receiver at this time. Some people fall asleep or go out of body during healings, and should be left undisturbed. In some lighter sessions, the healer and receiver may chat while going through the hand positions. A session done with other people present usually precludes heavy releasing or emotional work. Use intuition as to when conversation is okay, and when it is not. If psychic information arises, share it with the healing's receiver in a compassionate way.

Some healers like soft music playing in the room when they do Reiki. Use nonvocal, Classical or New Age type music played at low volume, not hard rock or hip hop. Keep lighting low; take the phone off the hook or shut the ringer, and close the door to distractions. Do self-healing when you will not be interrupted or distracted, too. You deserve the time and space for healing as much as someone else does. Since the first Reiki position is over the eyes, wash your hands before starting a healing. Center yourself, calm your mind and begin.

Loose clothing is the most comfortable for both healer and receiver in a Reiki session; both remain clothed. Some healers like to take their shoes off if the floor is carpeted and the room is warm. The receiver of a healing takes her shoes off and her eyeglasses, if she wears them, leaving contact lenses on in most cases. Remove a heavy belt if she is wearing one. With Reiki, I do not feel it necessary to remove jewelry, but some healers may prefer to for the receiver or themselves. Have a blanket available in case the receiver feels cold. If placing crystals under the massage table, make sure they have been cleared.

Reiki can be used with, and is highly effective with, gemstones and crystals in laying on of stones. First, and of primary importance, the stones need to be thoroughly cleared before starting and after the healing is finished. Cleared crystals or gemstones can also be charged in your hands. With the receiver lying on her back, place the stones over her chakras and then begin the Reiki session. Information on laying on of stones may be found in many books, including my own *All Women Are Healers* (The Crossing Press, 1990). Basically, the colors of the stones are placed to match the colors of the chakras (orange stones are placed on the Belly chakra), but use your intuition. When using gemstones in a Reiki healing, the chances of the receiver experiencing an emotional release are much greater, and these are very intensive healings.

The Reiki hand positions are also primarily over the chakras. After the three head positions, this makes them easy to remember. The chakras are located on the etheric double energy twin of the physical body, one layer away from the physical body level. They are energy transformers, bringing Ki from the Earth and Heavens into the human or animal body. The chakras on humans are placed in a vertical line down the center of the body, front and back. A full Reiki session covers all of the chakras and all of the body's organs. In pets, there is a more triangular energy pattern, and only some of the chakras are along the center line of the spine. For more information on chakras in pets, see my books, *Natural Healing for Dogs and Cats* and *The Natural Remedy Book for Dogs and Cats* (The Crossing Press, 1993 and 1994).

While it is not crucial to know the locations of the chakras to do Reiki, it makes describing the placements easier. The chakra system used in the West was developed in India, which gives it a further Reiki connection. It is important to note, however, that many cultures developed similar systems. It also makes sense energywise to know why your hands are on a particular part of the body. Each chakra regulates the organs in its area. I will describe the centers only very briefly, as there are many excellent books on the chakra system. A Reiki healing begins at the head and moves down, so I will describe the chakras from head to feet.

The Seven Major Chakras [2]

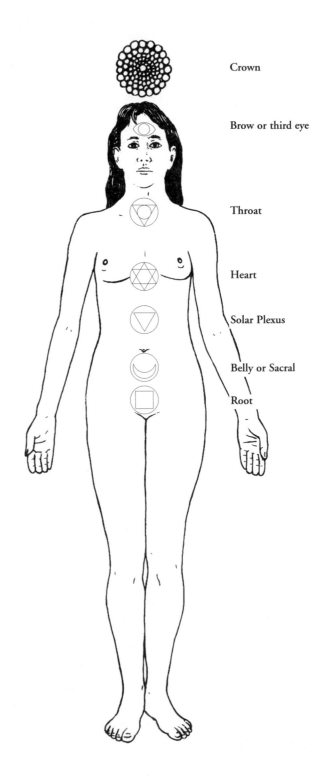

Crown

Brow or third eye

Throat

Heart

Solar Plexus

Belly or Sacral

Root

The three Reiki head positions cover the Crown and Third Eye centers. The Crown is located at the top of the head, slightly to the back of the highest part of the skull. Physically it is associated with the pineal gland. This is people's connection with spirituality and Goddess/Source, and is represented usually by the color violet or white. The Crown is the place of perception of spirit guides and the skill of channeling. The Brow or Third Eye is next, located above and between the physical eyes, and associated with the pituitary gland. This is the chakra of psychic perception, and understanding of the Oneness of the Universe. The color for the Brow is indigo, the blue-black of the nighttime sky. It is women's power center and represents the creation of personal realities. In physical healing the Crown and Brow are the brain, eyes and central nervous system.

The Throat chakra is located at the base of the neck, and is associated with the thyroid and parathyroid glands. Its color is light blue, and its function is communication both physical and psychic. In a world where speaking out is a risk, most people's Throat centers are in need of healing. Emotions are expressed at this level, and creativity is located there. Healing issues include anything with the throat—sore throats, stage fright, thyroid problems, throat cancer. Below it is the Heart, behind the breastbone or sternum, and associated physically with the heart organ or thymus gland. Two colors are often used for the Heart center; the primary one is green and the other is rose. Emotions come from the heart, as does universal love and love for others. Heartache and heartbreak (and physical heart conditions) are typical of modern society—most of us need heart and emotional healing.

Below the Heart and between the lower rows of ribs is the Solar Plexus; its color is solar yellow. This is men's power center, and the place where energy moving through the body is assimilated. Food is assimilated at this center—its physical correspondence is the pancreas gland or liver—as well as power issues and balances of power. Solar Plexus diseases include digestive problems, alcoholism, and food issues. The Belly or Sacral center is the spleen in men (purification) and the uterus in women, which also has a purifying function. Its location is a few inches below the navel. First impressions and old emotional pictures are stored in this center, and it is also the center of sexual choosing. Its color is orange. Healing at this chakra includes recovery from past abuse, and sexuality or fertility issues.

Developing Chakras: The Hara Line [3]

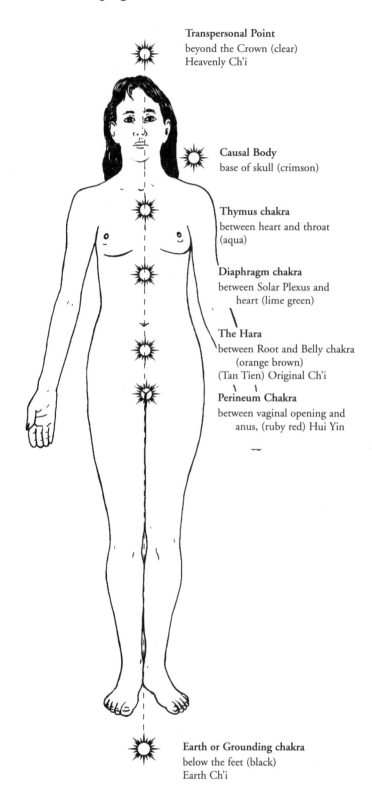

Transpersonal Point
beyond the Crown (clear)
Heavenly Ch'i

Causal Body
base of skull (crimson)

Thymus chakra
between heart and throat
(aqua)

Diaphragm chakra
between Solar Plexus and
heart (lime green)

The Hara
between Root and Belly chakra
(orange brown)
(Tan Tien) Original Ch'i

Perineum Chakra
between vaginal opening and
anus, (ruby red) Hui Yin

Earth or Grounding chakra
below the feet (black)
Earth Ch'i

The Root chakra, usually associated with the adrenal glands, is located at the genitals, It is represented by vibrant red. Known in the East as the Gateway of Life and Death, the Root is the place of birth and rebirth. This is the survival center, the ability to draw abundance from the planet. Root center healing involves basic issues of having enough food, shelter and clothing, of wanting to live or die, of grounding and of living on the Earthplane. These are the seven major chakras, and they are present on both the front and back of the body. There are said to be a total of forty-nine chakras on the human etheric double, with the others usually considered to be minor energy points. Each acupuncture point may also be called a minor chakra and there are hundreds of them. The small chakras located in the hands and fingers are not minor centers for healers. And those located on the soles of the feet—that can also transmit Reiki and serve to connect us to the Earthplane—cannot be considered minor, either. There is a chakra at the back of each body joint. The chakras are a major part of the electrical system of the body, the bridge between physical and non-physical Be-ing.

Besides the seven major and many minor chakras of the etheric double, there is another line of important energy centers. Beyond the Crown and above the physical body is the Transpersonal Point. Its color is clear (all colors), and its function is Goddess-Within. Other beyond-the-Crown centers may be developing in people at this time. Below the physical feet is the Earth or Grounding Chakra, whose color is black. This is people's connection with the planet, and with grounding us into the nourishment and magnetic energy of the Earth.

An energy line runs from the Transpersonal Point to the Earth Chakra. This line is probably beyond the etheric double and on the emotional/astral body aura layer. Barbara Brennan, in her book *Light Emerging* (Bantam Books, 1993), names this the Hara Line.[4] Mantak and Maneewan Chia describe it in *Awaken Healing Light of the Tao*.[5] It is also the basis for Duane Packer and Sanaya Roman's *Awakening Your Light Body* tape series.[6] Along this line are several more centers, which are part of the ancient Ch'i Kung system, but seem to be opening spontaneously for the first time in many people. I perceive their presence in more and more healings. The Hara Line is more important in Reiki II and III, but I will describe

the "new" centers now, though their uses are not fully clear to me at this time.

Among these include a red and gold chakra at the base of the skull, that appears to be involved with manifesting and is called the Causal Body. Between the Throat and Heart is another new center—its color is aquamarine and I call it the Thymus chakra. It plays a part in immunity and in protection from pollutants and chemicals. At the diaphragm, the new center is lime green in color. Its purpose lies in the purging of old emotions and toxins at every level. The last of these is the Hara itself, located between the Root and Belly chakras and sometimes called the Sacral center. In Ch'i Kung it is named the Tan Tien, and is known in Japan and China as the center of human energy and power—of Original Ch'i. Its Western equivalent is the Solar Plexus (though its color is gold, rather than yellow), but the Hara or Tan Tien is much more.

For Mantak Chia, the Tan Tien is the location of Original Ch'i in the body, the life force energy one is born with. This combines with Heavenly Ch'i (from the Universe) and Earth Ch'i (from the planet)—the Transpersonal Point and the Earth Chakra—to create the three forces that sustain and nourish all life.[7] Barbara Brennan defines the Tan Tien or Hara as the place of the "will to live in the physical body."[8] She describes the Hara Line as the line of intention and purpose for this incarnation. There is more about the Hara Line in Reiki II. The human Ki (or Ch'i) system is highly complex, and as people develop it becomes ever more so. For the Reiki I hand positions, however, all you need to know is the seven major chakras.

SELF-HEALING

From here we finally begin a Reiki session, and Reiki I has its greatest benefits in self-healing. I have had students tell me that they have studied many healing methods without finding information to help themselves, but this is where Reiki begins. The hand positions for self-healing are the basis for all the other Reiki positions as well. While I give them below in an organized manner, always allow intuition free play. If you are guided in a healing to put your hands somewhere not designated as a Reiki position, do so. Likewise, if you are guided to skip a position or to do it out of order. I ask that my students learn the given positions fully, use them until they thoroughly know them, and then to let their guides and intuition vary them when needed.

There is no incorrect way to do Reiki. Teachers vary on these positions, but everyone is right. Put your hands down and the energy goes where it is needed. Keep them on a position until the energy flow changes and you are directed to move to the next place. If you are unable to do a position, or it is uncomfortable to reach one or more, go on to the next. If you are unable to bend your arms and body well enough to do the back, do only the front. Do not cross your arms or legs in the placements. The basic instruction for Reiki is to put your hands where the pain is. When it is possible to do a full body healing session, this is optimal, but when it is not, do what you can.

The illustrations show the hand positions for self-healing, which are numbered for easy identification. Healing always starts at the head and moves to the feet on the front, and then continues from head to feet on the back. The first three positions are on the head. In the first, place your slightly cupped hands gently over (but not pressing on) your eyes. Hold the position until the energy sensations that develop stop, usually in about five minutes. This first position balances the left and right sides of the brain, and is wonderful for headaches and eyestrain. It also covers the Brow or Third Eye chakra.

Next (position 2), move your hands to the sides of your face. Your thumbs rest just beneath the ears, and your palms cover the cheeks. Again, wait for the energy cycle to complete. This is almost an instinctive way to place your hands, and it is extremely comforting. The third head position (3–3a) moves your hands to the back of the head, cupping the occipital ridge. This covers the Crown chakra, and also the Third Eye from behind, as well as reaching the Causal Body. Again, each position takes about five minutes.

Next go to the Throat chakra (4–4a). If putting your hands over your own throat brings on a panic reaction—it is less likely to on yourself—place your hands instead over your collarbone below it. When doing Reiki for others, almost always put your hands below, rather than directly over the Throat center. (The chakra is actually in the V of the collarbone, anyway.) Position five (5–5a) over the Heart is only done on oneself. Put your hands over the breastbone, or even over the breasts if healing is needed there.

The Solar Plexus is the next position (6). Place your hands in opposite directions with fingers facing over your lower ribs, just below the breasts. Anatomically, your right hand is over your liver and gallbladder and your left over your pancreas, spleen and stomach. You may hear some internal rumbling at this position. Again, each position takes approximately five minutes to complete the energy cycle, so relax with the process. The hands held in the same way move next over the middle abdomen at about the waist or just below it (7), then lower once more to cover the pelvic bones (8). The energy reaches the intestines from this position, and the Belly chakra.

The last of the torso positions is with the hands brought together in the center of the lower abdomen, one above the other, just above the pubic bone (9–9a). On yourself, you may cover the genital area if you wish. This position is the Root chakra and covers the uterus and ovaries, bladder and vagina in women, the bladder and testes in men.

Next move to the knees, ankles and feet. These are not Traditional Reiki positions, but I find them to be extremely important, particularly the feet. They serve to balance and ground you after the energy of the upper centers, reconnect you with Mother Earth, and also integrate and bring through the energy of the healing. For the knees and ankles (10, 10a, 11, 11a) first put your hands on both knees, then do the same at both ankles. You may have to reach to find a comfortable way to do the ankles. An alternate choice here is to put one hand on the right (or left) knee and ankle at the same time, then move to the other leg's knee and ankle. Do the feet last, placing your hands on the bottoms of the soles where the chakras are. Put one hand on each foot (12), or both hands on one foot then move to the other (12a). Again, keep your hands in place as long as the energy sensations continue.

Then go to the back. There is one position only for the head (13), but since you have done three head positions already this one is optional. Place one hand on the Crown of the head and the other at the back (Causal Body). It can be done alternatively with both hands at the Crown (13a). Next place your hands over the back of the neck or on top of the large muscles between neck and shoulders at the back (14). These muscles are tension–holders for many people. They constitute the

Reiki I Hand Positions
Self-Healing
The Front—Head Positions

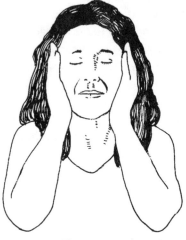

1. Over the eyes.

2. Over the cheeks, thumb is just under the ears.

2a. Alternate second position.

3. Back of the head, over the occipital ridge.

3a. Alternate third position.

Reiki I Hand Positions (continued)
Self-Healing

4. Over the throat.

4a. Alternate throat position.

5. Over the heart—breastbone (self only).

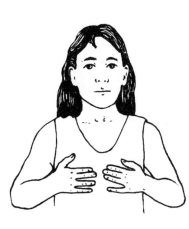

5a. Alternate fifth position (self only).

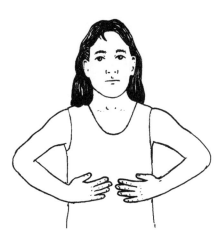

6. Over lower ribs below breasts.

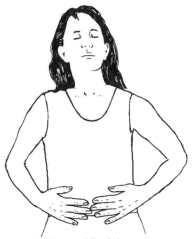

7. Over middle abdomen.

8. Over pelvic bones—lower abdomen.

9. Hands in center above pubic bone (not touching genital area).

9a. Alternate ninth position—over pubic area (self only).

Reiki I Hand Positions (continued)
Self-Healing—The Front—Knees, Ankles and Feet

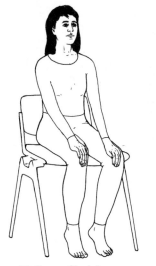

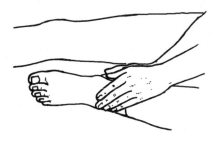

10. Front of both knees.

11. Front of both ankles.

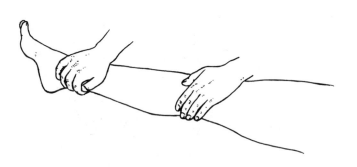

10a.–11a. Knee and ankle done together. Do both legs.

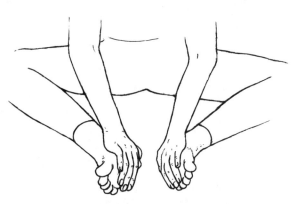

12. Bottoms of both feet—or 12a. Bottom of one foot then the other.

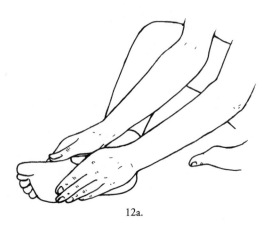

12a.

Reiki I Hand Positions (continued)
Self-Healing—The Back

13. Back of the head—one hand over occipital ridge, one hand over crown (top).

13a. Alternative head position for the back.

14. Back of the neck and over top of shoulder muscles.

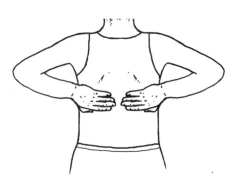

15. Over ribs, below shoulder blades, back of heart.

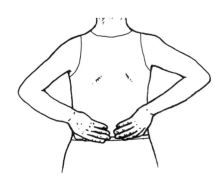

16. Middle back.

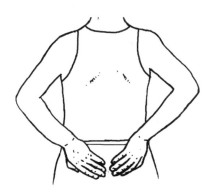

17. Lower back over sacrum.

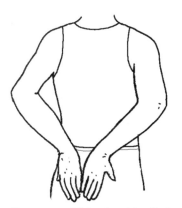

17a. Alternate or additional position for lower back.

18. Backs of both knees. (refer to figure 10, but do position from back).

19. Backs of both ankles. (refer to figure 11, but do position from back).

19a. Hold back of knee and ankle at once on same leg. Repeat with the other leg.

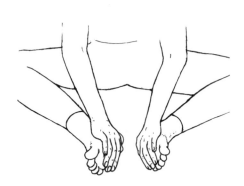

20. Bottoms of both feet.

Location of Major Body Organs—Front View

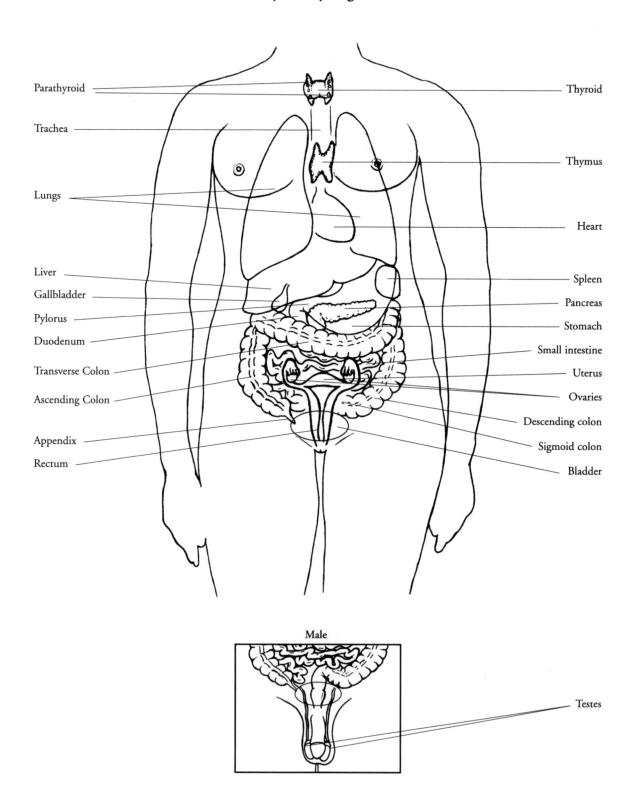

Parathyroid

Trachea

Lungs

Liver

Gallbladder

Pylorus

Duodenum

Transverse Colon

Ascending Colon

Appendix

Rectum

Thyroid

Thymus

Heart

Spleen

Pancreas

Stomach

Small intestine

Uterus

Ovaries

Descending colon

Sigmoid colon

Bladder

Male

Testes

Location of Major Body Organs—Back View

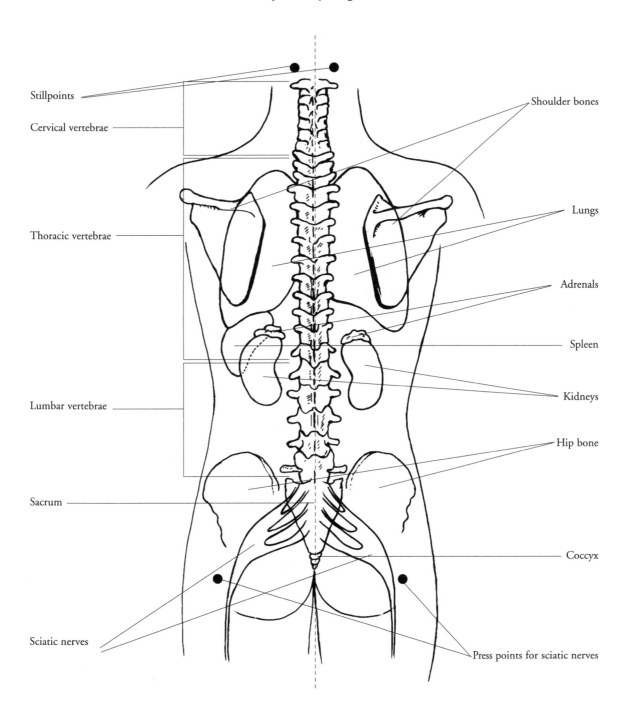

Stillpoints

Cervical vertebrae

Thoracic vertebrae

Lumbar vertebrae

Sacrum

Sciatic nerves

Shoulder bones

Lungs

Adrenals

Spleen

Kidneys

Hip bone

Coccyx

Press points for sciatic nerves

Throat chakra at the back, and are not sensitive as the Throat center front is.

Turn your arms around now, reaching up to below the shoulder blades (15), covering the back of the Heart. The hands point toward each other as on the front torso. Next move lower to the middle back, holding the arms and hands in the same way (16), and do one position lower yet (17). These positions cover the Solar Plexus and Belly chakras. An alternate or additional placement is over the lower back (17a) with hands positioned downward for the Root Chakra.

Repeat the knee and ankle positions (18–19 or 19a), but this time place your hands at the back instead of the front. To finish, do the bottoms of both feet again (20). This is the full Reiki self-healing session; the positions become familiar quickly. After completing it, drink a large glass of pure water and rest a while. You may feel spacey for a few minutes to an hour. Pay attention to the emotions and thoughts that have arisen during the healing.

HEALING OTHERS

The Reiki session for others is actually the same healing as a self-healing, with two exceptions. First, the hands reach out instead of being brought toward oneself, resulting in some change in how the positions are done. The healer needs to do the session in such a way that her own body is totally comfortable, or the reaching can cause considerable strain. Do not cross your arms or legs or allow the receiver to. Second, when doing healing for someone else, be aware of body privacy. Touching the breasts or genitals is an invasion of body safety unless the person is yourself or your mate. Be aware of this for children as well as adults. One out of three women in America has been raped and probably half to three quarters have been incested or otherwise violated. Reiki sessions are safe space—it can be no other way.

To begin the healing, do the head positions standing or sitting behind the person receiving the session. You will remain there through three head positions, the Throat, and probably the Heart. The hand positions are again illustrated and numbered. Begin with your cupped hands placed gently over the person's eyes, not pressing on them (1). Feel the energy sensation cycle and when the sensations stop, move to the next position. This first position balances the left and right sides of the brain. The woman receiving the healing may be restless through it, but she will become quiet when you move to the next position. Discourage talking for at least the time of the head positions, and if the woman continues, ask her to remain silent.

Position two (2) is over the cheeks, with your little fingers placed just beside the ears. Where position one covered the Third Eye, position two reaches both Crown and Third Eye chakras. The person receiving the healing most often becomes quiet, and may go to sleep or out of body. To do the next position (3), the healer lifts the receiver's head (the receiver usually helps), and slides her hands underneath. Cup your two hands under the curve of the back of the head, the occipital ridge. Where it feels comfortable for your hands is the place. Crown, Third Eye and Causal Body chakras are covered. The head positions treat the skull, brain, eyes, ears and central nervous system.

Reach forward to the Throat chakra (4). Because so many people panic when hands are placed over their throats, I never place my hands directly on it. Instead put your hands below the throat and over the collarbone. You can also hold your hands tent-wise above the throat without touching it, but this is an uncomfortable strain for the healer. In past lives, many people who are healers today died at the stake—we were usually strangled before the flames reached us, and therefore the phobia.

Extend your arms further forward or move to either side for the Heart (5–5a). Never place your hands over the breasts of a woman you are not intimate with, unless both of you have agreed to do so. (If the woman has cystic breasts or breast lumps you might.) Usually, however, place your hands above the breasts, or between them if there is room to do so, or skip the position completely. Again, wait for the energy cycle to climb and fade, a period of up to five minutes, then move your hands to the next position. You need to be at the woman's side instead of behind her now. The Solar Plexus (6) is located just under the breasts and covers the upper digestive organs (liver, gall bladder, pancreas).

With the torso positions, you have a choice of how to place your hands. They can be held as they were for self-healing, though facing out instead of in. To do this set them in a horizontal line across the body, the fingers of one hand almost touching the heel/wrist of the other. Alternatively, and sometimes more comfortably, place the hands side by side (thumb almost touching thumb). To find the positions with this, imagine the receiver's torso divided into four quarters and place your paired hands over each quarter. Do the upper right side, upper left side, lower right side, then lower left side. Bring both hands to the center of the lower abdomen last. (Start from either side; with Reiki it doesn't matter.) Do this on the back also if you choose to. The illustrations and my description show the first way, but an illustration of the second is shown on page 46. Both are correct—it is simply a matter of what is more comfortable to the healer.

To continue with the torso, position seven (7) is just below the waist and covers the Belly chakra, with the next hand placement just below it (8) above the pubic bone and over the pelvic area. Place the hands either horizontally or side by side. Next bring both hands to the center of the lower abdomen (9), just above the pubic bone (Root center). The hands are placed one above the other on the body. These positions cover all the abdominal organs, the digestive, eliminative and reproductive systems. See the drawings of the body organs; some knowledge of anatomy is helpful and necessary for Reiki healers, though medical terminology is not needed.

The knee, ankle and feet positions are even more important when you work on someone else than they are for self-healing. For the past half hour or more, the person receiving the healing has been lying quietly (unless she has had an emotional release). She may appear to be asleep or just "out there somewhere" and out of body. The hand positions on the legs and feet begin to bring her back to Earth now.

To do them, the healer must move again. In doing the torso positions the healer stood or sat on one side of the receiver. There is no need to move from side to side, just reach across the woman's body to her opposite side. Now move further down so you can reach her legs. Do the tops of both knees (10) and then the tops of both ankles (11). Alternatively, place one hand on her knee and the other on her ankle of the same side (11a)—this is the preferred way. Complete these positions by waiting for the energy sensations to fade, as usual.

Finish the healing with the bottoms of the feet (12). Do one foot at a time (12a–12b), or both feet at once, which is preferable. If you are continuing the healing by doing the back of the body, you may choose to skip the feet positions until the end of the session. Now ask the woman to turn over, and move to her head again.

With the receiver's head turned to the side, optionally do the one head position for the back (13). One hand is placed on the Crown and the other on the back of the head at the occipital ridge. When the sensations change, move to the next position, the back of the neck (14). I have not met anyone sensitive to the Throat position from the back. Placing your hands over the trapezius muscles, the big muscles where the shoulders meet the neck, is an alternative.

Move to the side again and do three positions down the back (15, 16, 17). The hands may be placed end to end or side by side as on the front torso. These positions cover the Heart, Solar Plexus and Belly chakras. They also reach the kidneys, and are wonderful for tension, stress, and back trouble. If the person has a particularly long back or much lower back pain, do one more position further down, where the buttocks begin. An optional way to do this is with one hand facing in each direction (18).

Next go to the legs and feet, and this time it is extremely important to do these positions thoroughly. They help the receiver ground—she has been "out" for a long time by now. Move lower toward her legs, and do Reiki positions on the backs of both knees (19) and the backs of both ankles (20). A preferred way to do this is to place one hand on the back of the knee, and the other on the back of the ankle of the same side (20a). Wait for the energy, then repeat on the opposite side. Make sure to do both sides.

The last position of the healing is the bottoms of the feet (21). Whether working on the front or back of the body, the feet are still held on the bottoms, where the chakras are located. You will feel streams of energy moving through the feet, and they may continue for several minutes. This position integrates the healing and completes it. The receiver of the healing will be far from grounded when she gets up from the session, but she will be functioning—without the feet positions she would be much too spacey for a while.

An optional way to complete the healing is to do a brushing off of energy. Hold one or both hands about eight inches above the receiver's body, palms facing downward. Gently but quickly sweep your hands at this height, moving in long strokes from the receiver's head to feet. Stroke first from head to torso several times, then from torso to legs, and legs to feet. Your hands are in the

Reiki I Hand Positions
Healing Others

The Front—Healer stands or sits behind person receiving healing

1. Hands cupped gently over the eyes.

2. Over the cheeks, healer's little finger rests lightly against ears.

3. Hands under the head—healer does the lifting.

4. Hands rest lightly over the collarbone—slightly below the throat.

The Front—Healer comes to side of person receiving healing.

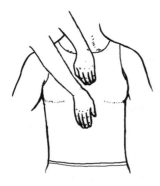

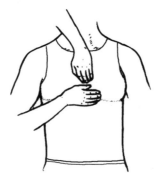

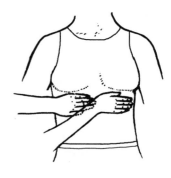

5. Between breasts—optional position. Use with respect not to violate women's body privacy.

5a. Alternate of fifth position.

6. Below breasts over lower ribs.

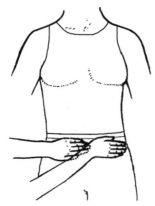

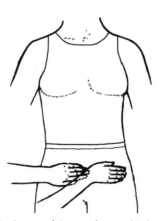

7. Just below waist.

8. Across pelvic area above pubic bone.

The Front—Healer moves further down the side.

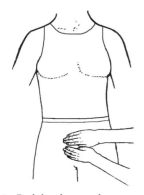

9. Both hands across lower abdomen above pubic bone.

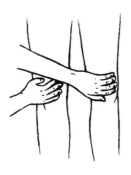

10. Front of both knees.

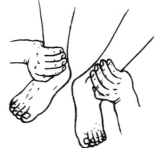

11. Front of both ankles.

11a. Ankle and knee at once. Do both legs. Preferred position—combines 10 and 11.

The Front—Healer moves to bottom, facing feet of person receiving healing.

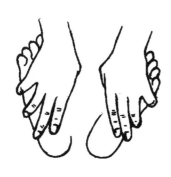

12. Bottoms of both feet.

12a.–12b. Alternate of twelfth position. Bottoms of both feet done one at a time.

The Front—Healer returns to the head of the person receiving the healing.

13. Optional head position–One hand on crown and other hand on back of head (at occiput). Person receiving healing will have her head turned to the side.

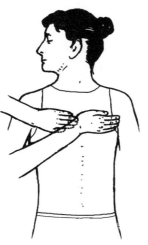

14. Back of neck. (Healer moves to receiver's side.)

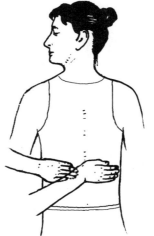

15. Over shoulder blades.

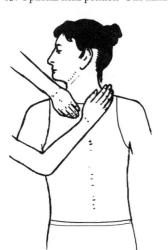

16. Middle back.

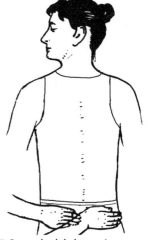

17. Lower back below waist—over sacrum.

Reiki I Hand Positions
Healing Others
The Back

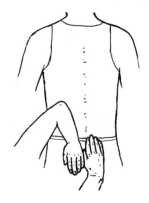

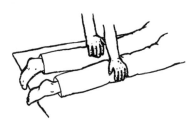

18. Over tailbone (coccyx)—optional position.

19. Backs of both knees.

20. Backs of both ankles.

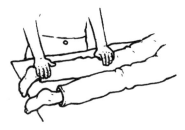

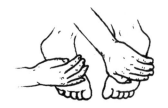

20a. Hold back of one knee and ankle together.
Do both legs.

21. Bottoms of both feet.

Optional Hand Placement Alternative
Optional hand placement alternative for torso and back. Place hands side by side instead of end to end.
Replaces hand positions 6, 7, 8 and 9 on front and 15, 16, 17 and 18 on back.

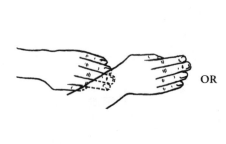

OR

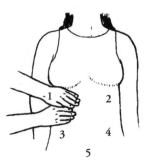

Front

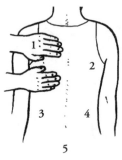

Back

receiver's aura and there is a sensation of flowing water, which she may perceive as well. The aura stroking, especially when done quickly, helps to ground the person and to awaken her fully. She will like the feeling.

Tell the woman receiving the session that you are finished, and advise her to lie quietly until she is ready to move. Do not hurry her to get up. When she is ready, show her how to first turn on her side and lift herself with her arms, as lifting from the neck is damaging to the neck and back. Once she is sitting up, caution her not to move too quickly, just to sit for a while, and bring her a glass of pure water. She may feel light-headed and spacey for as long as half an hour, and relaxed and in an altered state for as long as three days. The feeling is pleasant and enjoyable.

After a healing session, some people begin a physical detox process. This is quite safe, but the woman new to Reiki may need to know about it. It does not happen after every healing, maybe after one first-time healing in six. She may also do some emotional processing for the next few days or a week. Tell her to allow the images to happen, to see them and let them go without resisting them. Most people feel wonderful after a Reiki session and continue to feel better and better. Many of the positive changes in a Reiki healing remain permanently, though long-term difficulties are seldom resolved in one session. After doing Reiki, the healer feels wonderful, too.

There is a sacral-cranial massage movement that can be used with the third Reiki head position, when the receiver is lying on her back. It is called the Stillpoint, and using it has the effect of aligning the entire spine from top to bottom by its energy. No spinal manipulation is involved here in any way, and the procedure is fully safe. If done incorrectly, nothing happens. If done correctly, it can bring someone out of a migraine, stop a headache, relieve neck and lower back pain, align the jaw, and often have the effect of a full chiropractic treatment.

I once used it with a woman who had been in a car accident and had hit her head against the windshield. She was literally seeing stars and very disoriented. Doing the Stillpoint brought her out of it, and she had no further difficulty. I have used it for migraines frequently with wonderful results; it is also excellent for emotional tension. Use it safely even with people who have back problems. There are several ways to do a Stillpoint, on different parts of the body. Most massage therapists are taught

Reiki I

Locating the Stillpoint [9]

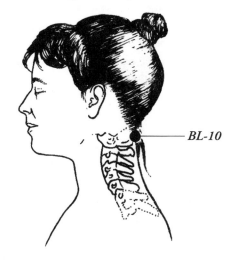

BL-10

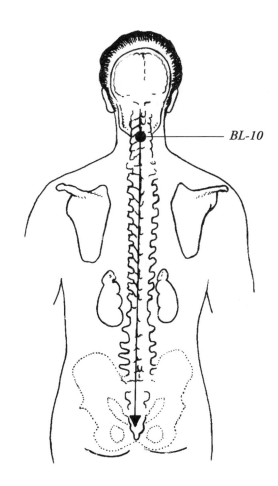

BL-10

the one described below, but they seem to skip over it, not realizing its worth.

To begin, find on yourself the two Bladder-10 acupuncture points. The pair is located on the back of the upper neck, on both sides of the spinal column where the boney structure of the head meets the neck. The points are two tiny depressions in the neck muscle under the skin. You know that you have found them by the strange sensation, which I describe as feeling like a thumbtack in the brain. It is not usually painful, unless your neck is out of alignment or the muscles are tense. Most of the time it will give you only an odd feeling. If you find one point, feel around for the other just across from it. Once you learn to find these points on yourself, try to find them on other people, until you become familiar with them.

When you are doing healing and your hands are under the receiver's head is the time to use this technique. Her head is resting in your palms. First find the points using the index fingers of both hands, one on each side of the neck. The woman can tell you when you have found these points, if you ask her help. It is important to be exactly on the points or nothing will happen. There are many pairs of such points along the line where the skull meets the neck, and most of them work. The Bladder-10 points are the closest to the spine but not directly over it.

Once you have found the points, keep your fingers on them and apply a light pressure. The woman receiving this feels your fingers on the oddly sensitive spots. Then watch her breathing. Placing pressure on the Bladder-10 acupuncture points balances the spinal fluid pulse, which beats at seventeen beats per minute. When that balance occurs, the woman's heartbeat, pulse rate and breathing become synchronized for a while. You know this by the woman's breath rate: at the start she is breathing normally, with a rhythmic up and down motion of her chest.

When the Stillpoint synchronization is reached—it may take a moment or several minutes—she may first sigh deeply, then her breath rate will drop. Instead of the up and down motion, her chest will become almost still. At that moment, apply slightly more pressure with your fingers to the acupuncture points and pull back on the points gently (about a quarter to half an inch). You may

feel her neck move slightly. This is a very gentle traction, with no force in the pulling. Hold that position steady.

After a minute or two, the healer starts to feel a slight pulsing in the tip of each finger that is placing pressure on a point. You will probably first feel one and then the other, before both points pulse at once. When you feel the pulsing on both sides, release the points and slide your hands out from under the woman's head. The Stillpoint is done; continue the Reiki session. Balancing the energy and the spinal pulse causes the vertebrae to slip into alignment. The bones may move into place. The healer has not done an actual adjustment, but the energy of the Stillpoint and Reiki have.

At the end of the session, the woman experiencing a Stillpoint is more spacey than after a normal Reiki healing. It lasts for about half an hour. The feeling is pleasant, and she is very relaxed, but she should not drive until it passes. Most people cannot do a Stillpoint for themselves, but it is possible. Try placing two tennis balls inside a sock and knotting the end to hold the balls together. Lie on a hard flat surface (floor) placing the tied-together tennis balls under the upper neck. Lean back on the balls for the traction. This may provide the pressure to do a Stillpoint alone.

There are two possible errors in doing this process. If your fingers are not precisely on the pressure points, the woman will not go into the synchronization and nothing else will happen. In the other instance, if you apply the pulling back pressure before the synchronization occurs, the spinal alignment does not take place, either. If you miss the synchronization—the woman goes into it and you do not pull back—wait until it happens again in a few minutes, keeping your fingers on the points. If the woman does not seem to be synchronizing and a lot of time has passed, ask her to take a very deep breath. That may put her into the place where you can apply the pulling-back pressure. Nothing happens at all if you make a mistake doing a Stillpoint. The healing does not occur, but there is also no harm done.

The procedure is of such great benefit to so many people and to anyone with migraines or back problems, that I usually teach it with Reiki I. It is not actually a part of Reiki, though definitely an important part of healing. Because it fits so well with the third head position, I feel it belongs in a Reiki book. A student from one of my classes wrote me:

The Stillpoint healing you did for my TMJ (Jaw Misalignment Syndrome) is nothing short of miraculous. Not only has my jaw stopped popping out of the socket, it no longer clicks when I open and close my mouth. Thank you very much!

The process is simple but it may take some practice to learn it. It is definitely worth the effort.

GROUP HEALING

The healers at Chujiro Hayashi's Reiki center in Japan worked in teams, and this still is an option today. By working with a group of healers, several hand positions can be done at once and the sessions take far less time. The person receiving the energy experiences a very strong burst of it and gets all the advantages of the full Reiki healing very quickly. A healing team that has learned to work well together can achieve many more healings than they could by working alone, and as a team they do the healing almost without effort. The companionship of other Reiki practitioners with whom to do healing is also a great joy. Each person on the team is needed and seems to find her own unique work in each session.

In a Reiki healing team, all the members must have at least first degree Reiki, but teams can include first, second and third degree practitioners. A team can consist of as few as two healers or as many as eight or nine. If there are more than there is room for them to work in, the extra practitioners stand behind the other healers. Each then offers the energy by placing her hands on the shoulders of the healer in front of her, who in turn has her hands on the receiver. So many healers working together for the person receiving it is wonderful—so many people who have Reiki to offer is the way the world needs to be.

To start group healing, one person stands or sits at the receiver's head. She does all three of the head positions—the space is too small for more hands—and she also is the director of the session. There can be as many more healers as there are other Reiki positions, one pair of hands on each position. With fewer healers, divide up the work. With two healers, one does the positions from the head to the Heart, moving down, and the other starts at the Solar Plexus and goes to the feet. If there are three healers, one works at the head, one at the torso, and the third does the leg and feet positions. When there are four healers, place one at the head, two at the torso, and again

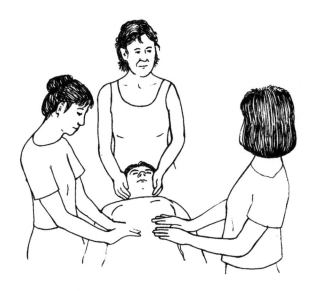

Group Healing[10]

one at the legs and feet. As many healers as can fit around the massage table or bed can participate in the session.

Sometimes in a team of three or more, one person remains at the final feet positions for the length of the healing. She places one hand on the bottom of each of the receiver's feet and remains there through the session. This can be a very interesting position. The healer feels in her hands all of the energy changes of the session as they move through the receiver's body. She may know where the energy is moving and where it is blocked. These sensations do no harm to the practitioner, though if much raw emotion is occurring it is best to stand aside. Keep your hands on the feet, but move your body out of range of the releasing energy. Much psychic information can also come through for the healer at this position. It may include past lives, this-life situations, guided directions on things the receiver needs to know or do, and occasionally diagnostic material.

I was fortunate to begin my Reiki healings in 1988 in a team with two gay men. We went to a hospital AIDS floor to do sessions for anyone who wished them. The healings were highly emotional. We worked mostly with men who were within days of their deaths. The hospital personnel were highly suspicious of us. I learned a tremendous amount about Reiki and group healing in the year that we did this. In one case, we did a session on a man who had had surgery a few days before. The doctors were looking for a tumor, we were told, and the young gay man never awoke from the anesthetic. He was in good weight and in good physical shape, not debilitated by the dis-ease. It puzzled me as to why he would have been operated upon—and why he was now in a coma.

When we did the healing, I had my hands on the feet positions for the entire session, while one of my friends did the head to heart positions, and the other the torso, knees and ankles. As the newest healer, I felt the other two were ignoring me. Suddenly I became aware of what was wrong, and I blurted it. I said, "This man isn't dying of AIDS, he's dying of liver damage. They overdosed the anesthetic." The social worker who had invited us to do the healing became quite upset, and she literally dragged me from the room. "Who told you?" she wanted to know. "It's on the chart, but no one was supposed to know." I hadn't seen the chart. The man regained consciousness during the session. We had met him previous to his hospital admission and he knew me by name. He died that night a few hours after the healing.

In another team healing in someone's home, I was one of seven healers doing the session with a woman who had hurt her elbow in a fall. She was in much pain and had an appointment for X-rays scheduled for the next day. When the healing began, I did not know why she requested the session. As an extra healer and a new Reiki I, I was directed to hold the woman's arm for my position. I did so, and in a few minutes felt tremendous pain coursing through my own hand and arm. This is the only time I have ever felt intense pain doing Reiki. I gritted my teeth and held on though it was very hard to do so, and the sensation finally faded.

Afterwards, I asked her if there was pain in her arm and she told me about her fall. Her elbow no longer hurt though she had been sure the bone was cracked. After the Reiki she could move it. The next day's X-rays showed nothing was wrong. My own neck, that had hurt badly before the healing, was suddenly without pain as well. The entire session probably lasted less than ten minutes, but much can happen quickly in a group session. When there are many healers, group sessions are more beneficial for physical than emotional healing, as there is little time for an emotional release.

The healer standing at the person's head is also the director or team leader of the session. In a group Reiki healing, everyone begins by holding their hands above the receiver's body, over their position or beginning posi-

tion. Who will do what position/s is agreed upon before starting. When everyone is in place, the leader at the head nods and all the healers place their hands on the receiver's body at the same time. The team members then watch the leader as she does her positions, while they also do their own part in the healing.

When she completes her first position, the leader looks to the others to see if they have finished their first positions also. When she gets the silent nod from everyone, the leader moves to the second position and each healer who also has somewhere to move does so at the same time. This continues through the positions. If there is no other position for a healer to move to when the team leader moves, she remains in her place. When the leader doing the head and throat positions has completed her own positions, she looks to the other healers. Once everyone has completed all of their positions, and the leader has received the nod from each, she also nods and everyone lifts their hands at once. With a little practice, the sessions move quickly and smoothly.

The receiver then turns over, and the session is done in the same way on the back. There is an addition or alternative to the standard back positions that works well in group healing, which is particularly helpful if the receiver has back problems. I thank Diana Acuna for sharing it with me; she calls the process "the Big H," and H is for Healing. To do a "Big H," the session's leader remains at the head, placing her hands at the top of the receiver's shoulders. The healers at the sides alternate their hands, placing them in a row along the receiver's spine. Use as many hands as are available. One further healer may remain at the receiver's feet. If there are only a few healers, the woman at the head may complete her position, then move to the side.

The result of so many hands in a row along the body's major energy channel is a tremendous flow of Reiki that moves down the spinal column and kundalini channel. The healers may feel the energy surging under their hands. Sometimes it feels as if the flow moves both up and down, and it can continue to do so for several minutes. Also try placing healers at the head and feet only and sending energy back and forth between them. For the last Reiki surge, make sure the flow goes to the feet.

At the end of this healing, the receiver may take a longer time than usual to return to the present—she will be spacey for a longer amount of time. Combined with a

Group Healing
"The Big H"

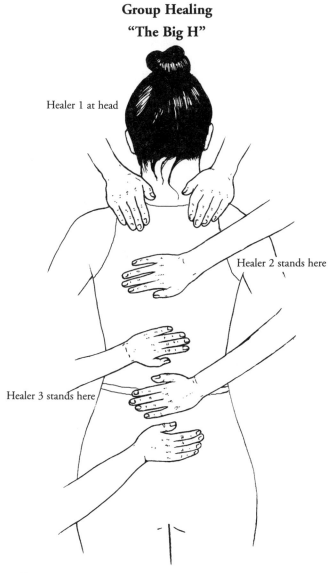

Healer 1 at head

Healer 2 stands here

Healer 3 stands here

Stillpoint, the "Big H" makes a wonderful session for someone with upper or lower back pain, disc problems, sciatica, spinal arthritis, neck injuries or leg pain.

There is one more aspect of group healing that needs discussion, and that is the social aspect. Doing group healings together is a great deal of fun. They can become a regular event by starting Reiki Shares with the healers in your area. To do this, someone with a large enough house invites as many Reiki healers as she knows, naming a date and time. When the women gather, bringing pot-luck dishes and massage tables if they have them, they will break into several groups. Each group does a team healing on each member, so that each person receives a

healing and also participates in several other sessions. When everyone has had her healing, they begin the potluck dinner and the social evening.

Here are some tips on doing Reiki Shares. First, develop a list of interested healers and do a phone tree. One person making all the calls gets tired of it quickly. At the first meeting decide upon a time and date that remains constant—such as the second Sunday of each month at two o'clock. If enough people have large enough living space, rotate the location of the sessions from month to month, rather than holding them in the same house. Decide at the beginning or end of each Reiki Share where the next one will be. Begin the healing early enough so that dinner isn't too late. Many people are made uncomfortable by very late dinnertimes, and some can even become ill from waiting too long. Begin the healing as close to the designated start time as possible.

All the healers in group healing teams need to be at least Reiki I's. People who are not may come only to receive healing, and should be allowed to do so. Where there is a teaching Reiki III at the Reiki Share, I encourage giving people who want it a Reiki I attunement without charge. This is particularly helpful for someone who has a chronic or serious dis-ease, especially cancer, HIV+ or AIDS people. Already attuned healers may like another attunement, too. If a guest wants to join in as a healer, the attunement gives her the tool, and every community needs as many healers as possible to do the work. This may be very much against Traditional teaching, but in the name of humanity and the planet, it is time for it. I also fully believe in giving children the attunement—they are growing up in a very difficult world. Many of them will surprise you with their ability as Reiki healers.

This ends the information on the Reiki First Degree, though the healing itself is only just beginning. Reiki is useful everywhere and every day. Once you begin using it, it becomes so much a part of daily life, that it *is* one's life. There are endless needs and uses for it—small or large injuries, times of stress and emotional upset, headaches, menstrual cramps, chronic dis-eases, sudden crises—for oneself, one's family and friends, and for pets, plants, and even cars and machinery. Remember to do healing for others only with permission. I went to an outdoor concert today, and while I was sitting on the grass with friends, I did healings almost from start to finish without missing any music. Once people know about Reiki, you will be asked often to "turn it on."

Reiki is a Goddess gift and a true miracle. The more it is used the stronger the healer becomes, and the more benefit she brings to herself and others. Use it wisely, frequently, and well, and have gratitude for it. The best expression of gratitude for Reiki that I can think of is to use it every day. I hope, too, that many more people will go on to Reiki II and III, and that this book and the information that follows will help to make that happen. A discussion of Reiki II begins with the next chapter.

1 Bodo Baginski and Shalila Sharamon, *Reiki: Universal Life Energy* (Mendocino, CA, LifeRhythm Press, 1988), pp. 93 and 96.

2 Ajit Mookerjee, *Kundalini: The Arousal of the Inner Energy* (Rochester, VT, Destiny Books, 1991), p. 11. The crown chakra is pictured here above the head.

3 These are as I perceive them. Others may perceive differing colors or give the centers differing names. The term Hara Line is by Barbara Ann Brennan, *Light Emerging: The Journey of Personal Healing* (New York, Bantam Books, 1993), p. 29.

4 *Ibid.*

5 Mantak and Maneewan Chia, *Awaken Healing Light of the Tao*, p. 22.

6 Duane Packer and Sanaya Roman, *Awakening Your Light Body* (Oakland, CA, LuminEssence Productions, 1989), Audio Tape Series.

7 *Ibid.*

8 Barbara Ann Brennan, *Light Emerging: The Journey of Personal Healing*, p. 29.

9 I thank veterinarian Robin Cannizzaro for identifying the names of the points, and massage therapist Diana Grove for explaining the process.

10 Bodo Baginski and Shalila Sharamon, *Reiki: Universal Life Energy* (Mendocino, CA, LifeRhythm Press, 1988), p. 84.

THE SECOND DEGREE

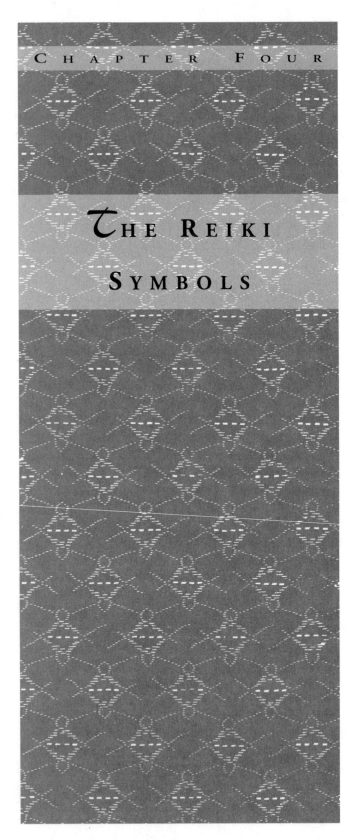

CHAPTER FOUR

The Reiki Symbols

Many people come to me for Reiki III who have little understanding of the Second Degree that precedes it. They have been shown the Reiki II symbols, told to memorize them, and received the attunement, but have been given no other training. One woman said her Reiki II class took half an hour, and my own Reiki II training was similar to this. Some Traditional students were drilled for days on drawing the three symbols, but were still given little understanding of what the symbols are used for or can do. By the time these people reach me for Reiki III, they have forgotten how to draw the symbols and often even the symbol names. I need to teach them Reiki II before we can go on to Reiki III.

Traditionally, Reiki II's are not permitted to keep copies of the symbols, but must learn them in class. They are asked to promise that they have not made drawings to take home, and at the end of the class weekend they ritually burn the pages they have studied from. Once home they invariably forget. Human memory is rarely perfect, and even those who use the symbols regularly may in time distort them. I have seen at least four versions of the Hon-Sha-Ze-Sho-Nen, the most complex of the Reiki II symbols. If you have ever played the party game of telephone, the message at the end of the circle is very different from what it was at the beginning. By depending on fallible human memory in the passage of time, the symbols risk being lost entirely.

These are some of the reasons I have chosen the controversial act of printing the Reiki symbols and discussing them fully in this book. If this is not done soon, they will be lost forever or changed beyond recognition. While information in a book is not "written in stone," at least it is written in a way that it can be accessed and standardized. I feel also that many or most Reiki IIs have gotten only half of the training in how to use these symbols. Much of the material has already been lost.

I learned from a channeling session by Suzanne Wagner that there were once three hundred Reiki symbols, twenty-two in common use. A total of five remain today in Reiki II and III, though these five comprise a beautifully unified system. The remaining symbols still exist in Tibet in a few libraries in remote monasteries. However, Tibet has been taken over by Communist China, and its spirituality and learning are being systematically destroyed. Most of what little remains is that

54 CHAPTER FOUR

which has been smuggled into India by fleeing monks, but many of the monasteries and more of the ancient texts have been lost forever. Putting what information is available into print is a way of preserving what remains of it.

John Blofeld, in his book *The Tantric Mysticism of Tibet,* describes current Tibetan thinking on its mysteries:

> For more than a thousand years, these techniques…were handed down from teacher to disciple and carefully guarded from outsiders. A few years ago, tragedy struck Tibet sending its people fleeing in thousands across the frontiers. Since then, the Lamas have come to recognize that, unless their homeland is recovered within a generation, the sacred knowledge may decline and vanish. Hence they are eager to instruct all who sincerely desire to learn. In this one respect, Tibet's tragic fate has been the world's gain.[1]

Reiki is one of the endangered mysteries, both because of the Chinese occupation of Tibet and the technique's dilution in Western teaching.

The Traditional argument for keeping even the names of the symbols secret is that they are sacred. Indeed they are, but sacred and secret are no longer synonymous. For people to learn the sacred it must be within their access. We no longer have the luxury or time for years of private study with a learned scholar or guru/teacher. There are few places remaining in the world for the teachers to be trained and few people who can devote their lives exclusively to the sacred path. The tradition of oral teaching no longer remains.

People today are mostly solitary. They learn from the mass media or from books, and this is where the information needs to be found to be reasonably available. The planet and all people are in a state of extreme moral and physical crisis at this time. To change this situation or even to survive it requires spirituality and a key to the sacred, and people must find that sense of the sacred where they can in their own cultures.

Therefore, I am publishing the whole Reiki system as I know and teach it. My teaching methods are modern—they are an integrated energy system that works in an optimal way. I am ending the secrecy to bring the sacred to those who need and want it. This book and the information in it from this point on are a radical act. Reiki II and III symbols, information, and methods have never before been put in print—or not since very ancient Sanskrit times. There will be those who disagree with my doing this and will try to discredit me; they will say that my methods are not Reiki, when indeed they are. I can only ask for their understanding of why I have done it; honest soul-searching must recognize the need. My spirit guides have been urging this book for several years, and its writing is proceeding faster than anything I have ever before written. The words flow as fast as I can type and when I stop at night the flow continues. It's time to put the secrets into print and make Reiki available to all, as it was designed to be.

My training has been both in Traditional and modern Reiki methods, and I will explain any divergence from Traditional teaching as it arises. Where I have diverged in my teaching, it is always because the nontraditional method exceeds both in strength and simplicity the older ways. Some of the changes have also come about through deeper information—understanding why something was done in a particular way or how it was done at the beginning—material derived through study or spiritual guidance. Many times in teaching and throughout the writing of this book I have been told "do it this way" by my guides. I have never found these new ways to be wrong. We live in a world that is changing, and Reiki is changing, too.

One generally given reason for hiding the Reiki symbols and the Reiki II and III teaching is that it may be used for harm if allowed into the wrong hands. In my guidance and experience, and in guidance by others as well, it becomes quite clear that the material cannot be misused. As I stated at the very beginning of this book and as Mikao Usui also learned, the information does not activate by itself. It requires the Reiki attunement for the degree to activate the healing methods and the information. The attunements can be passed only by a trained teacher who has been attuned herself.

Reiki was also carefully designed, and the guides and leaders of our planet's past who brought it here knew what they were doing. Reiki was conceived as a mistake-proof healing system. If it is used for other than positive means, nothing happens and no harm can occur. Remember too that energy is a neutral force—fire can cook dinner or burn down a city, and energy's intent returns to the sender. What you send out returns to you for good or ill. The intent to harm anyone with a system designed for healing, whether it succeeds or not, becomes part of the karma of the sender. Likewise, as a system designed for helping and healing, the intent to do good overrides any loss of information. By doing your best to use Reiki for the good it was intended, the Reiki guides fill in what is missing.

The Reiki guides are a factor that manifests with Reiki I, but for most people they first become conscious in the Second Degree. These are a group of discarnate healers that take part in every Reiki healing. The Reiki I practitioner is probably not aware of them, but with Reiki II they begin to make themselves known. In Reiki III they are running the whole show! While only a few of my Reiki I students are aware of spirit guides, by the time a student has had Reiki II for a few months she is working consciously with guides in every healing. This was the most major change for me in my own healing work with Reiki II, and it broadens the work considerably.

Working consciously with spirit guidance makes every healing a joy and a wonder. Until the guidance becomes conscious, it may appear to the healer as a heightened intuition. The healer doesn't know "how she thought of it," "it" being a key piece of information for the healing. "It" may also give her a new tool for future sessions or for self-healing. If you don't know what to do in a healing situation, ask for help and the answer will appear or will simply happen. As a result more complex situations arise with Reiki II than in Reiki I. Because of your positive intent to do your best at doing Reiki, you are given all the tools and information you need. If a technique is in error—a symbol is misdrawn for example—the Reiki guides will fix it. Often you can psychically watch it happen.

I have no fear that Reiki can be degraded or used for harm, either through misuse or bad intent. The guides simply will not allow it. I have questioned the Reiki guides thoroughly in many sessions about putting this information in a book and have been given full approval and every help I needed to locate the necessary material. Some of the symbols in fact are already in print,[2] and are easily known and available to Buddhist scholars as well (see Reiki III). Reiki once belonged to everyone. The Reiki guides want it to be so again. The very fact that you are reading this book indicates that they want you to have this information.

Second Degree Reiki, as I teach it, consists of information on three symbols and how to use them, healing karma, distance healing, non-healing uses of the symbols, and contact with spirit guides. I also include in Reiki II the Kundalini/Hara exercises and techniques that are involved in my nontraditional method of passing attunements—they are actually a bridge between Reiki II and III. Along with this information, Reiki II includes an attunement. When I teach a Reiki II class, the symbols are contained in written handouts to take home.

The symbols are the essence and formula of Reiki. They are the keys to using and passing on this healing system. All things profound and life-affirming are simple, and Reiki is an extremely simple method, comprised essentially of the symbols. They are the formula Mikao Usui found in the *Sutras*. Three are taught in Reiki II and two more in the Third Degree. The symbols are readily known in Buddhism, where they are not secret or withheld information. A full discussion of the symbols and the Path to Enlightenment is made at the end of this book. Reiki II begins the use of these profound energy keys and keeps them simple with further information left for later in the teaching process.

It has often happened that after passing Reiki I attunements, one or more people in the class will tell me, "I saw some strange writing." When I ask these people to draw for me what they saw, they usually draw one or more of the symbols. Despite the complexity of some of the symbols, I have had some students draw them all and draw them correctly. These symbols are placed in the aura in the Reiki I attunements, and they are already a part of every Reiki healer. Often the student who draws them before she has seen them in written form will tell me that what she saw looked familiar. When students see the symbols in writing for the first time with Reiki II, many remember having seen one or more of them before. Some students have already started using them. Before you see the symbols visually in Reiki II, you are already channeling them with Reiki energy through your hands.

Once you obtain the symbols visually, they become part of direct sessions and self-healing as additions to it, and the basis for distance healing. In direct healing, you are able to put your hands on yourself or the person you are doing Reiki with. In distance healing, the person or animal need not be physically present. To add the symbols to a Reiki hands-on session, simply visualize them (imagine they are there). Hold them in your mind and they will activate. You can draw them in the air with your hand before beginning the session or a position, draw them on or over the receiver's body, or draw them on the roof of your mouth with your tongue. Use them in this way for direct healing; information on distance healing is included in the next chapter.

The first of the symbols is the Cho-Ku-Rei, the use of which is to increase power. In Reiki it is known as "the light switch." I referred to Reiki earlier as electricity.[3] The light is switched on when you put your hands down to heal. When you add the Cho-Ku-Rei, the light is boosted from a fifty watt bulb to five hundred watts. Reiki II as a whole boosts your healing ability from a 110 current to a 220 power line, and Reiki III takes it from alternating current to direct.

By visualizing the Cho-Ku-Rei symbol, your ability to access Reiki energy is increased many times. You will probably use it with every healing. The Cho-Ku-Rei concentrates Reiki in one focused spot by calling all the energy of the Goddess Universe into the healing. The spiral and pathway shape of this symbol is the design of the Labyrinth, an initiation space at the ancient Goddess temple of the Palace of Knossos on Crete. In the archeology of this planet, spirals always represent Goddess energy.

The arrows and lighter lines on the symbol sketches describe how the figures are to be drawn. *The symbols must be memorized and you must be able to draw them exactly.* I was taught to draw the Cho-Ku-Rei clockwise, moving from left to right, while the Traditional Cho-Ku-Rei is drawn counterclockwise. I have tried it both ways, and many of my students have also, and they agree with me that the clockwise direction increases energy as the symbol is intended to do. Counterclockwise does not.

In any metaphysical or energy work, including Wicca, clockwise motion in the Northern Hemisphere is the direction of invoking and increase, and counterclockwise motion is the direction of decrease and dispersion. In the Southern Hemisphere it is the opposite. Intent is paramount here. Try it both ways and make your choice. If you determine for yourself that one or the other of these directions increases power, keep using that method, as increase is the intent of this symbol. Pick one way and use it consistently.

I have been guided to use the Cho-Ku-Rei counterclockwise on only one occasion. At that time I was doing a healing for a woman who had an abdominal tumor. Though I used the Cho-Ku-Rei clockwise as usual

Second Degree Symbols

Cho-Ku-Rei /cho kü ray/
Increase power

Sei-He-Ki /say hay key/
Emotional

Hon-Sha-Ze-Sho-Nen /hón sha zá sho nén/
For absent healing

Drawing the Symbols

The lighter arrows show how to draw the symbols. They must be drawn exactly and memorized.

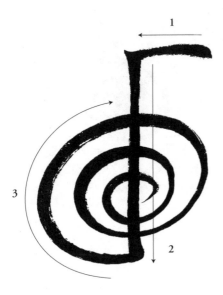

Cho-Ku-Rei
Increase power—"The Light Switch"
(clockwise)

Sei-He-Ki
Emotional healing, purification, protection, and clearing

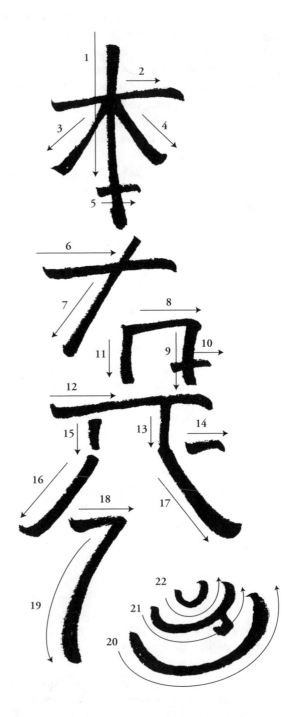

Hon-She-Ze-Sho-Nen
Distance healing, the Akashic Records, past–present–future

through the healing, I was directed to draw it counter-clockwise while my hands were over the tumor area. Since this direction from right to left means dispersion to me, it made sense. It is only very rarely in situations of that type that I have used the symbol "backwards." In using the symbols, intent is extremely important; if your will is for increase, the symbol will give you increase, whichever direction it is drawn in. Doubled Cho-Ku-Reis, one drawn in each direction, are used for manifesting—more on this in the next chapter.

The Sei-He-Ki is next, and this symbol is Traditionally designated for emotional healing. I was taught to use it specifically when someone in a healing session is upset, distraught, or emotionally disturbed, but at no other times. It was defined for me as "God and man coming together," which somewhat offends my feminism. Why not "Goddess and woman coming together" or "Divinity and people"? Another definition might be, "As Above, So Below." The symbol brings divinity into human energy patterns and aligns the upper chakras.

It is interesting to note that I have seen fewer variations and versions of the Sei-He-Ki than of the other symbols. There is only one alternative drawing style that elongates it. Although there are fewer versions of this symbol, there is more divergence in the uses. The symbol is Traditionally described for mental level healing as well as emotional healing, but I feel that this is in error. It is the Hon-Sha-Ze-Sho-Nen that targets the mental body. There is further material on the symbols later on in this book which will make this distinction clearer.

The more healing work I do, the more certain it becomes that virtually all physical level dis-ease has an emotional coordinate. Whether the emotional state or past emotional trauma causes the dis-ease, as Louise Hay and Alice Steadman posit, or the dis-ease itself brings about the emotion and mind-set is irrelevant. The point is that dis-ease and painful emotions go together, and healing the dis-ease means also healing the emotions that go with it. Human life is filled with emotional pain and with traumas large and small, and most people are taught that expressing their feelings is inappropriate. Instead of allowing oneself to feel the pain and then release it, the emotions get stuck inside. Where pain remains within and has no other release, it manifests as physical illness.

Reiki energy goes to where healing is needed, to every level of the physical, emotional, mental, and spiri-tual bodies. By using the Sei-He-Ki, the emotional aspect is specifically addressed and this is often the key to the healing. A painful emotion or trauma that has been held within is brought to the surface. The receiver of the healing reconnects with the pain long enough to finish it and let it go. With the emotion released, the physical dis-ease often vanishes. Anger, frustration, fear, grief, and loneliness are more often the source of human dis-ease than any bacteria, virus, or organic malfunction. With this in mind, I use the Sei-He-Ki with most healings.

Like people, animals manifest dis-ease as a way of handling emotions they cannot otherwise release. They feel and experience the same emotions that humans do, but they do not have the same levels of understanding and control of their lives as humans do, Therefore, pets have increased frustration and fear. A dog or cat that is particularly bonded to her person may also manifest the person's dis-ease or emotions, sacrificing herself in the process. Pets take upon themselves the job of clearing their people and homes of disturbing energy. If the family is in crisis, the animal picks it up and may not be strong enough to transform it. The Sei-He-Ki is as helpful for animals' emotional pain as for humans', releasing it so dis-ease can heal.

In the healing situation or out of it, the Sei-He-Ki has further uses. It can be invoked for protection and purification, to clear negative energy, to release spirit attachments, and to guard a room against negative emotions, dis-ease or entities. I was not taught these uses, and believe they are no longer generally known. This is another piece of information that may be in danger of being lost. Discussion of these uses, and others for the Sei-He-Ki, is given in the next chapter. I have focused this introduction to the symbols on their basic uses for hands-on healing, the healing familiar from Reiki I. In that context, I use the Sei-He-Ki in most healing sessions, as a help in releasing the emotional sources of dis-ease.

When the receiver in a healing begins an emotional release, the Sei-He-Ki is highly important. If she is attempting to release emotions but can't seem to speak or cry, the symbol will help. Use the Sei-He-Ki by visualizing it, saying the name in your mind, drawing the symbol on the roof of your mouth with your tongue, or drawing the symbol with your hand in the air or over the receiver's body. It can be drawn on the receiver's Crown at the start of a healing, if you know that emotional issues are primary to begin with.

Invoking the Sei-He-Ki focuses Reiki energy on the emotional body, and intensifies its effects. It helps the receiver to target the emotions specific to her needs for that healing, and to release them as quickly and easily as possible. Use the symbol once at the beginning of the healing, and/or at the time it appears to be needed. If your intuition doesn't remind you of the Sei-He-Ki at all, assume it is not needed for that healing.

A.J. Mackenzie Clay, in his book *The Challenge to Teach Reiki* (New Dimensions, 1992) put the Sei-He-Ki in print for probably the first time. His drawing matches the visual representation that I was taught. Clay describes the Sei-He-Ki as "activating the Source within."[4] He also defines it as awakening and purifying the kundalini, repatterning the brain, and healing the mind-body connection through the subconscious. In his next Reiki book, *One Step Forward for Reiki,* Clay shows the symbol paired, two Sei-He-Ki symbols facing each other and drawn upside down. He feels that this use of the symbol integrates the left and right halves of the brain.[6]

A version of the Hon-Sha-Ze-Sho-Nen has also been published by A. J. Mackenzie Clay in *The Challenge to Teach Reiki* (page 9). This is the symbol with the most variations and versions, perhaps because of its complexity to remember and draw. Like the other Reiki symbols, it is written in Japanese and meant to transmit a picture. The Hon-Sha-Ze-Sho-Nen appears in the shape of a tall pyramid, and resembles the human body. It is also known in English as "The Pagoda," but the older "Stupa"—a Tantric Buddhist representation of the chakras or five elements in statue or building form[7]—is probably more correct. I have learned that the symbol spells a sentence that translates to mean, "No past, no present, no future."

Most healers are taught only that this symbol is for distance healing. This is true, but is just the beginning of the uses for this very powerful figure. The Hon-Sha-Ze-Sho-Nen is the energy that transmits Reiki healing across distance, space and time. It is always used in distance or absentee healing, and also is used for healing in a hands-on way—both for others and oneself. The most intensive use of the symbol is in direct healing sessions. In scope, this is the most powerful and complex of the Reiki II energy keys and perhaps of any of the Reiki III symbols as well.

Doubled Symbols

Cho-Ku-Rei
clockwise

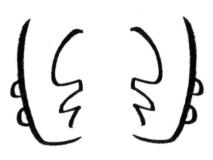

Sei-He-Ki [5]

Hon-Sha-Ze-Sho-Nen
Drawn side by side, one figure slightly behind the other.

The Hon-Sha-Ze-Sho-Nen is also an entrance into the Akashic Records, the life records of each soul, and therefore its most important use is in healing karma. The Akashic Records describe the karmic goals, debts, contracts and life purpose of each soul's many incarnations, including the present lifetime. By use of the symbol in healing, present life traumas can be reprogrammed so that they literally change the future. Past life patterns can be uncovered and released, and karmic debts resolved. All of this happens in direct hands-on healing sessions, usually in a series of healings. The method can be used for self-healing as well.

Here are some examples of the use of this symbol for karmic release, starting with this lifetime. A woman receiving a Reiki session was incested as child, and she is now doing recovery work to heal the damage. This particular woman has done the work long enough that she has a full overview of what happened to her, and this is a necessary prerequisite for releasing her past. The Hon-Sha-Ze-Sho-Nen works with the conscious mind, the mental body, rather than the subconscious that is the focus of the Sei-He-Ki, and is therefore the next step in the process. After feeling the emotions, the Hon-Sha-Ze-Sho-Nen offers people new choices and actions. When doing healing with someone who does not understand the full picture, who may not have gone through the emotions yet, continue Reiki healings with the Sei-He-Ki until she has reached this point.

In the session, the woman talks about what happened to her and her realization of how the incest has affected her life. The first way to use the Hon-Sha-Ze-Sho-Nen here is to draw or visualize it while asking her to describe herself as a child. Next, while continuing the hands-on healing, ask her to go to herself as the child and to do healing for her child-self. Ask her to take the Reiki energy to the hurt little girl, and to tell her she is no longer alone. Continue visualizing the Hon-Sha-Ze-Sho-Nen while this is happening, and probably the Sei-He-Ki as well. The child may ask something of her grown self; have the woman give her what she needs. This sounds simple but can be a deeply moving and powerful healing. The receiver may need a few quiet days afterwards to help her integrate the session.

Then perhaps in another healing, take the woman to her child-self again, this time to the day or evening before the first incest happened. Ask her to describe her day, and

what the child is doing, feeling, thinking. Next, ask her to imagine and describe what that day or night would have been like if her perpetrator had not come into her room. Begin using the Hon-Sha-Ze-Sho-Nen at this point. If she had not been incested that night, what would the night have been like? Ask her to describe it.

Lead the woman further into a new life. What would the next day have been like, if she hadn't been incested the previous night? What would her life have been like six months later if the incest had not occurred? What would her life have been like a year later? How would she have been different five years later? Ten? How would she be different today? How would her life be different five years from now if she hadn't been incested at all? Gradually encourage the receiver to imagine her life as if she had not been incested. This process can be used for any major life-changing trauma.

Once you have brought the woman up to the present, ask her to bring the changes into the present and the future, and make them part of her life. Send lots of Hon-Sha-Ze-Sho-Nens at this point. She may balk and say, "But it happened, how can I pretend that it didn't?" There is no attempt here to deny reality, but to change and heal the mental damage that remains today. Tell the woman, "Of course it happened, but you've just created another reality. Which reality would you like to have for your life?" The woman will likely choose the imagined/visualized one. Tell her then to bring it into the present and make it hers, and then to see her future. Again, repeat the symbol.

At the end of this healing, allow the woman to rest for a longer time than usual. Her whole mental body is rearranging and will continue to do so for probably a week. During that time, she needs to give herself as much space alone and as quietly as possible. She may need to sleep more than usual and should do so if she feels the need. She may see a series of old pictures of her incest experiences moving in front of her at quiet times like scenes in a movie. The way to deal with these is simply to watch them and let them pass, not to fight them or resist. If emotions come with the pictures, they are fleeting. Again experience them passively, they quickly move through.

The effects of this healing are life-changing. With the old emotions released (emotional body, Sei-He-Ki) and pictures recreated (mental body, Hon-Sha-Ze-Sho-

Nen) the woman moves forward in her life. She has freed the incest experience from her Akashic Records and resolved the karma. Though nothing can change the fact of the incest she suffered, the healing has changed the mental pattern and therefore released the damage. New pictures reprogram the brain. The typical incest recovery healing process is long and difficult, and this form of healing can take years off the process. What is perhaps even more important, it prevents the trauma from becoming a karmic pattern that repeats again in other lifetimes.

Sometimes it is patterns left from past lives that need to be released and healed. A woman came to me with severe chronic depression, telling me she had been depressed all of her life for no reason. She had been on psychiatric medications that didn't help, but had side effects. She was presently trying holistic means. In a healing session, I asked her to go to the first time she had been so depressed, thinking to find some early life trauma. Instead, she described being a man in Greece in the third century BCE, humiliated and bankrupt. Depressed, he had thrown himself off a high cliff into the sea to drown.

I began to use Hon-Sha-Ze-Sho-Nen symbols. I asked her to go to the day before the suicide and to imagine another way of healing her situation. She said she would have needed a lot of money, but couldn't ask anyone for help. I suggested to her, "Imagine your rich father gave you the money with a big hug." She did, described herself paying her debts and of spending a quiet evening, her reputation regained. Continuing the symbols, I asked her to imagine what her life was like a year later—she was the father of a baby boy. I asked her to describe her life five years later—she was elected to City government.

"What was your death in that lifetime like?" I asked her. "See it without emotion, as if in a movie." She described her death in her bed of old age, surrounded by children and grandchildren. By that time she was one of the most respected men of her community. I asked the woman to bring the healing she had just given herself in that lifetime into her present life. I completed the Reiki session, and again the woman needed several days or a week to integrate the healing. After it, she was never depressed again.

In another session with the same woman, I asked her to go once more to that lifetime and to describe it. She described an entirely different scene than she had at first—there was no suicide, no humiliation, no bankruptcy and no depression. I asked her if there were other past lives where she had been depressed or had committed suicide. She took me to four other lifetimes in that session, and very quickly we changed the scenario for each. Because the primary situation in Greece had been healed, the lifetimes that repeated the pattern healed more quickly. Again, she went through a week's integration process where pictures and emotions surfaced and were released. She allowed herself to sleep more than usual and said she felt "as if her molecules were rearranging."

When we next did healing, I took her back to each of the last session's lifetimes, and again the pictures were very different. I asked if there were other past lives where she had been depressed or suicidal, but no more came forward. The karmic pattern had been healed. A situation recurs until it is released from the Akashic Record in some way. Buddhists describe all reality as an "action of Mind" and that is also their definition of karma. By changing the patterns consciously (in the mental body) once the emotions have been processed (the woman felt the depression and knew it was a pattern), the karma of the situation was resolved and released. This woman's life is very different since the process.

This is a major hands-on use for the Hon-Sha-Ze-Sho-Nen. More information on the basis for it and why it can be done is given in Reiki III. The sessions above are very intensive work, typical of what the healer becomes ready for in Reiki II. She will not be given such situations until she is ready to lead someone through the process. Remember that the method can also be used for oneself. You can do the healing alone if necessary, but doing it with someone else as a guide is more positive. The time for such healing comes only when you are ready to do it. It is important to have as much information as possible about the situation before starting. The emotions have to be processed or at least recognized before healing on the mental level can happen. The woman who has just this week realized that she was incested as a child is not ready yet.

By changing the past and bringing those changes into the present, you also change the future. Each present moment was the future until it reached the now, and then it becomes the past. By changing a past event, the present and future also respond. This creates a domino effect that can be used for great good. When visualizing change in this life or a past life trauma, make very sure that the changes are ones you want to become part of your present and future. Create new solutions only in positive ways, and visualize only positive alternatives. Those who work with mental healing directly or in distance healing soon learn that "All time is now."

The Hon-Sha-Ze-Sho-Nen is also the mechanism for transmitting healing across space in distance/absentee healing work (more on that in the next chapter). The translation of the name Hon-Sha-Ze-Sho-Nen into "No past, no present, no future" gives the key to its many uses. When I was taught Reiki II, I was also told that the meaning was "Open the book of life and now read." Another meaning I was given was the Buddhist greeting Namaste—"The Goddess in me salutes the Goddess in you." However it is defined, the symbol heals the past, present and future in this and other lifetimes. Using the symbol doubled, two images drawn side by side, accesses and heals the future. One figure appears almost behind the other in the visualization.

These are the three symbols for Reiki II, with two more to follow in the Third Degree. The Cho-Ku-Rei focuses on the physical body in healing, the Sei-He-Ki on the emotional body or subconscious, and the Hon-Sha-Ze-Sho-Nen directs Reiki energy to the mental body or conscious mind. In direct healing it is not uncommon to use all three symbols, though this is not always the case. Use the symbols in healing when it occurs to you to do so—if you are not guided to use them in a particular healing they are not needed. If you use only one symbol, that is fine—it is also correct to use more than one. Let your intuition, which with Reiki II becomes strong and clear, guide you. They can also be drawn and placed on or beneath the massage table you work from.

The symbols must be memorized, and it may take some time to do this. They must be memorized in such a way that you can draw them, following the guidelines on the diagrams. Each line must be done precisely in order, and the symbols drawn exactly as they appear in the illustrations. Once you have become familiar with them, even if they have not yet been fully memorized, they can be "sent whole" in healing. Say them by name in your mind and visualize them as clearly as possible, and the symbols appear with every line in place. This happened for me as quickly as a few hours after receiving my Reiki II training and attunement. It took me several weeks to memorize the symbols fully enough to be able to draw them.

I was taught to visualize the symbols only in violet, but I find in healing that the colors tend to change. Whatever pure bright colors they manifest in are correct. Practice drawing them with your hand in the air, using your whole hand rather than a pointed finger. The chakras from which the energy flows are primarily in the palms of the hands. If you have had Reiki II from me or from any of my students, you will have had the Reiki symbols placed in both hands. If you have had it Traditionally, you may have been asked which hand is your "healing hand" and had the symbols placed in only one palm.

While visualizing the symbols to practice them or in healing work, try placing your tongue against the roof of your mouth behind your teeth. This connects the two major Kundalini/Hara energy channels of the body and increases the sending power of the symbols. There is more information on this and more use of this information, in Chapter VI, *Opening the Kundalini*. Reiki works with the human electrical system, and this is a part of it.

I have been shown an interesting variety of Reiki symbol drawings, particularly of the Hon-Sha-Ze-Sho-Nen. When a student comes to me for Reiki III, I tell her to use whatever version of the symbols she is already using. All of the versions work—or as I think more likely, not a single one of the symbols that we have is correct and the Reiki guides alter all of the symbols to work. Intent is highly important in using the symbols. The Reiki guides want this healing to manifest in every way possible on the Earthplane at this time. They help to make it happen in every way they can. If you have drawn a symbol wrong, don't start over—they will fix it. Do not, however, use this as an excuse to memorize them sloppily. The guides do not tolerate laziness, but they gladly support honest effort. As with the Reiki I hand positions, the best way to learn the symbols is to use them.

Always treat the Reiki symbols with respect. They are sacred representations of very ancient energy, and embody the energy in themselves. Traditionally, students are made to promise that they will not show the symbols to anyone uninitiated into Reiki II. I feel that they cannot be used for harm, and they will not activate without the attunements. However, they still must be used with discretion. I have sometimes shown the symbols to Reiki

Alternative Reiki II Symbols and how to draw them
Usui Traditional Reiki

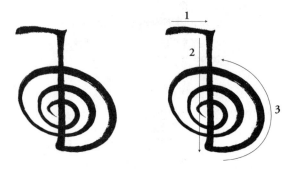

Cho-Ku-Rei
"Put the power here" or "God is here" (counterclockwise).

Sei-He-Kei
"Key to the universe" or "Man and God becoming one."

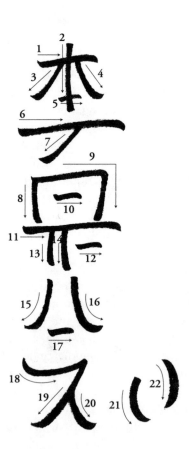

Hon-Sha-Ze-Sho-Nen
"The Buddha in me reaches out to the Buddha in you to promote enlightenment and peace."

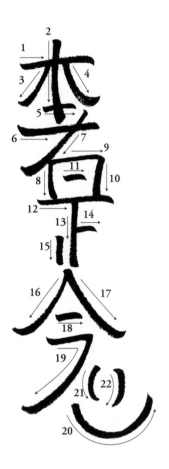

I students who have seen them during attunements. As a new Reiki I, I began to see parts of symbols and asked what I was seeing; my teacher gave me misinformation. Lying about them is inconsistent with healing ethics and is unnecessary. My suggestion here is to show them when it is appropriate and only to people of integrity, but that secrecy is not required.

The next chapter goes further into the uses of the Reiki II symbols. It discusses distance/absentee healing, non-healing uses for the three symbol keys, and working with spirit guides. The beginning healer of Reiki I has now become an experienced practitioner, ready for more advanced work.

1 John Blofeld, *The Tantric Mysticism of Tibet,* p. 9.

2 A.J. Mackenzie Clay, *The Challenge to Teach Reiki* (Byron Bay, NSW, Australia, New Dimensions, 1992, pp. 9–11, and *One Step Forward for Reiki* (Byron Bay, NSW, Australia, New Dimensions, 1992), pp. 38–45.

3 I owe this metaphor to Sherwood H.K. Finley II, "Secrets of Reiki: Healing With Energy in an Ancient Tradition," in *Body Mind and Spirit,* March–April, 1992, pp. 41–43.

4 A.J. Mackenzie Clay, *The Challenge to Teach Reiki,* pp.11–12.

5 A.J. Mackenzie Clay, *One Step Forward for Reiki,* p. 45.

6 *Ibid.*

7 For a series of photographs of stupas, see Pierre Rambach, *The Secret Message of Tantric Buddhism* (New York, NY, Rizzoli International Publications, 1979), pp. 56–61.

8 Version of the Distance Healing Symbol, published by A. J. Mackenzie Clay in *The Challenge to Teach Reiki,* p. 8.

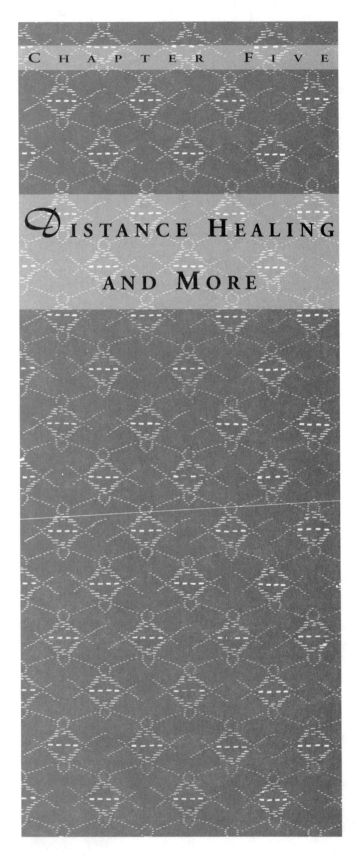

CHAPTER FIVE

DISTANCE HEALING AND MORE

Along with increasing the power and focus of hands-on healing, the Reiki II symbols make absentee healing possible. This means doing Reiki for someone who is not physically present, someone you cannot put your hands on for the session. Doing this type of healing, as simple as it is, opens psychic abilities, and psychic growth is one of the results of becoming a Reiki II healer. Second Degree Reiki primarily works on emotional and mental levels, where the First Degree healed the physical body. Distance healing happens on the mental body level, the conscious mind, as did the karmic release work of the last chapter. If, as the adage by Dion Fortune says, "Magick is the act of changing consciousness at will," then Reiki II is surely magick. It is magick with real results in the world.

The healer who works frequently on this level also becomes aware of realities beyond the physical plane. This is consistent with the Buddhist concept that all reality is created by Mind from the Void. Tantric Buddhist mental training includes the development of complex visualizations, whole worlds created in meditation and inhabited by Goddesses and demons. These become the adept's teachers in a world beyond her own. With the Reiki II initiation, contact with other realities begins, and the healer learns to access other worlds for information and help in healing. The Reiki guides are manifest on this level, as are spirit guides. The Reiki II healer moves beyond the limits of her body.

This expansion and new focus can be something very different for the healer. After the Reiki II attunement, she goes through a profound process of change. If Reiki I changed her life—and it did—Reiki II changes who the healer is in relation to herself and her world. The changes are highly positive, but may be disconcerting. For about six months after the attunement, all of the healer's outgrown emotional and mental patterns are challenged. What is no longer positive is cleared from her emotional and mental bodies; she becomes someone who feels differently and thinks differently than she did before. What these changes mean is wholly individual. They heal whatever needs healing at this level in the person's life, and they come about by expanding her awareness of new realities.

The process of emotional/mental clearing is not always easy. One woman may decide that her primary relationship is no longer right for her and leave her partner. Another may finally deal with the abuse or incest memories that she has pushed aside for years. Someone else may choose to stop working for other people and go into business on her own. Dreams that seemed only fantasies now become daily life, and what were once unacceptable risks become things to reach for routinely. Everyone is stretched by Reiki II, everyone grows. At the end of a year or so, the healer looks at who she was and who she is now. She is amazed to realize that she is stronger and more whole, though the path getting there seemed chaotic. She is pleased with who she has become.

It is best to wait some time between Reiki I and Reiki II training; three months is considered optimal. Learn the First Degree thoroughly, do healing and self-healing sessions, and give your body time to adjust to the new energy before going on. If you learn nontraditionally, however, there may not be time to do it this way. When I travel to teach, I usually offer all three degrees in a weekend. Most of my students have no other access to the training, and many of them do two or even three degrees in this time. Reiki I and II together work very well, as long as the new healer understands and is willing to accept the speed of the life changes that follow.

For the beginning healer who has had no previous background in metaphysics or energy work, it is better to take the training slowly. Three months—or more, or less—may be necessary to make a new healer comfortable and competent with Reiki I. Each person is an individual with individual needs. If the First Degree begins a deep healing and cleansing process, the healer may want to complete it before attempting Reiki II. Traditionally, it is only highly committed healers who go beyond the Reiki I at all.

For someone who has spent years doing energy work of other types than Reiki, who has trained her psychic abilities, and considers herself an intermediate or advanced healer, two degrees in a weekend (or even three) may be fully comfortable. This is someone who is ready for them. Only the individual can judge where she is, and I let my students decide. No one has ever been harmed by Reiki energy, though some may be overwhelmed.

The major teaching of Reiki II is distance or absentee healing. If your mother in New York has an earache, and you want to help her from Florida, distance healing is the way. There are as many ways to do distance healing as there are healers, and absentee healing is not something invented by Reiki. What makes Reiki's use of distance healing unique is the Reiki symbols, as well as some

specifically Reiki techniques. When teaching Reiki II, I go around the circle and ask each person who has done distance healing to describe what she does. If there are eight people out of fifteen who do this type of healing, they will offer eight different methods. All of their methods are effective. Because only about half of each group has ever done healing this way, I will explain further how it's done.

Absentee healing is basically a process of visualization in the meditative state. Visualization also means imagination. To visualize, create a representation in your mind of someone who needs healing. In other words, imagine that person. In the West, such representations are usually in pictures, but this is not the only way. Visualization means use of any of the senses which include sight, sound, touch, and fragrance—taste is seldom used in healing. One way I learned to visualize for healing was in creating roses.[1] Make a rose in your imagination using any of the senses, and give it the name of someone you know. Send Reiki to the rose and watch it bloom, then let the rose dissolve. This is the essence of a psychic or distance healing.

Sometimes hearing how others do distance healing reminds people that they already know how. "I send them energy," one person might say, "Is that distance healing?" It is. Sending energy, sending love, sending light or colors, praying, thinking of someone, and imagining someone well are all distance healing techniques. Lighting a candle above the photograph of someone who needs healing is another method, or placing the picture in the hands of a Kwan Yin or Mary statue.

Most ways of doing psychic healing begin with a representation of the person to be healed. If you have no photograph, use any object that reminds you of the person. You can also make the representation in your mind by visualizing, and this is usually how distance healing works. It takes a quiet undisturbed place to do this, but only a short amount of time. This quiet place is called meditation and is the other half of the absentee healing technique. Meditation for distance healing does not mean a deep trance, only a light state of concentration. Once you are experienced in visualizing, you can do it anywhere, but in the beginning use a meditative space.

This consists of a quiet room with no one else in it where you will not be disturbed. Close the door, take the phone off the hook, and lower the lights. Lighting a candle is a good habit. It is beautiful and creates a soft glow, and in time just lighting the candle stimulates the meditative state by association. Sit quietly in a chair with legs and arms straight, or on the floor in a lotus or half-lotus position, if that is comfortable. Take a few deep breaths to quiet yourself, look at the candle flame, and imagine the person you wish to do healing with.

The person will not appear clearly. You may see a silhouette, a fuzzy outline of the person, light or colors. Any representation gives you what you need. The image will not be photograph-clear. If your dominant sense is not vision, the person may appear as the sound of a cello or the fragrance of lilacs. She may manifest as the familiar feeling of her hug, or her hand on your arm. You will recognize her in whatever way she comes, and the recognition is enough.

Next, you must have permission and this is of vital importance. The ethic for Reiki I was that healing could only be done with permission, and this is no less true for Reiki II healing at a distance. If your mother with the earache has already asked for healing on the telephone, no more is needed. If she has not, and you think she might refuse if you asked her, ask her now "on the astral" of your visualization. You will receive some answer. It may be her voice saying yes or no, or she may turn toward you (yes) or away from you (no). You will know and are ethics-bound to respect her wishes. Often someone who refuses (or who you think might refuse) on the physical plane welcomes healing when asked in this way. Use this method with someone in a coma, also. If you receive permission in the meditative request, proceed. If not, withdraw quietly with love and end the session.

If you are not sure of the answer, send the healing with the clear intent that it be accepted by free will only. Add that if the person refuses the energy, it can go instead toward healing the Earth or to someone else who needs it. Unwanted Reiki energy may be recycled in this way for positive use, while still not violating anyone's free will. To force unwanted healing on anyone is totally against healers' ethics. People and animals have the right to hold onto their dis-ease if they choose to do so.

With permission to continue granted, I next send the person light. I do not designate a color, but let the light become whatever color is needed. All the colors are positive, as long as they are bright and beautiful. Black is positive also in healing, the velvet black of a night sky with stars or of Mother Earth's fertile ground. There are many reasons why someone might need black, and black sent with love and healing intent is never negative. It is comforting, protective and grounding. The color (or no-color) to use less of is white. It is far more effective to send a color that focuses on the receiver's needs than to send white as a blanket for everything.

Some of the colors that appear in distance/psychic healing are not Earthly colors. They are hard to describe in words and as far as I know have no names. They are incredibly beautiful. These are the astral colors that are complementary to each of the Earthplane's basic (chakra) colors. They often appear when using Reiki II for distance healing, and are the main reason that I choose not to designate color when I send light. Naming Earth colors limits what can appear; such naming also may prevent the appearance of the astral complements. I would also rather the person receiving the healing, or her higher self or guides, choose the color/s that are most effective for her needs.

Let the colors fill the person's aura and then send the Reiki symbols. Send them whole, simply by willing their appearance. They seem to fly through space to scribe themselves down the length of the receiver's body. Remember that the Hon-Sha-Ze-Sho-Nen is the symbol that transmits Reiki across space and time—use it in every distance healing. The Cho-Ku-Rei increases the power of the healing energy, and the Sei-He-Ki treats the emotional components of dis-ease. I generally send all of the symbols in most absentee healings. The symbols also take on color, and I choose not to limit this—the color becomes what the receiver needs.

Once you have sent the symbols wait for a moment longer. You may hear a message from your guides or the person receiving the energy with direction to do something more. "Fill her aura with gold," might be one such message. Guided messages are always positive and life-affirming, refuse anything else. When this is finished, visualize the person recovered and well. For your mom with the earache, you might imagine hearing her say her earache is gone. For someone with a broken leg, watch her running happily, without a cast, and with a big smile on her face. Then withdraw from the meditation (dissolve the rose) and return to present awareness. The process takes seconds, a far shorter time than explaining it.

Everyone who does psychic healing has her own methods, and this is mine. No two people who visualize do so in the same way, and all of the methods are correct. The concentration to visualize and meditate comes slowly at first, but develops steadily with practice. The skill is like exercising a muscle—the more you use it the stronger it gets. I tell new Reiki II's to do these healings nightly. Eventually, you will be able to slip into the meditative state anywhere and do healings even on the bus. The more you practice, the deeper the meditative state gets—it is best not to do it while driving.

This simple process of imagining or concentrating on the person, sending her light and Reiki symbols, seeing her well and returning to now has profound effect. Healing done in this way can be as effective as a hands-on session, but takes seconds instead of more than an hour. Note, however, that healing done from this mental level resonates more with the emotional-mental bodies of the receiver than her physical body. Energy at these levels filters down to the physical, but is not focused there. It may take some time (usually a few minutes to a few hours) for physical level pain to be affected when healing is done in this way. In the meantime, though the healing reaches the source of the dis-ease, hands-on work may still be needed.

The person receiving absentee healing, whether she knows about it consciously or not, is likely to feel it happening. If she is very open to energy and psychically aware, she may know exactly what you did and at what time. She may not have full consciousness, but may be thinking of the sender while the healing is happening. She may suddenly feel peace, or see a color, or start feeling better. Her earache may stop at the time of the healing, and it may not return. When you first begin doing distance sessions you may think you are "just imagining it"—making it all up. A few confirmations will quickly change your doubts and give you great respect for the process.

The Reiki symbols add effectiveness and increase the power of psychic healing tremendously. Whatever method of distance healing you use is positive. Continue using it. Just add the Reiki symbols, and it becomes a Reiki healing. Psychic healing methods can be as simple as creating roses, or far more complex. Ask to see the chakras, and the healing can be done by clearing and balancing them. If a chakra is out of place, put it back. If it is "dirty," wash it—visualize window cleaner. If it is bro-

ken, use super-glue. If something is clogging a center, remove the gunk. Add the Reiki symbols to each center, particularly the Sei-He-Ki, and watch them clear the chakras one by one.

Likewise, some healers "see" anatomically and fix what may be wrong, using such metaphors as above. If the receiver has a wound, imagine a needle and thread to sew it up. If she has a broken bone, try "Goddess Tape." Metaphors work as well as imagined surgery can—what is visualized occurs. Make sure to visualize only in a positive way; the image of wellness at the end of the session is a safeguard. Again, use the Reiki symbols over pain or dis-ease areas and they channel the energy to heal the dis-ease.

In doing distance healing, be open to what you see— sometimes things are different from what the healer expected to treat. In healing a headache, for example, the Reiki symbols fly directly to the woman's abdomen. The energy knows where it is needed, let it go without limiting it. Do healing for the person instead of her dis-ease by designating the session to heal Jane, not Jane's headache. This frees the energy to do all the good it can do.

When a healing is done, return to the present and forget about it. Dwelling on it keeps the energy with the healer instead of releasing it to go to the receiver. As with direct sessions, judge the frequency of absentee healings by the seriousness of the situation. For something as simple as a headache or earache, once may be enough. For more serious dis-eases, repeat the healing as often as every few minutes, but between sessions let the energy go. Once or twice a day is usually enough for most non-critical conditions.

By using the Hon-Sha-Ze-Sho-Nen, you can direct the healing to repeat as often as you want it to. You can also tell it to repeat at designated times (once an hour on the hour, or twelve o'clock twice a day). Renew it by repeating the distance session at least daily, however. When asking Reiki to repeat, put a limit on it. Designate the healing to repeat for as long as the person needs it, or until some specific goal is met, or it will continue endlessly, unneeded.

Any of the distance healing techniques can be used when the person is present, too. Do the healing seated across the room from the receiver in cases where a hands-on healing is inappropriate or there isn't time for a full session. Use it when touch would cause pain, as in a burn patient, or when there is a risk of infection to the receiver or healer. Do it for sleeping pets when the animal won't otherwise cooperate with hands-on healing. This is a good method for use with animals in the wild, or with farm animals that are not pets. The same techniques can also be used for healing oneself—instead of visualizing someone else, visualize yourself in the meditation.

Besides adding the Reiki symbols to other ways of doing distance healing, there are four specifically Reiki methods. These are also visualizations or focusing techniques. In the first, imagine that you are there with the person receiving the healing, doing a hands-on session. This sounds simple enough, but is actually the most difficult of the four methods. It takes a long time to do the Reiki positions, and therefore the healer must hold the visualization for a long time. Most distance healing takes a matter of seconds, and unless you are very experienced, an extended visualization of this sort is extremely hard to do. An option that helps might be to grow some extra pairs of arms, like those shown on a statue of Kwan Yin or Tara. This shortens the time considerably, but it still takes major effort. Yet, the few times I have done healing in this way have been very loving and highly effective experiences.

A second Reiki way to do distance healing is to imagine the person/animal/planet shrunk down small. Hold the image in your hands between your cupped palms. Distance healing can be done for animals as well as people, of course, and the Earth needs all the healing we can send her. An alternative to this is to take a small globe, the kind they sell as marbles or key-rings, and hold it in your hands to send it Reiki. A photo can be held for Reiki energy, too. With the receiver's image cupped between your palms, send the symbols and the Reiki hands-on healing. This is probably the easiest of the four methods.

The next two techniques use a focusing object, rather than a visualization. In the first of these, sit in a straight chair and imagine that your knee and upper leg are the receiver's body. The roundness of your knee becomes the person's head, your thigh is her torso, and your hip represents her legs and feet. Do the healing as if your hands were actually on her body, holding her image in your mind while doing so. Use your left knee to represent the person's front, and your right knee for her back.

The last of the four methods is my favorite. Use a teddy bear, doll, pillow or photograph of the person as a surrogate or focus. Do the healing on the bear, then imagine giving the healed bear to the person receiving the distance treatment. Tell her, "Take what you can use from the bear." This method is particularly good if when in asking permission, the response is, "I'm not sure" or "What do you want to do?" Show the receiver on the bear, then astrally give it to her.

I did this once for a friend who had hurt her back but was unfamiliar with healing. She wasn't sure she wanted to accept it, so I did it on a soft teddy bear I keep for the purpose. I imagined giving her the bear and "saw" her holding it before I ended the meditation. This was the last thing at night. The next day I was sitting on the couch reading when I got an image of the woman holding the bear up by the arms. I asked her, "What's happening?" and she said, "I'm taking it from the bear."

I used the bear in healing with her often, until she decided to accept the energy from me directly.

To summarize, add the Reiki symbols to whatever way you already do distance healing. Distance or psychic healing is a visualization in the meditative state that takes moments to complete. There are four Reiki ways to do absentee healing:

1. Imagine being there and do a hands-on session.
2. Imagine the person shrunk small and hold them in your hands for healing.
3. Use your left knee and thigh to represent the front of the person's body, and your right knee and thigh for the back. Do a hands-on healing.
4. Use a teddy bear, pillow, doll or photograph as a surrogate.

The process of distance healing becomes easy with practice and grows strong with frequent use. Never underestimate the good it can do. Remember to add the Reiki symbols to the healing.

I have been told in several different channeling sessions that in the early days of Reiki, everyone had a symbol that was her own. This personal symbol sometimes appears to Reiki II's who use the energy frequently, and often occurs first during attunements. The figure appears again and again, asking not to be ignored. Usually these personal symbols are highly positive for self-healing work. Sometimes they have other meanings. If an energy of this sort comes to you, meditate on it and practice sending the symbol. Quickly or gradually, you will develop a sense of

Reiki II: Distance Healing

Imagine that you are there with the person receiving the healing, and do the healing as if you were. To speed the process, you can also imagine yourself with several pairs of extra arms!

Imagine the person/animal/planet shrunk small enough to heal in your hands.

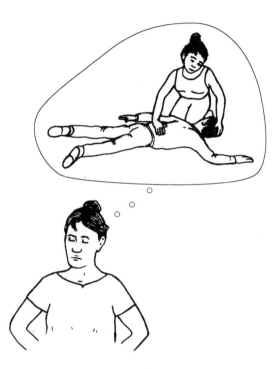

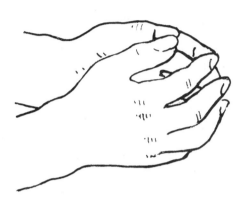

Imagine your knee is the receiver's body, and do the healing as if it were. Focus on the person receiving the healing. Use the left knee for the person's front, and the right knee for the back of her body. Your knee is her head, your thigh her torso, and your hip her legs and feet.

Use a teddy bear, doll, pillow or photograph of the person as a surrogate. Do the healing on the bear, then imagine giving the healed bear to the person receiving the distance treatment. Tell her, "Take what you can use from the bear."

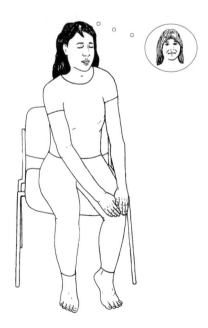

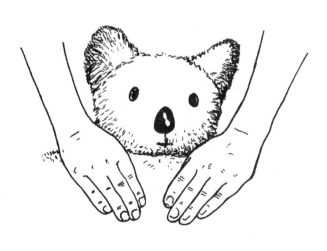

what the symbol is and how to use it. Occasionally, these are not personal symbols, but symbols that are shown in Reiki III.

The Reiki II symbols have more uses than strictly for direct or distance healing. Draw the Cho-Ku-Rei over food to increase the nutrition and offer thanks for the meal—it may have been the first way that blessings over food were done. If you have any doubt about the quality or freshness of the food, do a Sei-He-Ki over the plate for cleansing and purification. This is useful at picnics when the potato salad may have been out too long, but don't depend entirely on Reiki. If something seems questionable, don't eat it. When using both symbols, do the clearing (Sei-He-Kei) before magnifying the energy (Cho-Ku-Rei).

The Cho-Ku-Rei and Sei-He-Ki together also clear crystals. Use the Sei-He-Ki first to clear the stone by holding the crystal or gemstone in your hand and visualizing the symbol drawn over it. Let the symbol sink in and repeat until you know that no more is needed. Then send the Cho-Ku-Rei in the same way, until the crystal is bright and glowing. While using the Cho-Ku-Rei, designate the gemstone's use to program it, as for healing or for protection. A crystal or semi-precious stone can also be programmed this way for healing a particular person. Clear and charge the stone, then give it to the person it is meant for. Other objects than crystals can be used in this way, also. When the use is for healing, I like to add the Hon-Sha-Ze-Sho-Nen to the energies in the stone or object.

The Cho-Ku-Rei and Sei-He-Ki can be used together similarly over medicines—to boost the healing properties while reducing possible side effects. Again, use the Sei-He-Ki first to energy-boost only the cleared and positive properties. With a homeopathic remedy, use the two symbols to increase the healing and decrease or eliminate aggravations. Herbals or flower essences increase in effectiveness by holding the bottle between your hands and sending the Cho-Ku-Rei into them. I make my own flower essences and gem elixirs, and add Reiki into the infusing and bottling process.

There is no more powerful aid to manifesting abundance than the Cho-Ku-Rei. In using it, make sure to be totally positive and ethical in what you ask for, and to ask carefully for only what you really want. The Universe is comprised of abundance, with every goodness available for those who ask and are ready to receive. Receiving is

not easy for most people, especially women—we have been taught that we do not deserve to have or to ask for good things. Of course we do. While many situations of poverty and lack are karmic—and patriarchal—manifesting is a skill that can be learned.

The ethics of manifesting, especially with such a powerful aid as Reiki, are simple and clear. If you must ask for something in such a way that it deprives someone else, it is unethical. You can have money, or anything else you want, without taking it from someone else. If what you deem to be good for you harms anyone else in any way, it is also not ethical. In asking for a job, for example, it is wrong to ask for someone else's job; ask instead for the best possible employment of your own.

Most of the questions in manifesting involve love affairs. You want someone's love, but s/he is in a relationship with someone else. To ask for that relationship to end is unethical, as is "making" the person want you. To ask instead for the best possible relationship for you, without designating a specific person, is the positive way. It is also unethical to ask for or visualize a specific person unless that person agrees. (Then it is wonderful to do these rituals together.) To ignore this is to violate free will and can have karmic consequences, as well as consequences in the relationship and in this lifetime.

One way to positively manifest a relationship is to make a list of all the qualities you wish for in the best possible mate and use the list for a visualization focus. Make the list in the meditative state, as in distance healing. Then take the list between your hands and do Reiki on it, adding the Cho-Ku-Rei. If you are drawn to do so, also place the Sei-He-Ki and Hon-Sha-Ze-Sho-Nen into the list. At the end of the meditation, place the list under a lit candle or on an altar if you use one. Keep the same list for further meditation. Doing this with the waxing moon, from the New Moon to the Full, also adds to the energy.

Another way of manifesting is to visualize yourself in a joyful, fulfilling relationship but not giving the lover's image a name or face. Feel her kiss or hold her hand. Hold the image in your mind and send the Cho-Ku-Rei, or a pair of them side by side (doubled Cho-Ku-Reis). See the symbol inscribed across the image. This can also be done to manifest other things. If you want a new apartment, make a list of what you want. Do not limit your wish-list to what you think you can afford; go all out. See yourself inside the new apartment, with a lease or a key to show that it is yours. Send Cho-Ku-Reis, or doubled Cho-Ku-Reis to the image.

This meditative process can be used to bring into your life whatever you need. Visualize yourself in these images, but bring in someone else only if you are certain it will not violate that person's free will. The Wiccan adage warns, "Be careful what you ask for, you might get it." Ask with clarity. Picture exactly what you wish to have, not what you think you can have. Most people receive too little because they ask for too little. Before asking for something, build a careful picture of it, then ask how it will affect your life.

When doing manifesting work, I like to use an affirmation derived loosely from Marion Weinstein's book *Positive Magic* (Phoenix Publishing, 1981).[2] This is the only book currently available on the subject of Wiccan or metaphysical ethics and is highly recommended. The affirmation can be revised to fit almost any situation; and I phrase it as follows: "I ask for these things, or their equivalents or better, according to free will, harming none, and for the good of all." Using it puts positive intent into any manifesting and corrects any ethical mistakes. It is no substitute for clear ethics, but it helps.

The Sei-He-Ki also has many uses, far more than most Reiki healers are taught. Use it in changing negative behavior patterns and habits—to stop biting your nails or quit smoking, for example. Whenever there are cravings, visualize it. It is wonderful for clearing any sort of energy blockage in direct or distance healing—as in a sluggish chakra or organ. The symbol cleanses negative energy, including spirit attachments. Where the negative energy or pattern may be karmic, add the Hon-Sha-Ze-Sho-Nen.

Use Sei-He-Kis at the corners and over the windows of a house to clear the energy of a room or home. Do a house-blessing by first using the Sei-He-Ki to clear the energy in each room, then place Cho-Ku-Reis throughout the house to bring and increase the qualities of a peaceful home. Some of these qualities to invoke include love, harmony, friendship, prosperity and wellness. Do the clearing outside too, around the house and the perimeters of the property.

Sometimes an older house may hold the energy of someone that once lived there. The person is no longer alive, but her energy and image still remain. This is what is called a discarnate entity or popularly a "ghost." They are souls that are caught in the wrong dimension, who need help in moving on. Seldom negative or harmful, entities can sometimes be mischievous. They may not know that they are dead. Psychically aware people may see them, or intuit that something is amiss. People may feel that they are not alone in a room or that they are being watched—but no one is physically there. The energy of the house feels wrong.

In cases of this type, first thoroughly smudge the house with sage, or sage and cedar incense. Fill each room with the smoke and place Sei-He-Kis in each corner and over the windows and doorways. Tell the entity, "I'm here to help you move on. You don't belong here any longer." At some point, you will feel its presence. Send the Sei-He-Ki to the entity, and invite in its spirit guides, asking them to take the person home. Be gentle and polite. Even if the entity blusters and refuses, it can do no harm. In order to leave the spirit may need to see its mother, mate or a religious figure it believed in. When in doubt, I call in Mary as the Earth Mother to take them home.

Occasionally spirits trapped on the astral plane can enter people's or animal's bodies and manifest as diseases. These are called spirit attachments. As a healer becomes more experienced she begins to encounter them. The process for removing these is similar to releasing entities in a house. The difference here, however, is that these spirits know they are doing wrong and may be afraid to "go home." I ask in Mary as the Earth Mother again, telling the attachment: "Go to the light. Your job is done and now you can go home. You will not be punished, you will be welcomed and healed. Go to the light, the Mother is waiting for you." Use lots of Sei-He-Kis. You will feel the energy release, and the healing sometimes causes a long-standing health or emotional problem to clear.

The theory about spirit attachments is that they have indeed completed a job, having caused the person harboring them to undergo a learning experience agreed upon before incarnating. Now the learning has been accomplished, and the dis-ease or pain is no longer needed. Such entities inhabit the lower astral realms where they are stuck and can go no further. This is not where they belong or need to be. By entering a body from which they will be released in a healing, they find the way to go to where they belong. The person harboring them and the healer releasing them have both done the attachment a service. Many entities are leaving the lower astral realms in this way. Spirit attachments are not something to be afraid of. If they appear in a healing, it is because they are on their way home.

Once a room, house or person's energy is cleared, use Sei-He-Kis for protection. Also use it on your car and for pets. It can be done in an absentee healing. The symbol seals the space or person's aura from encroachment by any form of negativity. If someone has had surgery or other physical or emotional trauma, the Sei-He-Ki can be used to repair tears in the aura from anesthetics, pain or fear. When sealing the aura after clearing spirit attachments or other negative energy, I often am called upon to use the Hon-Sha-Ze-Sho-Nen along with the Sei-He-Ki. Such entities can be karmic attachments, which the symbols can clear fully.

Karmic attachments are situations, dis-eases, or negative energy brought from other lifetimes for the purpose of being healed now. They can include past life emotional patterns, but are usually negative symptoms, habits, or dis-eases from the past. Sometimes they are fixations upon people carried over from other lifetimes. A karmic attachment is not a positive relationship but something that needs clearing so the person can fulfill her life in harmony. Using the Hon-Sha-Ze-Sho-Nen in a healing situation that seems to have no coherent cause can release such attachments, freeing the person from much unexplainable negativity and pain. It is hard to give definite advice here; just go by guidance and intuition. Reiki often releases these things without the healer or receiver being aware of them.

With so much discarnate activity happening with Reiki II, some help from the other side is in order. We were not meant to come to Earth alone; everyone has a series of spirit guides assigned to us for help and healing. The human soul energy is not a single line, but a multi-strand braid like the DNA molecule. When a person incarnates, she is only one strand of the braid. Another strand that remains out of incarnation is a separate entity, and may be the person's life guide or guardian angel. Each soul can incarnate several Be-ings at once, though they rarely meet each other. Other spirits from the incarnated individual's soul group can also act as her guides. This is only a partial explanation for a very complex process.

Each of us has a number of spirit guides. Everyone has a life guide, who remains with her throughout the incarnation. This is usually a guide who helps an individual accomplish her life's work. A concert musician, for example, may have for a guide someone who was once a violinist. My own life guide was formerly an Ojibwa shaman, and he helps to write my books. Another of my guides is Theresa of Avila, who says she was also one of my past lives. She takes care of my body and teaches me healing methods. A guide I call Mother is the Goddess Isis.

Other guides come for a specific purpose and leave when that purpose is fulfilled. Some remain in contact for a long time, while others may stay only for a day or a week. Some guides appear in groups. For the past few years, I have worked with a group of guides that are named Bharamus; they tell me that their purpose is to teach me to be happy. There are at least six entities, males and females with different identifiable voices and images, who comprise this group. Some archetypes are not precisely guides, but may act in that role. Kwan Yin, Mary and Brede all appear in my healings at various times, and they welcome being invited into them. They will appear at need for anyone who calls.

Spirit guides are fully positive Be-ings. Any entity that directs you to do something against your will, or that you know to be wrong, is not a guide. A guide does not tell you what to do and only offers an opinion when asked. They do not violate free will or make your choices for you, or intervene in lessons or decisions. They are instrumental in supervising and overseeing learning processes, providing protection, bringing gifts, aiding your life's work, and helping any work you do for others. A healer always has guides to help her in her healings.

A Reiki spirit guide is assigned to every healer from the time of her First Degree. As soon as the energy begins to flow in a healing, the Reiki guides appear. If they are needed in the session, they take part. By the time a healer receives Reiki II, their presence is hard to ignore. One guide with Reiki I becomes several with the Second and Third Degrees. I have frequently done healings that felt like the room was full of people. Sometimes I see them, and sometimes I only feel their presence. Sometimes the receiver of a healing thinks my hands are still on her when they've long since been removed. Sometimes she feels several pairs of hands, when only mine are there.

Often I am given information in a healing that I have no logical way to know. When such information arises, it is because it is important for the session. I have never found such information wrong, and virtually every time that the message seems "odd" to me, the receiver confirms its validity for her. Most of my psychic information comes by clairaudience—I hear it in words—and since this is my best perception, this is how it is given. It is as if someone who knows much more than I do is standing beside me, offering what I need to be the most effective healer, and cheering the receiver and me on. When I feel their presence, I know that the healing is an important one. Much in the way of emotional release, past life resolution and entity clearing happens in such healings.

For someone who has never worked with guides, meeting spirit and Reiki guides can be a gradual awareness. For a Reiki II healer, it is almost inevitable that she will start working with guides. When in a healing, you hear a voice directing you to "send gold" or "look at her belly chakra," it is definitely a guide. (I once thought the voice I heard was my guilty conscience, and discovered it to be Theresa instead!) They make healing a joy and a wonder, and their presence causes miracles to happen, both in Reiki and in daily life. Personal spirit guides add a dimension to living that needs to be experienced. We were not meant to come here unaided, and by interaction with guides we are no longer isolated and alone.

To begin working with spirit guides, first be aware of them. When you hear that quiet voice, pay attention to it. When there are extra hands in the healing, thank them. At the start of a Reiki session, invite them in—state the request for "all positive healers and guides who wish to help." Once they know you are aware of them, and trying to make clearer contact, they begin helping you to do so. Once you begin to acknowledge their presence and thank them for it, they become more noticeable. Ask to be shown how best you can work with them in healings. In personal meditation, ask their purpose for being with you. Some people hear guided information, as I do. Others may feel their presence, while still others receive visual impressions—you can see them, or see colors or light forms in the room. Some guides come with a fragrance of flowers or incense.

Make conscious contact with your guides in meditation. It is extremely simple to do, and tremendously rewarding. This requires a deeper relaxation and concentration state than is needed for psychic healing. Find a time when you will not be disturbed and work in a very protected space. Light candles and incense if you wish—the fragrance of sweetgrass draws positive spirits and candlelight is a good meditative focus. Cast a circle if you are Wiccan, or make the affirmation that "only positive energy enters here." Go through a step-by-step process of relaxation, clenching and relaxing your body's muscles from feet to head. Once completed, though you feel relaxed already, repeat the process again. Lie on the floor with your knees raised and bent, so your feet make contact with the Earth.[3]

Once completely relaxed, make the following affirmation with your mind: "I am ready to consciously meet my life guide." Lie quietly and be open to what comes. Listen carefully, for the presence has always been with you and is so familiar you may miss it if you aren't completely open. When you make contact—which may happen by sound, vision, fragrance or touch—ask for information. If you hear your guide and want to see her, ask for that. Ask her name, who she is, what her purpose is in your life. There may be several guides present; ask them to come forward one at a time rather than all at once. It may take several meditation sessions to meet them all.

When I first did this meditation, from Laeh Maggie Garfield and Jack Grant's *Companions in Spirit* (Celestial Arts, 1984), I was amazed at how simple and easy it was to contact guides. Three appeared for me the first night, all eager to talk with me. I heard them in my mind and saw one very clearly, with two others only as bright forms. Each night after that I used my bedtime meditations to talk with them and learn more about them. As they told me their purposes, I included them in my life more and more. Two of the three initial guides are still with me. One left to reincarnate, and a second is only rarely present now. The third is Grandfather, the shaman who is my life guide and who works primarily though my writing.

Some years later, I asked to meet my Reiki guides in much the same way. They are a group who were instrumental in the decision to write this book and have fully guided all that comprises it. Many of my questions about Reiki's past were answered by these guides, as well as my ongoing questions on Reiki teaching. When I teach Reiki, I feel it is they who do the teaching and who pass the attunements. In healing sessions they are present and active. Their primary purpose in working with healers is to protect Reiki, and to use it for the best good of all. They want Reiki to be universal again, as it once was before.

If you are new to working with spirit Be-ings, I recommend first getting to know your own guides. Begin with your life guide, then meet and get to know the others who come forward. Do the meditation for meeting guides to open the dialogue and continue it until you reach an understanding of what guides are and how they operate in your life. With this understanding and some knowledge of how personal guidance operates, do the meditation again and ask to meet your Reiki guides. Ask how you can learn to work with them for healing, and any other questions you might have. When doing healing sessions, invite the guides to join in, and be flexible as to how you can work together. Your life and healing work both broaden considerably with this contact. It is a richness not to be missed, a vital part of Reiki and of being a healer.

Only one more thing needs to be discussed in this section on Reiki II, and that is using Reiki for healing the Earth. Our Mother needs us now in ways she has never needed us before. Take time frequently to send Reiki to the planet. One way to do this is to put your hands on any representation of the Earth. Use any type of Earth globe, or hold in your hands one of the tiny globes used on keychains. I have a yo-yo made in the shape of the oceans and continents, and there are blow-up beach balls and stuffed-toy planets. Focus your intent not on the toy, but on healing the Mother herself. Put your hands on the ground and send energy and love directly into the Earth.

Another way is by distance healing. Visualize the Earth from outer space and send Reiki energy and symbols that way. Visualize a particular country or trouble-spot, or group of people, or endangered forest or animal, and send the healing there. Visualize earthquake faults, developing hurricanes, flood areas, and pollution disasters, and send the energy for calming and clearing. There is no end of people, animals, plants and places that need protection, cleansing, energizing, release, or karmic assistance. Pick an Earth Goddess or planetary protector and send her energy and love. Send it also to the people you know who are working for peace, and for planetary change and restoration.

As a Reiki II practitioner, you are part of the healing of people and the Earth. Ability comes with responsibility. In Reiki I you were given the skills for self-healing, and this comes first. With Reiki II, there is a process of emotional and mental cleansing and releasing, and an increased ability to help others. The next step is healing the planet—we are each metaphors of her body. I ask all my Reiki II students to think seriously of what they can do for the Earth, as part of their Reiki II healing work.

The next chapter focuses on opening the electrical system of the human body, and is a bridge between Reiki II and III. For those not planning to take the Third Degree, the material to this point may be all you wish to work with. For those going on to Reiki III, the material that follows is a prerequisite for it in my method of teaching. I hope that more and more Reiki II's will go forward to become Reiki Masters. Teaching Reiki is another way of healing people and the Earth.

1 Amy Wallace and Bill Henkin, *The Psychic Healing Book* (Berkeley, CA, The Wingbow Press, 1978), pp.99–101.

2 Marion Weinstein, *Positive Magic: Occult Self-Help* (Custer, WA, Phoenix Publishing Co., 1981). See Chapter VIII, "Words of Power, The Work of Self-Transformation," pp. 199–254.

3 The following process is from Laeh Maggie Garfield and Jack Grant, *Companions in Spirit* (Berkeley, CA, Celestial Arts Press, 1984), pp. 38–43.

From this point, my methods of teaching Reiki move from the Traditional into the fully modern—though they are not modern at all. The exercises and information that follow are not used in Traditional teaching, but make possible the nontraditional Reiki III information that follows it. I offer this material as part of Reiki II partly because it is a bridge between the energies of the Second and Third Degrees, and partly because the student needs some time to work with it before beginning Reiki III training in earnest. The information and exercises are also vital to understanding how Reiki works, and while this only begins to be a focus in Reiki II, it is very much the focus of the Third Degree.

The material of this chapter is very ancient, going back to the Sanskrit and Tantric Buddhist teachings. These teachings were old at the time of Jesus, and he brought some of them to early Christianity. For almost two thousand years they have been lost to the West and are now being reintroduced as some of the planet's oldest knowledge and civilizations are threatened with extinction and loss. They are methods known by various names in different Eastern countries. I do not know when or how these exercises were integrated to become part of advanced Reiki teaching. Nor do I know who developed the attunement method I use that employs them. The material may actually have been an original part of Reiki, since Mikao Usui seemed fully trained in Buddhist learning and aware of the ancient *Sutras*.

By understanding the energy channels of the body, the healer understands how Reiki enters and moves through her. By working to expand these Reiki channels, she increases her ability as a healer. By learning to control the energy flows, the healer becomes a Reiki adept now able to transmit that energy to others. That transmission is the Reiki attunement process, and the energy exercises of this chapter train your body to carry it. The ability to contain and transmit heightened amounts of Ki and the techniques to make use of the energy are what comprise the Reiki attunements and make a Reiki Master. The exercises of this chapter begin that process.

The nature of this energy and how it moves through the body is the nature of life itself. Channeler Barbara Marciniak, in her awareness-raising book *Bringers of the Dawn* (Bear & Co., 1992) calls the life force energy "Light" (what in Japan is called Ki) and defines it as "information." She states that human DNA, the carrier of

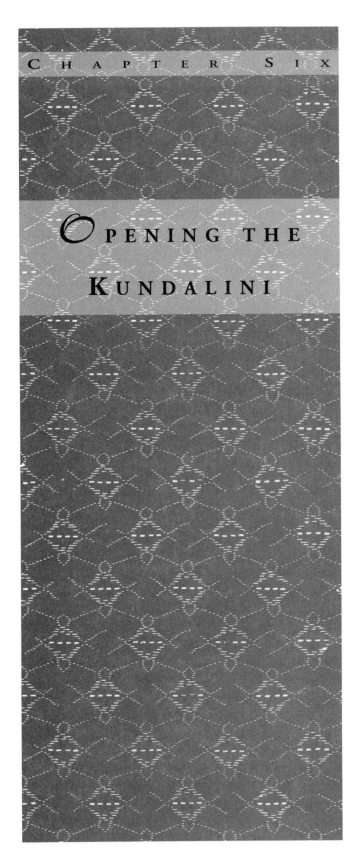

CHAPTER SIX

OPENING THE KUNDALINI

"Light," or Ki or information, was once twelve-stranded where now it is only a double helix strand. In the nature of human evolution today, we are learning to tap into the coded information/Ki and to reconnect with what we have lost. Remember the discussion of the soul as a multi-strand braid in the last chapter. I believe Reiki to be a vital part of that reconnection process.

Says Barbara Marciniak:

> It is time for you to move through the challenges and unlock the history that is inside of your body by allowing the light-encoded filaments to rebundle, forming new helixes, and by allowing yourself to be receptive to what this new information in the DNA is going to plug in to you....
>
> The light-encoded filaments are a tool of light, a part of light, and an expression of light. These light-encoded filaments exist as millions of fine, threadlike fibers inside your cells, while counterpart light-encoded filaments exist outside of your body. The light-encoded filaments carry the Language of Light geometry, which carries the stories of who you are....
>
> As the DNA begins to form new strands, these new strands will travel along a nervous system in the body that is being developed at this time, and memories will come flooding into your consciousness. You must work to develop this nervous system, to pull light into your body....[1]

This energy work of reconnection is happening right now, and primarily happening in those people aware of Ki (or Light) and how to use it. The methods of opening and channeling Ki are very ancient (Vajrayana Buddhism, Hinduism, Ch'i Kung) but being rediscovered at this time, as the need is being rediscovered. Sanaya Roman and Duane Packer are working with the process in their *Awakening Your Light Body* tape series. By opening the Light or Ki channels and learning how the life force works, new information begins to open as well. This new information is the greatest potential for human growth since the Tantric God/dess Shiva brought Reiki to this planet.

The life force (Ki) is being accessed in new ways with ancient methods, and its vehicle for transforming humanity is—as one of its several avenues—Reiki. There is a saying that "There is nothing new under the sun." We are returning home to ancient ways, as the route to becoming modern. Reconnecting human DNA and reclaiming our heritage as Light Be-ings (Light in the definition of Ki or information), is almost a metaphor for Reiki. Returning Reiki to as many on the planet as choose to open themselves and use it, is returning the twelve-stranded DNA and the Ki/Light/information we have lost.

Several ancient esoteric systems—energy channeling systems—are now being revealed for the first time in the West. For the first time the rules of secrecy and mystification are being set aside, as the urgent need for healing of people and the planet grows. Wiccan teachings, Hindu and Buddhist teachings, the early Christianity of the Dead Sea Scrolls, the methods of Kundalini and Tantric meditation, and of the Asian Ch'i Kung are newly available for anyone to read and understand. With oral tradition inoperative in the modern world in favor of books and television, and with a culture that is rapidly destroying its roots, such opening up is necessary for the survival of the learning. It is also necessary to respiritualize Earth people to give their lives value and meaning. Respiritualizing means saving the Earth, reconnecting the DNA, and learning who we really are.

Reiki plays a vital part in this process. The healing system reconnects people with their Earthly and Heavenly Ki (their connection to Earth and the stars), and reopens abilities humans have for many centuries forgotten. Learning the nature of these abilities, what they are, and how and why they happen, means learning the nature of the life force. The ancient energy methods being reclaimed and revised for a new time and culture are the keys to Reiki, and Reiki is the key to transmitting them universally to the Earth. No other method of working with Ki and the Light/information/energy system of the human body is so effortless and simple. Other disciplines take years of study and practice, Reiki takes only an attunement.

While it may not have been important a hundred years ago to know what the Reiki attunement and energy really do in the body, there is an urgency today that requires that we know. By making use of the Ki energy channels and developing them, we also reconnect the missing strands of DNA and reconnect our bodies, minds and spirits. By knowing how and why, we open the way to learning more. Though part of Reiki's magick and beauty lies in its simplicity, the information (Ki/Light) must be available to any who wish to understand it. In writing this chapter, I will do my best to present the information as I understand it.

The first concept is the circulation of Ki through the body. Ki is the life force energy, called Prana in India and Ch'i in China. In terms of Kundalini Yoga (from India), Prana means "breath," but also is defined as "a body of energy acting as the medium for carrying consciousness."[2] Consciousness is the animating force of Be-ing, without which there can be no life. In yogic traditions, Prana is always symbolized by the Mother Goddess, called Shakti-Kundalini, the feminine quality of existence that births consciousness into form. The study of the movement of Shakti-Kundalini through the body is called Kundalini Yoga, and the use of breath to regulate Prana is called Pranayama Yoga. Tantra Yoga is another method of working with the Prana/Ki energy channels.

Shakti-Kundalini in Asia is the Yin principle, represented by Earthly Ch'i. In Japan and China, the movement of Prana or Ki is based upon intention, the concept that Ki can be regulated in the body and moved by way of mind force. Buddhist teaching states that all reality is created through the action/intention of Mind upon the Void. The "Ki" in "Reiki" is the Goddess of consciousness, the life force energy, and the connecting link between the physical, energy and spirit bodies. The intention to move Ki is expressed when a Reiki healer puts her hands down to do healing—it turns the energy on. A more focused and conscious intention is required to pass the Reiki attunements.

Ki comes from the Heavens and the Earth, and is the enlivening force of Be-ing. Along with Heavenly and Earthly Ki, all people are born with Original Ki, the life force instilled in us at conception. While Earthly and Heavenly Ki are drawn into the body from without, Original Ki is inward, and is stored in the space between the navel and the Belly Chakra, in front of the kidneys (Door of Life), in the center of the body. The Hara is the Japanese name for this storage space. It is called the Triple Warmer in China and the Sacral Center in India.

Both Asia and India describe the energy channels by which Ki (or Prana or Ch'i) enter and circulate through the body. Both systems begin with a primary central channel, flanked by a pair of channels that move energy in opposite directions. These channels follow the line of the spinal column vertically through the body. They branch to become the body's entire electrical "wiring"

The Kundalini Channels and the Chakras [3]

"Ida and Pingala, as they rise from the region of the coccyx, entwine around the Sushumna, crossing from side to side at nodes between the chakras... The same spiral pattern is seen in the double-helix configuration of the DNA molecule..."

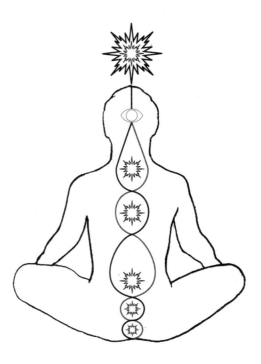

The double-helix configuration of the DNA molecule containing the genetic code of life.

The Hara Line [4]

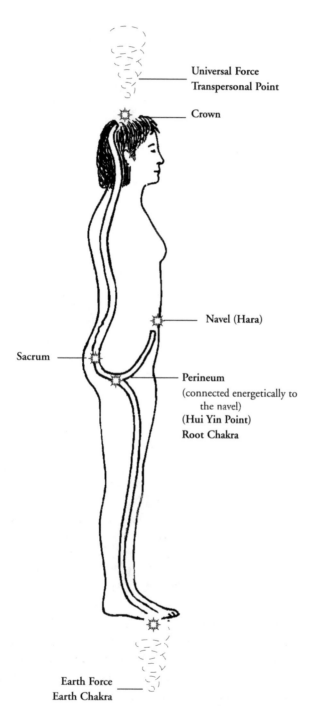

Universal Force
Transpersonal Point

Crown

Navel (Hara)

Sacrum

Perineum
(connected energetically to
the navel)
(Hui Yin Point)
Root Chakra

Earth Force
Earth Chakra

system. India describes the chakras as being rooted in the etheric central power line (Sushumna), and this line's energy is repeated on the bodies beyond the etheric double. There is a chakra system on each of the bodies, on the etheric double, the emotional body, and the mental and spiritual levels.

China considers the paired directional channels to be the main trunk of the acupuncture meridians. Branching from these primary channels are all of the large and small acupuncture lines, what in India are called the Nadis. These are the nerve channels of the etheric body, and they reach into the physical level. Divided further from the Nadis is the physical central nervous system, the autonomic system of the body. The meridians or nervous system channels end in the Seketsu (Japanese word), the reflexology points of the hands and feet. This network of branching channels is the bridge between the etheric double and the physical body, as well as between the etheric double and the higher vibrational bodies. Imagine it as a branching tree, and it becomes familiar as the Tree of Life, a symbol used in many cultures.

The three primary channels in India are called the Kundalini, generally considered to be located on the etheric double. The great central channel running vertically through the body, along the spinal column from Crown to Root chakra, is called the Sushumna. It is the connection between the energies of Earth and Universe, and contains a neutral energy charge. On the physical level, this is the spinal cord and central nervous system. On the etheric double level, the chakras are located along the Sushumna line. The pair of opposite moving channels are known in India as the Ida and Pingala, or sometimes as the Shakti and Shiva. These move in an intertwining path along the Sushumna, the energies crossing at the points between the chakras. Ida is feminine and has a downward movement on the front of the body, while Pingala is masculine and rises upward along the spine.

In China, Japan and other Asian countries the three channels are given different names and emphases to describe the same concepts. The central channel, with the focus on its position beyond the physical and etheric double levels, is the Hara Line in Japan. The pair of energy lines that move one on each side of it are called the Conception (or Functional) Vessel and the Governing (or Governor) Vessel. These are the Great Central Channels that are called Ida and Pingala in India. The Conception

Circuit of Ki in the Body [5]

The Microcosmic Orbit
Small Heavenly Cycle

Front View of the Small Heavenly Cycle

Side View of the Small Heavenly Cycle

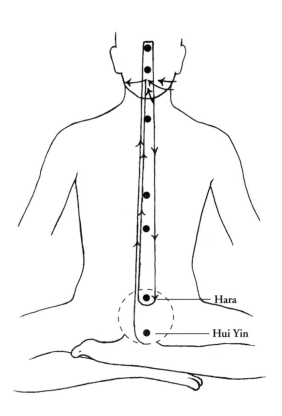

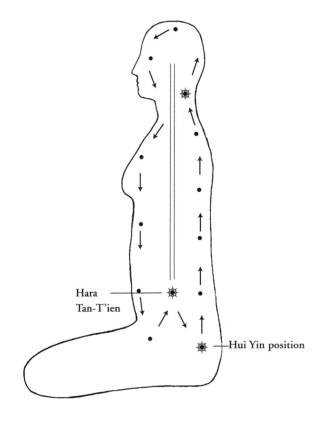

Vessel is feminine (Yin), and has a minus energy charge. It begins at the perineum or Hui Yin point (more on this later), and moves upward through the front of the body to end just below the lower lip. The Governing Vessel is masculine (Yang), and carries the opposite plus charge. It also begins at the perineum (between genitals and anus physically), and moves up the back of the body along the spinal cord. It ends at the top of the upper lip.

Where in India the energy points along the central channel are known as chakras (etheric double), in Asia key acupuncture points are instead mapped along the two central energy flow lines. The chakras are de-emphasized, and are considered minor centers. It is my belief and interpretation that this is because the emphasis of the channels is not placed on the etheric double where the chakras are, but on the deeper Hara Line. The Asian key acupuncture points correspond with the places between the chakras

where the Conception and Governing Vessel (Ida and Pingala) meet in their Ki circulatory movement. These points are also the "new" chakras described earlier, and they and the central channel (Sushumna on the Hara level) form the Hara Line. The movement of Ki or Prana in both systems is described as having a spiraling movement, and a pattern that resembles the life molecule DNA.

The discipline of moving Ki or Prana through these energy channels is called opening the Kundalini in India, and has other names and discipline systems in India and Tibet. In the Asian countries the discipline is called Ch'i Kung (or Qi Gong). There are some differences in how the energy is moved in these systems. Replenishing the life force is the major goal for doing so in Asia, and spiritual growth and transcending the body is the first intent in India and Tibet. In India, the process is that of moving the Prana energy upwards from the Root to the

Circuit of Ki in the Body, [6] (continued)
The Microcosmic Orbit (The Great Heavenly Cycle)
The tongue touches the roof of the palate to complete the circuit of the Governor and Functional channels

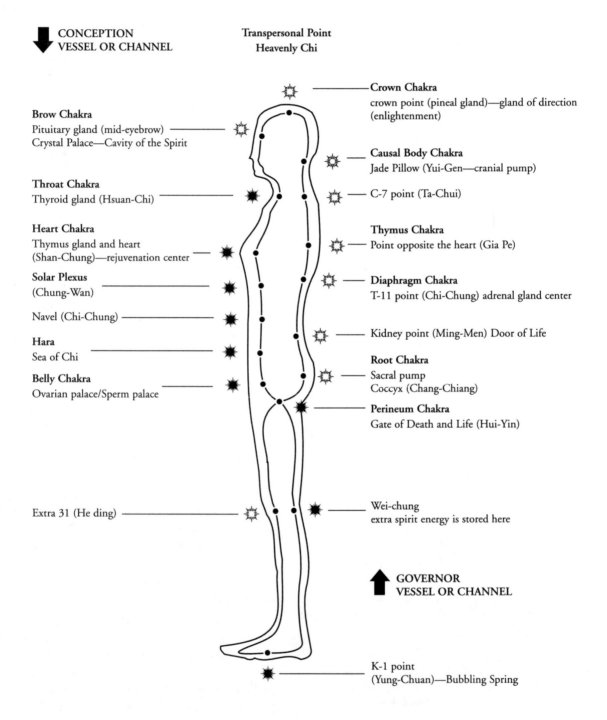

CONCEPTION VESSEL OR CHANNEL

Transpersonal Point
Heavenly Chi

Crown Chakra
crown point (pineal gland)—gland of direction (enlightenment)

Brow Chakra
Pituitary gland (mid-eyebrow)
Crystal Palace—Cavity of the Spirit

Causal Body Chakra
Jade Pillow (Yui-Gen—cranial pump)

C-7 point (Ta-Chui)

Throat Chakra
Thyroid gland (Hsuan-Chi)

Heart Chakra
Thymus gland and heart
(Shan-Chung)—rejuvenation center

Thymus Chakra
Point opposite the heart (Gia Pe)

Solar Plexus
(Chung-Wan)

Diaphragm Chakra
T-11 point (Chi-Chung) adrenal gland center

Navel (Chi-Chung)

Kidney point (Ming-Men) Door of Life

Hara
Sea of Chi

Root Chakra
Sacral pump
Coccyx (Chang-Chiang)

Belly Chakra
Ovarian palace/Sperm palace

Perineum Chakra
Gate of Death and Life (Hui-Yin)

Extra 31 (He ding)

Wei-chung
extra spirit energy is stored here

GOVERNOR VESSEL OR CHANNEL

K-1 point
(Yung-Chuan)—Bubbling Spring

Earth Chakra

Energy Flow through the Hara Line

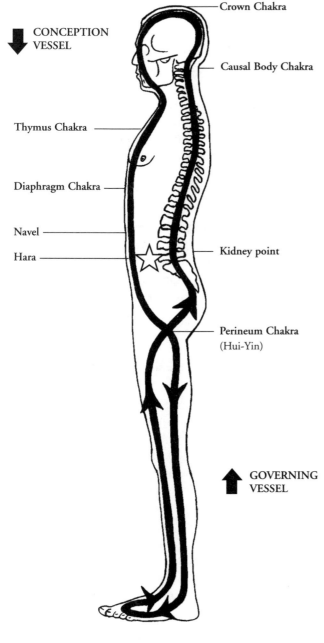

Transpersonal Point
Heavenly Chi

Crown Chakra

CONCEPTION
VESSEL

Causal Body Chakra

Thymus Chakra

Diaphragm Chakra

Navel

Hara

Kidney point

Perineum Chakra
(Hui-Yin)

GOVERNING
VESSEL

Earth Chakra
Earthly Ki

Crown chakras. Once Shakti and Shiva meet at the Crown, the energy is expected to release from the Crown or return along the pathway by which it came. In Asia, the downward path is given as much attention as the upward movement. This results in less negative symptoms caused by the backlash of more energy than the body can handle.

Unawakened Kundalini rests at the base of the spine, coiled in a spiraled serpent form, She is Kundalini Shakti—power consciousness. When she awakens, she rises along the Sushumna through the chakras to unite above the Crown chakra with Shiva—pure consciousness. The union is described as bliss and is the transcendence of the body and the fusion of Earth with heaven. For Tantrists, this is union with the Goddess and with the oneness of all life. The duality of the earthplane is resolved into the bliss of union and oneness, "As above, so below."[7]

In Ch'i Kung, where the energy pathway is directed in a circle rather than upwards only, the goal is for using the life force efficiently for health and long life. Spiritual awakening comes later. Practicing the energy circle daily is said to be a cure for almost any dis-ease because it heals energy blockages and weaknesses anywhere in the body, and brings Ki to all the organs. Ch'i Kung works with the Conception and Governing Vessels (the Ida and Pingala), instead of the central Sushumna that is focused upon in India. The circular path results in a grounded ending to each session, rather than allowing a heavy rush of Ki into the upper chakras. This prevents "overheating the brain," emotional problems and hallucinatory experiences, and provides a safety valve that using the Sushumna lacks. By moving energy through two channels in opposite directions, any excess energy is safely grounded or released.[8]

What does this mean in terms of Reiki? Reiki also works by bringing Ki/Ch'i/Prana through the body. The energy moves through the primary channels—the Hara Line, Conception and Governing Vessels—and through the branching energy pathways to the hands. The Reiki attunement opens and clears the three primary channels, and the chakras as well, directing and increasing the flow. It clears and opens the energy on both etheric double (Sushumna) and Hara levels. Each succeeding attunement after Reiki I increases the channels' capacities for holding and transmitting Ki—first in healing and then in passing attunements. It is by manipulation of Ki through the Conception and Governing Vessels that enough electrical energy is held in the Master's body to transmit the Reiki attunements. Reiki is a Kundalini discipline.

With Reiki II, the healer begins to manipulate this energy, increasing her body's ability to channel and hold it. In India, Tibet and Japan the discipline was only one part of the years of training in all the Tantric practices. By the time a Reiki II healer has become experienced with the energy level of the Second Degree, she has reached a place of attainment in her capacity to work with this energy. Whether she is conscious of it or not, the energy channels are open and flowing, and when she does healing, a strong amount of Ki passes through her. When she reaches Reiki III, however, she must learn to transmit the energy at will and become conscious of the process. This is the goal of the Ki Exercises that follow—to increase the body's capacity for holding this energy, and to make the process conscious. Later in Reiki III, the act of Mind and intent are added.

There first needs to be awareness of the energy flow pattern, which Ch'i Kung terms The Microcosmic Orbit. This is the basis in Ch'i Kung for all energy work, and I will discuss it briefly. I have chosen exercises in the Ch'i Kung method rather than in Kundalini Yoga because of the completed energy circuit used in Ch'i Kung which prevents problems from electrical overload and is vastly safer to do unsupervised. A lot of energy can be generated with it quickly, without discomfort or risk. Tantric Kundalini techniques also duplicate the exercises given here.

For serious work with the Microcosmic Orbit, I recommend two books by Mantak Chia: *Awaken Healing Energy Through the Tao* (Aurora Press, 1983), and Mantak and Maneewan Chia's *Awaken Healing Light of the Tao* (Healing Tao Books, 1993). My information on Ch'i Kung is mostly from these sources. The Microcosmic Orbit connects the Conception and Governing Vessel channels to make a completed energy circle through the body. It does so by two movements, both of which are vital for Reiki III. The first is to connect the channels at the bottom (Root chakra) of the body by means of the Hui Yin position, the closing of the perineum. The second movement connects the channels at the top of the body, and this is done by placing the tongue on the roof of the mouth behind the teeth. These are discussed more thoroughly later in this chapter.

The path of energy movement in the Microcosmic Orbit is the beginning and basis of the Reiki Ki exercises. It is done in meditation, similar to doing distance healing, but with the energy focused inward. Begin by placing your attention on the navel or Hara.[9] When warmth (Ki) begins to build at the Hara, move it by mind intent down to the perineum (Hui Yin, Root chakra) behind the genitals, then up into the spinal cord. Stop for a moment at the Kidney point (Ming-Men), then raise the energy/Ki slowly up the spine to the top of the head (pineal gland, Crown). Follow the energy flow, do not force it. Hold this energy at the Crown for up to ten minutes, then direct it downward to the forehead/Brow (pituitary, Third Eye). Flow the energy down the front of the body to the Hara/navel again. Hold it at the Hara until the warmth collects, then start the Orbit again, moving it next to the Root. Repeat the circle several times. Increase with practice to thirty-six Orbits per session.

When you are proficient with the above, include the legs and Earth connection.[10] From the navel, direct the energy flow to the Hui Yin (Root), then dividing it into two channels send Ki down the back of the thighs to the back of the knees. From there it flows down the calves of the legs to the soles of the feet. The K-1 acupuncture point (Yung-Chuan) on both soles is the location of the chakras in the feet. The point is called Bubbling Spring and is the body's electrical connection with Earth energy. Once warmth builds in the soles, move the energy to the big toes, then up the front of both feet to the knees, drawing energy from the Earth through the soles. Continue the flow up the insides of the thighs and back to the Hui Yin behind the genitals.

Return the flow up the spine and divide it again for the arms at a point between the shoulder blades. Send Ki down the inside of both arms to the middle of the palms, the place where Reiki flows from when healing. Concentrate on the sensation, then follow the flow along the middle finger and up the outside of the arms. When it reaches the shoulders it returns to the main circuit and flows up the spine and neck to the Crown again. Continue the energy circuit along the central channel, returning it to the Hara.

When finished with moving the energy, complete the Microcosmic Orbit meditation by grounding it. This is extremely important and must be done at the end of every session, whether you have done one energy circuit or many. With the energy at the starting and stopping place of the Hara, place your fist lightly over your navel area. Rub it in a spiral of no more than six inches width. Women move the spiral counterclockwise thirty-six times, then reverse it to go clockwise twenty-four times. Men move it in the opposite direction—clockwise thirty-six times, then counterclockwise for twenty-four. This grounds and collects the energy, preventing electrical overload and discomfort.[11]

The Microcosmic Orbit described above is the foundation for the two Ki exercises that follow. The exercises were taught to me as part of Reiki II in 1989. I had no knowledge at that time of their origin or of the Microcosmic Orbit, and was delighted to discover them in print while researching this book. These Ki exercises are known to both Kundalini Yoga and to Ch'i Kung, and are considered major practices in both disciplines. They were probably brought to China and Asia from India and Tibet.

The reason for doing the exercises is to increase the body's ability to receive and channel Ki. It requires a much increased energy capacity to pass the Reiki attunements, and the exercises are a preparation for doing so. If you are not planning to take Reiki III training, you may skip doing these—but I hope most students of Reiki will become Reiki III's. The exercises have much in the way of spirituality- and health-increasing value in themselves.

There is one final note before beginning the exercises, and this involves the sacredness of the body. While many metaphysical disciplines work to transcend the physical, it is important to realize also that the body is magickal and sacred. Buddhists believe that the resolution of karma can only be accomplished while incarnated, and certainly Reiki can be done only in body. In this age of the breaking down of civilizations to make way for a healed planet, there are too many things on Earth that pollute and damage the body, mind and spirit. Many of these are unavoidable—we have no choice but to breathe the air, drink the water, and eat contaminated food, as nothing else is available to us.

We do, however, have some control in other things. Many healers believe, as I do, that a smoker or recreational drug-user can never be a fully clear channel for Reiki, nor can an abuser of alcohol. Never do healing or pass attunements when under the influence of alcohol or drugs. These states at any time invite in negative entities and attachments unwelcome in healing. They are wholly negative for the healer. Never do healing or pass attunements when you are angry or more than slightly ill. If you wish to quit smoking or break addictions to alcohol or drugs, Reiki and the Microcosmic Orbit are powerful self-healing tools. Remember that as a Reiki practitioner, you are a sacred channel for the life force energy of the Goddess Universe.

Exercise One

Begin with the meditative state, and start the Microcosmic Orbit. Feel or visualize Ki as fire energy (Raku) and move it from the Hara (navel) to the Hui Yin (perineum), then up the spine to the Crown. Bring the energy down the front of the body to the Hara again. Directions are given from this point that are different for women and men. Do not visualize the Reiki symbols with this exercise.

For Women:

Begin with the root-lock, the Hui Yin position, which will be discussed fully in the next exercise. To use it for this one, begin by sitting on the floor with the heel of one foot pressed against the vagina and clitoris. Use a firm, steady pressure, which can also be achieved by sitting with a small pillow held between the legs, a tennis ball, or even a larger-sized crystal.[12] Place your tongue against the roof of your mouth behind the teeth. This position is the basis for most Kundalini Yoga and Ch'i Kung work, including the Microcosmic Orbit. Use of the pillow is a Zen (Japanese Buddhist) technique. You may feel heat or orgasm from the pressure.

Next raise energy in your hands, by rubbing them together or starting the flow of Reiki, until they are warm.[13]

Cover and press your uncovered breasts with the palms of your warmed hands, beginning to massage them in an up and outward direction. Do this eighteen times without stimulating the nipples, and become aware of the flow of Ki to the vagina, pineal and pituitary glands (Root, Crown and Third Eye). The upward rotation is called dispersion.

Stop with the fingers lightly touching the nipples and flow the energy from breasts, vagina, Crown and Third Eye into the Heart chakra. Repeat the set of eighteen massage circles two to four times, flowing Ki to the Heart after each set.

Then do the rotations in the opposite direction, moving down and inward instead of up and out. Gather the energy into the nipples, and move it to the spine at the back of the breasts. Next move it down to the Kidney Point. Do two to four sets of eighteen circles. The inward rotation is called inversion.

Move your hands from the breasts to the Kidney Point at the back of the body, behind the lower ribs. Massage and lightly shake the area nine to eighteen times, then stop. Do this set of motions two to four times, resting at the end of each set. Feel the heat in the kidney area.

Move your hands again, this time massaging the lower abdomen from the groin to the ovaries. Massage the liver and gall bladder area on the right side under the lower ribs, and the spleen on the left side. Do outward then inward massage motions, thirty-six times for each position. Massage the vaginal area next, to gather in the energy. Pause and feel the Ki expand.

Place the right hand on your vagina and left hand over your Heart center, and draw the resulting sensation of universal love into your heart. Draw in Earth energy and continue the Microcosmic Orbit, ending by gathering the energy into the Hara.

This completes the first exercise for women.

There are more benefits to this exercise than expanding the Kundalini channels. Most spiritual disciplines work in some way to direct sexual energy upward to the Crown. Sexual energy is Original Ki and its loss decreases life force vitality, shortening life spans and reducing optimal health. This energy is lost through menstruation, ovulation and the sexual act. The exercise above recycles this energy, increasing Original Ki for the benefit of body, mind and spirit. Combining sexual energy with heart energy develops compassion, and brings a sense of peace, well-being and delight.

The breast rotations also serve to balance women's hormonal processes, with sometimes dramatic results. Dispersion rotations can cause menopause symptoms to disappear, with the explanation that "the blood is turned back." Women with cystic breasts find that the dispersion rotations may reduce or eliminate the lumps. Doing only dispersion rotations may decrease breast size. Use rotations in the inversion direction to increase breast size, but avoid these if you have breast lumps or menopausal discomfort. For most women, doing both rotations (the

Ki Exercise for Women [14]
Exercise One

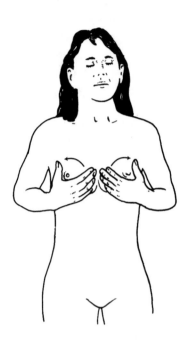

Massage breasts in an up and outward direction.

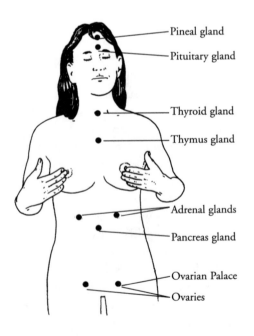

Touch the nipples and bring the energy into the heart.

Ki Exercise for Women [15]

Exercise One (continued)

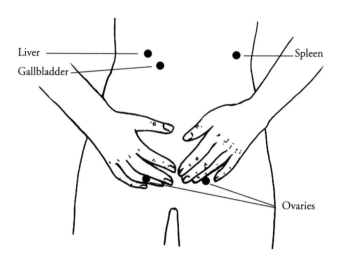

Liver

Gallbladder

Spleen

Ovaries

Massage the groin and waist.

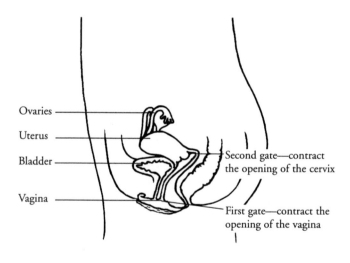

Ovaries

Uterus

Bladder

Vagina

Second gate—contract the opening of the cervix

First gate—contract the opening of the vagina

The Hui Yin position—Gate of Life and Death for Women

same number in each direction) balances the hormones without changing breast size.

Another possible result of doing these exercises daily is the "turning back of the blood" itself. For some women, estrogen levels can decrease enough to stop the menstruation cycle. In esoteric philosophy this is considered positive, as it means the sexual Ki has been recycled, diverted to the Crown. This is probably not reliable enough for birth control in most women. If menses stop and pregnancy is wanted, discontinue the exercises or go to a lower number of rotations (under a hundred per day). *There are no known ill effects from these exercises.* They stop the biological clock and enhance creativity and mental awareness.

The exercise may be done twice a day, morning and evening. Do no less than thirty-six rotations and no more than three hundred and sixty per session. Start with a smaller number and increase gradually.

For Men:

This exercise is also best done without clothing, and begun in the meditative state with the Microcosmic Orbit. Do not visualize the Reiki symbols while doing it, or the Raku (fire energy). To do so causes overstimulation and discomfort. If this happens, return the excess energy to the Earth, and use the Microcosmic Orbit finishing spirals to gather the Ki into the Hara. The Hui Yin position and how to connect the Conception and Governing Vessels for the Orbit are discussed later in this chapter. Also read Exercise One for women before beginning.

Start by raising energy in your hands; rub them together quickly or start the flow of Reiki.[16]

When your hands are warm, massage and lightly shake the kidneys nine to eighteen times. Stop and notice the warmth. Using mind power, inhale into the kidneys, then exhale the Ki into the Kidney Point. Do this two to four times. Become aware of the energy connection between the kidneys and the genitals.

Raise energy in your hands again. Cup the testicles lightly, without squeezing, covering them in your right palm. Massage the testicles eighteen to thirty-six times. Stop, and feel the Ki gather in the testicles.

Hold the testicles in the left palm, and place your right palm over the Hara. Using light pressure, massage with your right hand clockwise around the navel thirty-six to eighty-one times.

Ki Exercise for Men [17]

Exercise One

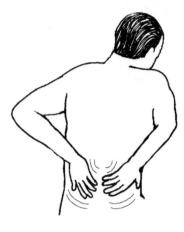

Massage and tap the kidneys.

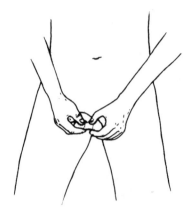

Massage the testicles.

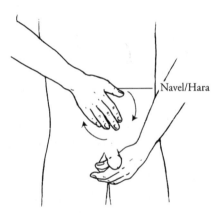

The left hand holds the testicles. The right
hand massages the abdomen clockwise.

Navel/Hara

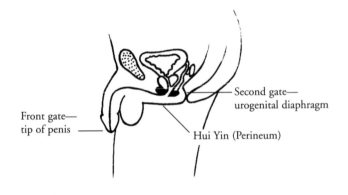

Front gate—
tip of penis

Second gate—
urogenital diaphragm

Hui Yin (Perineum)

Location of Hui Yin position for men.

Change hands and repeat, first raising energy in your hands again. Massage the Hara counterclockwise this time, thirty-six to eighty-one times. The right palm cups the testicles.

Move both palms to cover the genitals. Feel the stimulation in the organs and contract the muscles to gather the energy. Stop and feel the energy expand.

With the right hand on the testicles, place the left hand over the Heart center. Draw universal love energy into your heart.

Continue the Microcosmic Orbit, returning the energy to the Hara, and ending the exercise with the finishing spirals.

There are several purposes for this exercise. The first is in increasing compassion by connecting the heart and sexual organs. A second major benefit is in recycling sexual or Original Ki for longer life and fuller optimal health. The sexual organs themselves are strengthened. Prostate problems, premature ejaculation, and other sexual difficulties may be relieved. Circling energy through the Microcosmic Orbit heals all the organs and balances energy blockages anywhere in the body. Spiritual awareness is raised, and the mind, body and spirit are unified. The exercise also develops a heightened sense of inner peace, security and well-being. It sparks an increase in creativity, mental awareness and spiritual growth.

Exercise Two—The Hui Yin Position

The Hui Yin position connects the Conception and Governing Vessels at the top and bottom of the body. Without this position, Ki moves through the channels in opposite directions, in and then out in a straight line flow. Contracting the Hui Yin allows Ki to move in a complete circuit through the body, and is the propelling force for energy movement in the Microcosmic Orbit. The Orbit cannot be completed or Ki activated without it. This is also the means by which Ki is propelled through the Reiki Master's body to transmit attunements in the method of initiation I use and teach. The Ki exercises are not used in the Traditional Reiki attunement process.

In passing Reiki attunements, the Hui Yin position is one of the major differences between nontraditional and Traditional Reiki. In Traditional initiations, four attunements must be passed to each student in the First and one in the Second Degree. With the Hui Yin contraction, and the nontraditional method that activates the Hara Line, only one combined attunement is required for each degree. Reiki III involves a single attunement in both methods.

While both initiation processes work, I believe that activating the Hara Line to pass attunements is more powerful. Many of my students who have received the attunements both ways have commented on this, and I have felt it for myself. Also, the need to pass four attunements severely limits the number of students per class and increases the length of class time significantly. In order to bring Reiki to as many people as possible, and to teach at women's festivals where there are large groups, the fewer attunements needed the better.

The third reason for the newer method lies in its simplicity. There are four different attunements to learn for Traditional Reiki I, a different one for Reiki II, and another one again for Reiki III. With the method I use, only one combined attunement is required for each degree and it is done in the same way for all three levels. The necessity of learning the Hui Yin position for any

student planning to take Reiki III training is evident. I do not know who developed the method for passing attunements that I use, or who developed it with the Ch'i Kung exercises. Until now, Reiki has been an oral tradition.

The Hui Yin position is another example of turning sexual energy into spirituality, and of activating and replenishing Original Ki. It is a basic feature of Kundalini Yoga, Pranayama Yoga, Tantra Yoga and Ch'i Kung, and I have seen it discussed in a number of books on these subjects. By contracting the perineum, the Conception and Governing Vessels are connected at the bottom of the body. This results in the temporary closing of the Root chakra, or the Root chakra equivalent on the Hara Line. Instead of Ki leaving the body through the feet it moves upward, and sexual energy is diverted to the Crown.

In Kundalini Yoga, the position is known as the Root Lock or Moolbond. Placing pressure on the vagina as described in the first Ki exercise creates a posture called Siddhasana, the posture of accomplishment. It is considered the optimal meditation position for spiritual growth.[18] The pressure is made by placing the heel of the foot (or a pillow or other object) against the vagina or anus, or the perineum in between them. The closing of the Hui Yin (perineum point) brings Earthly Ki upward into the Hara, while at the same time drawing Heavenly Ki downward to the Hara, as well. When the two energies meet, they generate heat that moves to the base of the spine (coccyx, Root chakra), releasing Kundalini energy.[19]

Exercise Two teaches the student to contact the Hui Yin without external pressure, closing the perineum by muscular contraction. This is necessary, because it must be employed in passing the attunements while the Reiki Master/Teacher is standing and moving around. The position is absolutely necessary for passing Reiki attunements in the nontraditional method I teach. Also note, however, that for the student with handicaps that prevent her from using it, the Reiki guides intervene and the attunements may still be passed correctly.

First locate the physical muscles involved. They are between the genitals and the anus on both women and men, and are an acupuncture point known as CV-1 (Conception Vessel-1). They are the place of the episiotomy in childbirth, and of women's Kegel exercises. (Contracting the Hui Yin is a Kegel exercise.) On the *Awakening Your Light Body Tapes*, Duane Packer and Sanaya Roman calls this point on the Hara Line the N'ua

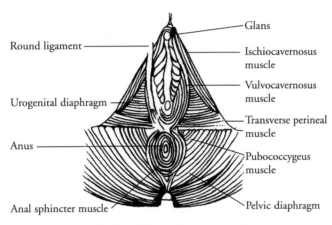

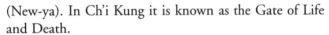

Muscles of the perineum (women)

Labels (left diagram): Round ligament — Glans — Ischiocavernosus muscle — Urogenital diaphragm — Vulvocavernosus muscle — Anus — Transverse perineal muscle — Pubococcygeus muscle — Anal sphincter muscle — Pelvic diaphragm

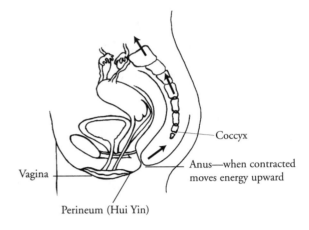

The Gate of Life and Death for women

Labels (right diagram): Coccyx — Vagina — Anus—when contracted moves energy upward — Perineum (Hui Yin)

(New-ya). In Ch'i Kung it is known as the Gate of Life and Death.

The second part of the position is to place your tongue on the roof of your mouth, just behind the teeth. This connects the Conception and Governing Vessels at the top of the body, as the perineum contraction does it at the Root. There are three possible placements on the palate to do this from, but the simplest is the furthest to the front, and called the Wind Position. Only light pressure is needed, just touch the palate with the tongue tip and keep it in place while doing the exercise. This also must be done while passing Reiki attunements.

From a seated position, begin working with these energies. Instruction is again given for women and for men. Do not visualize the Reiki symbols while doing the exercises at this time, wait for the attunement process in Reiki III.

For Women:

While sitting in a straight chair or on the floor, contract the muscles of the vagina and the anus.[21] It is probably easier to contract the anus muscles first; the vaginal muscles will follow. Contract the anus as if you were trying to draw your rectum up into your body. Contract the vaginal muscles as if trying to stop the flow of urine. If you have ever done Kegel exercises after childbirth, for bladder incontinence, or to stimulate orgasm, the exercise is familiar. The contraction happens anatomically in the

Pubococcygeus muscle. When both openings are contracted correctly, it feels like air is entering the body through the rectum. Hold this position for as long as is possible and comfortable, then release. Repeat it several times.

This may be hard to do at first for many women. Practicing develops muscle control, however, and the more you do it the stronger the muscles get. You will be able to hold the contraction for longer and longer amounts of time. Eventually, you will be able to hold the contraction as you go about your day, locking it into place and forgetting about it. Remember, however, that

Contracting the Hui Yin [22]

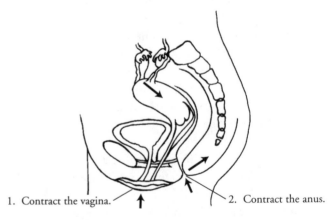

1. Contract the vagina.   2. Contract the anus.

3. Hold the area tight, contracting the entire pelvic floor.
4. Feel energy move to the coccyx and up the spine.

Hui Yin Tongue Position[23]

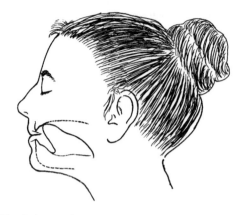

Touch the tip of your tongue against the upper palate.

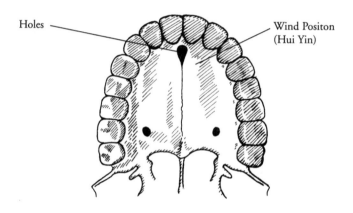

Holes

Wind Positon
(Hui Yin)

you are closing your Root chakra on the Hara Line by doing so. Release it frequently.

You must be able to hold the Hui Yin, your tongue at the roof of your mouth, and your breath as well, for as long as two or three minutes at a time to pass the Reiki attunements. This is the goal of the exercise, to develop the necessary muscular control. Begin initially to do the exercise with the breath held. When the vagina is fully contracted, you will also feel the cervix contract, closing an additional energy gate. Ki immediately begins to move upward in the body along the Hara Line, and energy can no longer move downward to leave the body through the feet and internal organs. Connection is made to Earth energy, which is drawn upward into the Hara.

Next, while holding the Hui Yin position at the base of the body, place your tongue on the roof of your mouth, in the groove behind the teeth on the hard palate. Now the energy circuit is closed and the Conception and Governing Vessels are joined at both ends. You will feel the Microcosmic Orbit begin almost immediately, and this tongue position with the Hui Yin is required to do the Orbit. Now Ki moves from the Crown downward, as well as from the Earth upward. The Hara is activated, and the energy cycles through the body in what feels like a moving figure eight. This figure is also the Egyptian symbol for infinity.

Practice holding all three parts of the Hui Yin. Contract the vaginal and anus muscles, place your tongue tip on the roof of your mouth, and take and hold a deep breath. Hold this for as long as you can. Eventually, you need to be able to do it standing up. Without holding the breath, practice the Microcosmic Orbit while connecting the two ends of the Conception and Governing Vessels into an energy circle. The position makes the Microcosmic Orbit possible.

For Men:

This exercise is done in the same way for men as for women, except that only the anus is contracted.[24] Draw the muscles up and in. The two gates for men are located at the tip of the penis at the urethral opening, and at the base. These are the places where sexual Ki is otherwise lost from the body.

Read the information for women, and do the exercise in the same way.

For men and women, practice both exercises twice a day, the first thing in the morning and the last thing at night. The more use of the Microcosmic Orbit with them, the better. As you practice them for longer periods, a sense of total well-being becomes part of daily life and many physical and emotional problems begin to clear. Doing the exercises releases endorphins in the brain, causing a natural "high." The second exercise is required for passing Reiki attunements, but the first removes energy blockages, increases spiritual awareness, and develops the body-mind-spirit connection. This is particularly true for men. For women and men both, the first Ki exercise may be important for healing reproductive difficulties and hormone imbalances.

I particularly salute the men who are developing spiritually in this era of a changing Earth. Awareness that begins with self-healing is a part of the healing of all men, and a part of making the Earth a better place to live on for all Be-ings.

This completes the information for Reiki II, with only the Teacher/Master's degree of Reiki III to follow. The Ki exercises are a bridge between the Second and Third Degrees. Before beginning to work with Reiki III energy, the student needs to know the symbols thoroughly and be able to draw them with every line in place. She needs to be proficient in doing distance healing, and in using the Reiki II symbols for direct sessions, as well as for non-healing purposes. With practice of the Microcosmic Orbit and the two Ki Exercises, the student is ready for Reiki III.

1 Barbara Marciniak, and Tera Thomas, Ed., *Bringers of the Dawn: Teachings from the Pleiadians* (Santa Fe, NM, Bear & Company Publishing, 1992), pp. 62–63.

2 Earlyne Chaney and William L. Messick, *Kundalini and the Third Eye* (Upland, CA, Astara, Inc., 1980), p. 23.

3 Ajit Mookerjee, *Kundalini: The Arousal of the Inner Energy* (Rochester, VT, Destiny Books), 1991, p. 21.

4 Mantak and Maneewan Chia, *Awaken Healing Light of the Tao* (Huntington, NY, Healing Tao Books 1993), p. 114.

5 Dr. Stephen T. Chang, *The Tao of Sexology, The Book of Infinite Wisdom* (San Francisco, CA, Tao Publishing, 1986), pp. 182–183.

6 Mantak and Maneewan Chia, *Awaken Healing Light of the Tao* (Huntington, NY, Healing Tao Books 1993), p. 170.

7 Ajit Mookerjee, *Kundalini: The Arousal of the Inner Energy*, (Rochester, VT, Destiny Books, 1991), p. 10–12.

8 Mantak Chia, *Awakening Healing Energy Through the Tao* (Santa Fe, NM, Aurora Press, 1983), pp. 6–7.

9 The following process is from Mantak Chia, *Awaken Healing Energy Through the Tao*, pp. 73–74. Also in Dr. Stephen T. Chang, *The Tao of Sexology, The Book of Infinite Wisdom* (San Francisco, CA, Tao Publishing, 1986), pp. 181–186.

10 Mantak Chia, *Awaken Healing Energy Through the Tao*, pp. 60–61.

11 *Ibid.*, p. 59.

12 This position is described in: Earlyne Chaney and William L. Messick, *Kundalini and the Third Eye*, pp. 32–35.

13 The remainder of this exercise is from: Mantak and Maneewan Chia, *Awaken Healing Light of the Tao*, pp. 382–389, and Dr. Stephen Chang, *The Tao of Sexology*, pp. 103–107. I learned the exercise in 1989, as part of my Reiki II training.

14 Mantak Chia, *Awaken Healing Energy Through the Tao* (Huntington, NY, Healing Tao Books 1993), pp. 383–384. Note: I was taught these exercises as part of my Reiki II in 1989.

15 *Ibid.,* p. 385.

16 Mantak and Maneewan Chia, *Awaken Healing Light of the Tao*, pp. 385–389 and Dr. Stephen Chang, *The Tao of Sexology*, pp. 72–76.

17 Mantak and Maneewan Chia, *Awaken Healing Energy Through the Tao* (Huntington, NY, Healing Tao Books 1993), p. 386–388.

18 Ajit Mookerjee, *Kundalini: The Arousal of Inner Energy*, p. 20.

19 Earlyne Chaney and William L. Messick, *Kundalini and the Third Eye*, pp. 32–33.

20 Mantak Chia, *Awaken Healing Energy Through the Tao* (Huntington, NY, Healing Tao Books 1993), p. 113–117.

21 Dr. Stephen T. Chang, *The Tao of Sexology*, pp. 105–106. I have seen this exercise in several sources.

22 Mantak and Maneewan Chia, *Awaken Healing Light of the Tao*, pp. 195, 289 and 291.

23 Mantak and Maneewan Chia, *Awaken Healing Light of the Tao*, pp. 147 and 227.

24 Dr. Stephen T. Chang, *The Tao of Sexology*, pp. 73–76.

THE THIRD DEGREE

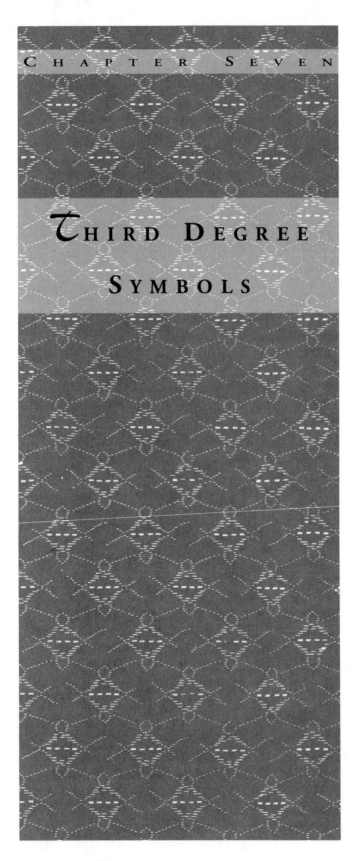

CHAPTER SEVEN

THIRD DEGREE SYMBOLS

The Reiki Third Degree is the most exciting part of this very amazing healing system. This is the teaching degree, where information is given on passing Reiki to others. Some teachers divide this degree into two sections, the Reiki III Practitioner and the Master/Teacher's Degree. The Reiki III Practitioner's teaching includes the Ki Exercises of the last chapter, along with the Reiki III symbols and their uses in healing. Some teachers call this an advanced Reiki II. (Traditional teachers do not use the Ki Exercises at all.) The Master Teacher's Degree includes information on passing the attunements and teaching the Reiki system. In my method of teaching, Reiki III includes all of the above, both healing information and the teaching degree.

There is a great deal of discussion in Traditional and modern Reiki circles as to who should have the Third Degree. In Traditional thinking, the Master Degree should be given only to people willing and able to dedicate their lives to Reiki. The candidate is screened carefully over a period of years, and several years must pass between Reiki II and Reiki III training. The student is not permitted to ask for Reiki III, it must be offered to her by an already initiated and teaching Master. Very few students are accepted for the teaching. Modern-method Reiki Teachers work at lower prices and more frequently teach the Third Degree with far less restrictions.

The fee for Traditional Reiki Master's training is $10,000 in this country, and $15,000 in Canada and England. There are no scholarships or lowered rates for Reiki III or any other degree. The student is required to apprentice with her Master for a period of at least a year. Once she begins teaching, it must be with the Master's presence for an additional period of time, and during that time the Master receives the class fees. She is permitted to teach only Reiki I at first, and then is allowed Reiki II. It can take several years before the new teacher is on her own.

For some time before and after Mrs. Takata's death, it was thought that only the Grand Master could initiate a Reiki III. Her students, though Reiki III's themselves, could teach only Reiki I and II. I have been told by Traditional people that the teachers themselves did not know they could initiate Masters. When the teachers discovered they could indeed make Master/Teachers, many more Reiki III's began to be trained. Hawayo Takata initiated twenty-two Reiki III's in the last ten years of her life (1970–1980). A few years ago there were a total of two hundred and fifty Usui Traditional Reiki Masters in the United States, with about seven hundred and fifty worldwide. There are probably many more now.

Some Reiki III's trained Traditionally have begun to question the cost and exclusivity, and the fees have been lowered by a few teachers. Some have also begun to revise and modernize the teaching methods. The result is that there are beginning to be many more Reiki Masters and that Reiki methods are evolving. My own Reiki II and III training came from such teachers and methods. These Masters are discovering that Reiki brings as much prosperity and benefit at lower prices, and that having more teachers benefits Reiki as well. There seems to be little or no dialogue between the Traditional organizations and modern Reiki Master/Teachers.

According to Phyllis Furumoto in an interview by William Rand, Mikao Usui taught Reiki in a very loose manner and without dividing it into degrees. Chujiro Hayashi developed the Traditional teaching methods and Hawayo Takata set the American payment system. The Reiki Alliance made many more rules after Mrs. Takata's death.[1] Ms. Furumoto, Takata's granddaughter, was named Grand Master by the Reiki Alliance. She states that "as Grand Master, she has no additional Reiki power, no additional symbols, attunements, techniques, and no authority over other Reiki practitioners."[2] Furthermore:

> So often it seems that many Reiki Masters and practitioners are overly sensitive to things like lineage, certificates, and membership in the "right" organization. The important thing is: Do you know within yourself that you are connected to Reiki. If you do, then nothing else matters.[3]

The Reiki symbols were also mentioned in this interview, and Ms. Furumoto recognized the differences today in different teachers' Reiki symbols. She said that the symbols do not have to be drawn alike by every teacher or practitioner; they have only to be recognizable. What is important in the use of the Reiki symbols is their intention. She compared the variants to differences in people's handwriting; no two people write the same. Almost everyone, however, can read others' writing no matter what the differences are.

In my own teaching when students come to me with different-appearing symbols, I show them mine and tell them to use what is comfortable for them. I have seen four different versions of the Hon-Sha-Ze-Sho-Nen and several choices follow for the Reiki Master's symbol. All of the many versions of the symbols work, and work powerfully and adequately. So too for the variant methods now evolving of teaching Reiki. The Traditional system is to be honored for bringing Reiki to the West, and for maintaining it as purely as possible.

Modern teaching systems have their place as well. They help to further adapt Reiki for a very different time and culture than developed it. Remember that this healing system probably was developed in India and Tibet, came to China with Buddhism and then to the rest of Asia, and came to the United States from Japan. The written formula predates Jesus by at least one thousand years. It is at least three thousand years old. The system may have been brought to Earth from other planets to begin with. Reiki has undergone a long process of adaptation and change over several thousand years.

Some (but not all) Traditionally trained teachers and practitioners refuse to accept any methods but their own. They do not honor the Reiki I training of modern-method students who come to them for further degrees. They may even refuse nontraditionally trained healers to join in their Reiki Shares. A few of my teaching Reiki III's have been harassed by these people when they advertise their classes. nontraditional students may be told that they "don't really have Reiki," or have been "taught wrong." If modern symbol drawings don't match the Traditional teacher's versions, the students are told that "those aren't Reiki symbols and they won't work." None of this is true. Such attitudes are certainly against any healer's ethics, and they are certainly "not Reiki" either.

The fact is that the simple Reiki attunement can make a beginner into a qualified healer with an afternoon's class. Healers are terribly needed, and the more healers who can be offered to the planet the better. Everyone is in pain in these Earth change days, and the Earth is in pain. To make Reiki universal again, as it once was and as it needs to be once again, many more teachers are desperately needed in all the Reiki methods. It is not moral to keep any healing system in these times exclusive, and no method is "better" or "more Reiki" than any other.

In my opinion, Reiki teacher's training cannot be restricted to only those people who can dedicate their lives to Reiki. The world doesn't work that way any longer. Few people can spend years of time for long apprenticeships or $10,000 for the training. Depending upon Reiki as a way to make a living is not appropriate for everyone's situation. In my teaching, I offer Reiki III to almost any person of integrity that wants it and has completed the other two degrees. For someone with the dedication, or with exceptional healing talent, I often waive my low prices. I teach about half of my students, perhaps more, without charge. This goes for all three degrees.

There is an ethic with each of the three degrees of Reiki, as I teach it. In Reiki I and II, the simple ethic is to give healing only to those who want it, whether directly or by distance, and not to violate free will. In Reiki III, the ethic is money. Reiki brings prosperity, long life and well-being to all. These are not values that can be bought and sold. While a teacher or healer has the right to make a living from her work, she also has the responsibility to make healing affordable. In my own private teaching I currently charge $75 for Reiki I, $100 for Reiki II, and $300 for Reiki III. When I teach full weekend groups I charge a flat fee or percentage of proceeds far below the private individual cost. I do not personally charge to do healing work, but again feel that healers have the right to make a living. I ask that my students' charges be reasonable, and that there be scholarships.

When I first began teaching, I went through a period of about three weeks of wanting to keep Reiki to myself, of wanting to make money from it and to have the Master status mean more than simple teaching responsibility. I was appalled at myself for thinking in this way, but the thoughts were there. I had always wanted Reiki III for the purpose of teaching as many people as possible at low or no cost and finally could not allow this lack of perspective to continue. After some soul-searching, the mind-set disappeared in a few weeks' time. Yet I have seen other modern teachers with positive intent lose their purpose in just this way, not long after beginning to teach. I tell this now to warn my students that the ego process could happen for them, also. Resist it and remember why you became a Reiki teacher.

As with Reiki II, I offer my students full information (much of it in handouts) to take home after Reiki III training. I expect serious students to do the work and feel that though I can and will teach them, they must do the learning themselves. I make Reiki III publicly available in three-degree weekends and rarely refuse a student. Not all of my Reiki III's become serious teachers, but most are serious healers. They have the teaching skill available when they choose to use it. I ask my Reiki III's to seriously consider teaching, and even those who tell me they have no wish to teach usually end up doing so. They may not offer classes, but they give Reiki to their families, or to those who need the energy. This is very different from Traditional methods of choosing a Reiki III student, but I feel that it works in these times.

When I teach Reiki II, I tell my students that I sincerely hope they will go on to Reiki III. I ask them to only do so if they have a commitment to healing themselves, others (including animals), and/or the planet. I do not limit my teaching, but take as many students per class as I can physically attune. The student herself determines her commitment—if she joins the class I assume she has made one. Sometimes students talk to me about their decisions, but often they do not. I do not ask for any specific time space between the degrees.

In teaching full weekends, I offer Reiki I, II, and III in three days' time—an exhausting process for all concerned, including myself. In Reiki I, I tell students to decide for themselves whether they can handle more the next day. If they are very much affected by the energy, or feel overwhelmed by the information (not often in Reiki I), it would be best to wait for Reiki II. If they feel ready, they are welcome to go further. In Reiki II, I am more emphatic, warning people about the six month emotional clearing process that follows Reiki II. People with ongoing emotional traumas may wish to wait.

If a student has had no other healing experience than Reiki I yesterday and today's Reiki II, I urge her to wait and take Reiki III at a later time. If a student is an experienced healer or psychic before Reiki training, or has at least had Reiki I previous to the weekend, I leave it to her own choice. Most people have a clear awareness of their limits. It is much more positive to allow time between the degrees, at least a few months, but the availability of teachers does not always allow for this. The student herself will know whether or not she is ready, and I honor her knowing and accept it. When I leave a city after a Reiki weekend, there will be at least several people ready to teach within a few months.

Reiki III teaching begins with the introduction of two additional symbols. Both are used in the attunement process, but only one is used for healing. Everything in

Reiki III drives to the passing of attunements, and the symbols are part of this process. The two Third Degree symbols are called the Dai-Ko-Myo and the Raku. The Dai-Ko-Myo is used for healing, and it is also the symbol that transmits the Reiki attunements. The Raku is used only in the attunement process, for no other purpose. It was not used by Mrs. Takata. The Dai-Ko-Myo is unique in that it has two very different variant drawings, one that is used Traditionally and one that is not. In my teaching I have chosen the modern symbol, though I have no idea where it came from.

Dai-Ko-Myo

Traditional version.

When I first began my quest for Reiki III, an acquaintance sent me the Traditional Dai-Ko-Myo symbol in the mail and I used it for my first year of teaching. The Traditional symbol itself has been shown to me in a number of variations, but with one basic form. A. J. Mackenzie Clay pictures a version in his book, *One Step Forward for Reiki* (New Dimensions, 1992). After I had been teaching for some time, my Reiki II teacher, from whom I had learned most of my teaching information, asked me which Dai-Ko-Myo I was using. When I sent her a copy of my symbol, she asked me to try a modern one. I was reluctant, since what I was using was working, but I agreed to try her new symbol. Once I did so, I never returned to the Traditional form.

The new symbol required no memorization—it was as if I had always known it—and my first thought upon seeing it was, "Of course, it's the Goddess' spiral." In using it for attunements, I discovered it to be far more powerful and vastly more easy-flowing than the original

Dai-Ko-Myo

Traditional version with arrows showing how to draw.

Dai-Ko-Myo. When I used both on students and asked them to compare them, everyone liked the newer symbol better. It felt clearer, simpler, stronger to them, as it did to me. After working with it for a while, and switching back and forth for a while, I decided to stay with the modern Dai-Ko-Myo.

In a channeling session with Suzanne Wagner, a student asked about the new symbol form. I was not present at the session, but heard the tape. The Reiki guides who participated in the channeling said that the new

Dai-Ko-Myo

variations

Tibetan Master Symbol (left) and Sunyata Reiki Master Symbol (right)

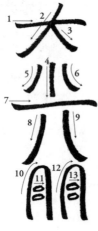

Dai-Ko-Myo variation[4]

Dai-Ko-Myo more closely fits the vibration of today's teaching needs. The older symbol fits the energy of an older time. They stated that there would possibly be people for whom I would wish to use the Traditional symbol when attuning or healing, and that I should follow my intuition. For the most part, however, they advised that the new symbol is to be used primarily. Both Dai-Ko-Myo's are shown in this chapter. I ask my students to try them both, and choose which best fits their energy and needs.

Nontraditional Dai-Ko-Myo

Once you know the Reiki III Dai-Ko-Myo, it is to be used in all healings. Sent distance, I find that it travels rapidly from the healer's Heart chakra to the Heart chakra of the receiver. Often it is the only symbol required in a healing, though for distance work always use the Hon-Sha-Ze-Sho-Nen, too. Used reversed, it pulls negative energy out of the bodies and releases it. The Dai-Ko-Myo's focus is healing the soul. Each of the Reiki symbols targets one of the vibrational bodies. The Cho-Ku-Rei resonates strongest with the physical body level, the Sei-He-Ki with the emotional body, and the Hon-Sha-Ze-Sho-Nen with the mental body. The Dai-Ko-Myo works on the spiritual body level.

This is extremely powerful healing. It heals dis-ease from its highest source, from its first cause. The spiritual body levels contain the blueprint or template from which the physical body is derived. Healing at this level makes for profound changes, the type commonly labeled "miracles." Reiki healers see "miracles" with every session, and the Dai-Ko-Myo invokes them frequently. Life changes occur here. As with the other symbols, send the Dai-Ko-Myo in direct healings when your intuition tells you to do so. I use it the most frequently of all the symbols.

Nontraditional Dai-Ko-Myo

How to draw

For distance healing, I often use all four symbols. Begin with the Dai-Ko-Myo as first source, then send the Hon-Sha-Ze-Sho-Nen. Next add the Cho-Ku-Rei, and then the Sei-He-Ki, and finally repeat the Dai-Ko-Myo last. The symbol often turns an astral rose color when sent, and sometimes metallic gold. It is not static in the sending, but moving, spinning and vibrant. I perceive it as carrying Goddess/Source energy directly and strongly through the medium of the healer to the receiver. It carries everything the receiver needs. This is the most powerful healing energy available to us on planet Earth, and certainly the most positive.

For self-healing, use the Dai-Ko-Myo in the same way it is used for others. Trace it over your Heart chakra, and visualize it with the other symbols. There is also a Ch'i Kung exercise using this symbol for self-healing and to increase the flow of Ki through the body. It stimulates the Hara Line Thymus chakra, and enhances physical immune function. Do the exercise twice a day as follows, from a straight-backed standing position.

First, find the point in the illustration. It is located on each shoulder blade in the boney hollow at the back. Raise Reiki energy in your hands, or rub them together until they are warm, then begin massaging the point on one shoulder with the finger tips of your opposite hand.

Use a clockwise motion. Massage for about one minute, then begin visualizing the Dai-Ko-Myo. Continue massaging for up to three hundred rotations. Find the same point on the opposite shoulder and repeat.

Do the exercise on both shoulders three times. To end, make a loose fist with your right hand. Lightly and gently tap your chest just above the breastbone twenty-five times, visualizing the Dai-Ko-Myo all the while. Do the complete exercise twice a day. I do not know the origin of this exercise, but tapping the thymus has been shown to stimulate and strengthen it. For an entire book on strengthening the thymus gland, see John Diamond, MD, *Your Body Doesn't Lie* (Warner Books, 1979). Diamond calls a similar exercise to the above "The Thymus Thump."[5]

The Dai-Ko-Myo has other uses. Visualize the four symbols to clear and charge crystals, to program them, and to ask them to become self-clearing. To do so hold the crystal or gemstone between your palms, sending it Reiki energy. First visualize the Dai-Ko-Myo, and then the Sei-He-Ki for clearing the stone of all previously absorbed negativity and pain. Next send the Cho-Ku-Rei, using it to program the crystal—to focus it for a purpose, healing for example. If the stone is used for healing for oneself or someone else, also add the Hon-Sha-Ze-Sho-Nen. Last, visualize the Dai-Ko-Myo again, asking that the stone become self-clearing from this time forward. This means

Dai-Ko-Myo Immune Energizer

that the stone will work to clear itself, though also clear it otherwise as frequently as possible. (It will need clearing far less often; test with a pendulum to see.)

When making flower or gemstone elixirs, I add the Dai-Ko-Myo and the Cho-Ku-Rei to the water and flowers (or stones) while they are infusing in the sun. I've been told that my elixirs are extremely powerful, and I'm sure the Dai-Ko-Myo is why. Use it also to charge medicines, herb tinctures, homeopathic remedies, etc. Often it is the only symbol needed. I use the Dai-Ko-Myo virtually every time I use Reiki, usually at the beginning and end of any symbol sequence or session. The energy runs strong and very deep. The Dai-Ko-Myo is the symbol that transmits and passes the Reiki attunements from the teacher to the student. Information on the attunement process is given in the next chapter.

Like the other symbols, the Dai-Ko-Myo must be memorized. The student needs to be able to draw it precisely, with every line in order and place. This is much simpler with the spiral form Dai-Ko-Myo than with the older symbol. A clue for me that the older Dai-Ko-Myo was not resonant with my energy was how very long it took to memorize it, several weeks. The modern Dai-Ko-Myo was mine from the moment I first saw it. No memorization was needed, I already knew it. Again, all of the variations for this symbol available to me are printed in this chapter. Use whichever of the symbols feels best to you. All the versions work.

It is interesting to note the Ch'i Kung definition of the spiral, which has also always been a symbol for Goddess energy. A clockwise spiral moving from its center has the property of condensing Ki at the core of the figure. The modern Dai-Ko-Myo is drawn in this way, from the center outward moving clockwise. By reversing the spiral in a counterclockwise direction, inner Ki expands to connect with Ki beyond the body. When the expansion is complete, the direction automatically reverses, bringing Ki within. Spirals create energy vortexes that draw in other energies. Nature moves in spirals, from ripples in a pool to hurricanes, and they are used in Ch'i Kung to gather and condense Ki for increased health and healing.[6]

The spiral in Wicca is the labyrinth of initiation. It is the passage of the Wheel of the Year, and the place of emergence and rebirth. Clockwise spirals invoke creation energy, while counterclockwise spirals designate dispersion and unwinding. Starhawk, in *The Spiral Dance*, (Harper and Row Publishers, 1979), compares the double spiral to a maze or labyrinth leading to the center of creation, the Buddhist Void:

> As you move through the spiral, the world dissolves, form dissolves, until you are in the hidden heart where birth and death are one. The center of the spiral shines; it is the North Star, and the arms of the spiral are the Milky Way, a myriad of stars slowly revolving around the still center point....You are in the womb of the Goddess, floating free. Now feel yourself pushed and squeezed, moving out of the spiral, which is now the vaginal passage of rebirth. Move clockwise though the double spiral of your DNA.[7]

The modern Dai-Ko-Myo is a double spiral.

The other Reiki III symbol is the Raku. Mrs. Takata did not use this Sanskrit symbol, but most or all American Reiki Masters use it today. Most Masters seem to have very little information on this figure, and do not realize its importance. It is only used in passing attunements, never in healing work. The symbol looks like a lightning bolt. Its definition was given to me as "banking the fire." At the end of the attunement, the Raku is used to ground the receiver of the Reiki energy. This is all most Reiki Masters know about this symbol but in fact it does

Raku
The lightning bolt, banking the fire. (For passing attunements only.)
Arrow shows how to draw.

much more. It activates the Hara Line, helping the student to bring the Reiki energy through her Ki channels, and grounds it in the Hara center (Tan Tien or navel).

During the attunement process also, the aura of the Master and student are joined, and something more happens while the auras merge. During these few moments, the Reiki guides use the energy to lift negative karma from the person receiving the attunement and the Reiki degree. The teacher doing the process receives what is released through her own aura and grounds it; she is usually totally unaware of this. The Raku at the ending of the attunement separates the auras. It also leaves both Master and student with far more Original Ki energy than they each had before. This release of karma during the attunement process explains the physical and emotional cleansing and reorganization that often follows.

With all of the symbol variations now existing, it is interesting to note that there is only one variation for the

Raku, Serpent Version

Raku. This is simply to soften the jagged line of the lightning bolt, making it a wavy line instead. Used this way, the symbol becomes the Serpent Kundalini Power. Since the lightning bolt, however, is also the Vajra of Vajrayana Buddhism—the symbol of the adamantine (diamond) path of Mahayana Buddhism in Tibet—the jagged form of the drawing seems more correct. The Raku is the small form in the opening between the ends of the Dai-Ko-Myo's double spiral.

Modern Reiki III's around the country also bring me whole sheets of "new" Reiki symbols. They say they are reclaiming some of the ones that have been lost. Many of these are Buddhist or Sanskrit energies that are positive in themselves but are not Reiki figures. In Laurel Steinhice's channeling, we were told that other symbols would be

returned to Earth. The first would be a symbol for turning on the energy centers in the eyes, allowing Reiki to be used as a laser. Many healers, as they develop psychically, learn to do this without a conscious symbol. The modern Dai-Ko-Myo seems to be the only nontraditional form that is actually a Reiki symbol, but some of the others are shown below.

While I do not consider these to be Reiki symbols, some of them bear discussion. Om is a Sanskrit symbol,

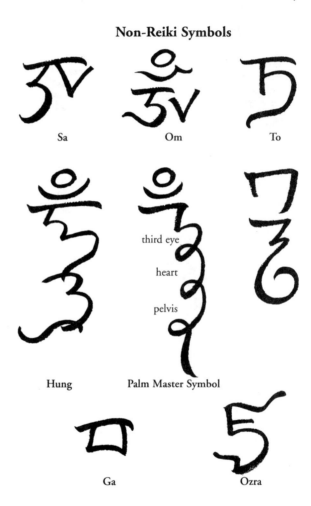

Non-Reiki Symbols

representing the sound that created the Universe. Several other Sanskrit symbols are pictured, all with healing energy. The Palm Master symbol represents the passage of energy through the chakras and Sushumna, and may be an initiation form. Tantric Buddhist statuary shows many similar symbols carved into the palms of the hands of the Buddhas. One series of symbols is called the Womb Pattern, and the symbols themselves are called Bijas—seed

Johre

White Light

Lon Say

Infection Negativity

Zonar

Infinity, timeless, eternity. Works well with past-life, karmic and interdimensional issues.

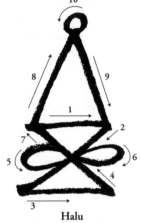

Halu

Love, truth, beauty, harmony, balance and a deeper Ray of Healing. Halu is Zonar amplified in power. The tall pyramid on the top is symbolic of high mental energy.

Len So My

Pure Love

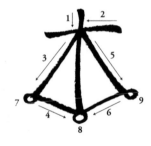

Harth

Love, truth, beauty, harmony, balance. This is the symbol for the heart from which healing and love flow. It is a three-dimensional pyramid.

Yod

When drawing this symbol, simply draw the large sweeping line, symbolizing the hands of God (into which the Ark of the Covenant is flowing). We do not own this energy; we are caretakers of the heart energy.

sounds. They are considered to be the language of the Absolute. The true meanings of Bijas, which play an important part in Tantric Buddhist ritual, are divulged only to initiates. Bijas which are drawn on Stupas can also be used to represent the five elements. Stupas are statues or buildings, forerunners of the Pagoda style, that display the elements intrinsically in their shapes.[8] The Hon-Sha-Ze-Sho-Nen much resembles a Stupa.

Another set of symbols, containing the Harth, Zonar, Halu and Yod, was given to me in California. They were designated to be used along with the Reiki symbols. While the intent of these is clearly positive, I had a very bad experience with one of them. When I showed a woman these symbols, she selected Harth and began to use it negatively, constructing black psychic pyramids for what she described as protection. These were placed over my aura and house and over other people's. They were not positive in any way. Instead, the pyramids enclosed what they were supposed to protect, stifling the person or place inside them. No psychic energy could leave the constructs, and this disrupted the daily exchange and in-and-out flow of normal energy. When negative energy was cleared from inside them, it did not dissipate but kept returning because the symbol trapped it in.

I felt uncomfortable with this symbol from the beginning and asked the woman not to use it, but she persisted. The pyramids were a full-fledged psychic attack and became the source of much stress and negativity in my emotions and home. When I finally realized what was happening, I worked with another healer to clear them. The black pyramids—and there were many of them—were almost impervious to any attempt to dismantle and remove them. After many futile attempts, we found that Rakus sent from the Third Eye could be used to break the pyramids apart, but they almost immediately reassembled themselves. Finally, we dismantled them, used the Raku intensively to disintegrate them, and ran light screens underneath to lift and carry them off the planet. It took several months to clear my home and self completely of this energy.

My suspicion is that the symbol was distorted to a negativity it was not meant to have. Yet, since that time, I have stayed away from experimenting with "new" symbols unless I understand them fully. I do not tell my students to avoid these unknown energies, only to proceed with much caution. Real Reiki symbols cannot be used negatively, they have a built-in protection. I was told in a channeling session that there were originally three hundred Reiki symbols, twenty-two of which were in daily use. They are archived in libraries in Tibet and India. When it is time for the West and Reiki to have them back, we will be given them in such a way that they can be known without doubt as truly Reiki forms. We will also be taught how to use them. The one preview to these seems to be the personal symbols that are given psychically and inwardly to individuals. These may be used, or at least investigated, safely.

Another form being used as an additional Reiki symbol is called the Antahkarana. It is a meditation and healing symbol from Tibet, mentioned by Alice Bailey and other authors as having been used in ritual for thousands of years. Placed under the massage table during healing, it focuses and amplifies Reiki or other healing energies. It

The Antahkarana [9]

is also said to connect the physical brain with the Crown chakra, and to have positive effects on all the chakras and the aura. Meditation on the symbol automatically starts the Microcosmic Orbit, sending Ki through the central energy channels and the body. During meditation, the symbol seems to shift and change, evolving into other images. The Antahkarana can be used to release negative energy from people or objects and can be used to clear crystals.[10]

I have seen holographic representations of the Antahkarana imbedded into square wooden plates. It seems to be used mostly in the Midwest, as the several people who have shown me the symbol are all from that part of the country. The form feels positive and sacred. It is not one of the lost Reiki symbols, but it is positive in its own use. It is said to be a symbol that cannot be used in negative ways; its energy has been proven by many healers for many years beyond its ancient history.

One other set of psychic healing symbols deserves note. This is the series of eleven symbols developed by Frank Homan in his book *Kofutu Touch Healing* (Sunlight Publishing, 1986). These very modern-looking symbols are carefully presented in the book, along with a series of physical body hand positions that are also the Reiki positions. The symbols are again not Reiki forms, but they are valid healing symbols that definitely work. The number and complexity of them makes them somewhat difficult to remember. I felt them not to be as strong as Reiki symbols or as focused, but they are valid. Some students may be interested in working with these. They are positive.

These are the symbols for Reiki III. The two Reiki symbols are the purpose of this chapter, and the student needs to choose between modern and Traditional versions of the Dai-Ko-Myo. The Raku is also presented, and there is more discussion of both symbols through the rest of this book. I have presented a survey of other symbols, non-Reiki symbols, as well. My thought on this is that the new Reiki Master will be as inundated with new symbols as I was, and may need a road map along the way for dealing with them. These non-Reiki symbols are not discussed further in this book. Once familiar with the Reiki III symbols and their healing uses, it is time to begin using them to pass attunements. The attunements and initiation process are the major "miracle" of the Reiki healing system.

1 William L. Rand, "A Meeting with Phyllis Furumoto," in *Reiki News,* Spring, 1992, p. 2.

2 *Ibid.,* p. 1.

3 *Ibid.*

4 Another version of the Third Degree Reiki Symbol, published in *One Step Forward for Reiki* by A. J. Mackenzie Clay (NSW, Australia, New Dimensions Press, 1992), p. 38.

5 John Diamond, MD, *Your Body Doesn't Lie* (New York, NY, Warner Books, 1979), pp. 50–53.

6 Mantak and Maneewan Chia, *Awaken Healing Light of the Tao,* pp. 119–121.

7 Starhawk, *The Spiral Dance: A Rebirth of the Ancient Religion of the Great Goddess* (San Francisco, Harper and Row Publishers, 1979), p. 82.

8 Pierre Rambach, *The Secret Message of Tantric Buddhism* (NY, Rizzoli International Publications, 1979), pp. 60–67.

9 In 1991 I was sent a xeroxed first edition or manuscript copy of William L. Rand's *Reiki: The Healing Touch, First and Second Degree Manual.* The material contained an Appendix that was not subsequently published as part of the current edition of that book, which I also now have. This material on the Antahkarana, including the drawing, came from pages 8–13 of that Appendix.

10 *Ibid.*

At the beginning of teaching Reiki I, students often ask what an attunement is. I tell them that I can describe it only as a miracle, and if after they receive it they can give me a clearer definition, I want to hear it. So far no one receiving or passing them has come up with any better description. The attunement has to be experienced—it cannot be described in any left-brained way. No one knows how or why the Reiki attunement works, why the combination of hand motions, breath and Kundalini control has the profound effect that it does. Those who have received the Reiki attunements know that they are life-changing. They are a lifetime's high point for many people, and most of us who pass them are totally in awe of the process.

The attunement is the difference between other touch healing systems and Reiki. Other systems may use hand positions over the chakras and work with Ki energy, but only Reiki has the extraordinary benefit of the attunement process. In Traditional Reiki training, there are four attunements for Reiki I, and single additional attunements for Reiki II and III. Each of the four in Reiki I is different. In nontraditional methods, the same combined attunement is used once for all three degrees, a single attunement powerful enough to take the place of several different processes. Both ways work beautifully. Receiving either way of doing the attunements creates a healer.

Reiki attunements open and expand the Ki-holding capacity of the Hara Line and clear the channels of energy blockage. They clear and balance the Hara Line chakras and the chakras on the etheric double. During an attunement, Heavenly Ki energy carrying the five Reiki symbols moves from the Crown to the receiver's Heart. Earthly Ki is drawn through the legs and lower centers from the Hara to the Heart as well. Original Ki in the Hara center is replenished and refilled, and any obstructions to the energy's full use are removed. All this happens in a matter of something less than a few minutes.

The attunement is a kind of karmic payback. During the process, negative karma is lifted from the receiver, as if in reward for becoming a healer. This happens because the Master/Teacher's extremely heightened energy level while passing the attunements boosts the level of Ki in the person receiving them. This happens automatically, without the Master causing or willing karmic consequences—it happens through her, not from her. No ego

CHAPTER EIGHT

PASSING ATTUNEMENTS

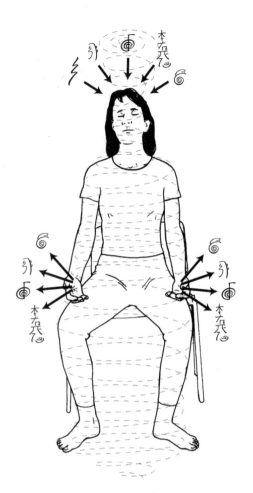

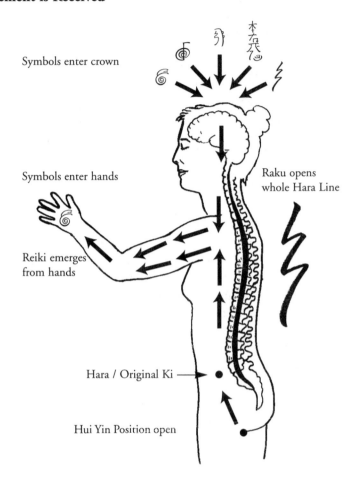

Symbols enter crown

Symbols enter hands

Reiki emerges from hands

Raku opens whole Hara Line

Hara / Original Ki

Hui Yin Position open

is involved. The Master does the simple physical motions, and everything else follows of itself.

The attunement process may be the most profoundly sacred thing on Earth today. From the time of performing the simple motions, a new healer is created—or *awakened* may be the better word. The ability to do Reiki is part of the human genetic code, wired into our DNA. The attunement turns on the light in a darkened house, reconnecting capabilities once universal but now mostly lost. Reiki is a major force in the evolution of the people of this planet. The attunements heal our broken DNA, reconnecting us to the "Light" of the information that has been lost to Earth's people.

Each person receiving the Reiki attunement experiences something different. She may see colors, feel sensations, watch pictures of herself from past lives, connect with spirit guides, or be filled with bliss and joy. Some

people break into tears or giggles. Others say they felt nothing but stand there with red faces and gigantic smiles. The energy opening is evident just by looking at them. Most people immediately develop the very hot hands of a Reiki healer, though some may take the length of the class time to do this. It can happen later when they first put their hands down for healing. I have felt the hot hands happen even on passing attunements to infants, and even when the symbols are not placed directly in the baby's hands. A woman came to a book signing I did once, and she shook my hand. "You have Reiki," she said. I asked her how she knew, as I was not teaching yet. "Because your hands are hot," she told me, "I can feel it. You at least have Reiki II." I had Reiki II at the time.

The person giving the attunements feels something different each time as well, but the overall feeling is one of intensive joy. The process turns the body into a light-

How an Attunement is Passed

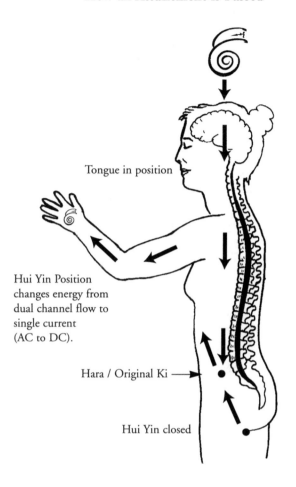

Tongue in position

Hui Yin Position changes energy from dual channel flow to single current (AC to DC).

Hara / Original Ki

Hui Yin closed

ning rod for Ki energy that first moves through the Master/Teacher before being transmitted to the student. It is a physically demanding process, requiring breath control and the ability to hold the Hui Yin position for long periods. There is no time for thought while passing an attunement, only for the energy moving through. There are no other considerations than the physical movements; the energy takes care of itself.

Passing attunements is a Kundalini experience, affecting both etheric and Hara levels. Ajit Mookerjee, in *Kundalini, The Arousal of the Inner Energy,* describes the ascent of Kundalini as an "explosion of heat which passes like a current through the Sushumna."[1] Some of the sensations are described:

> Inner sounds are heard, resembling a waterfall, the humming of bees, the sound of a bell, a flute, the tinkling of ornaments, and so on. The head may start to feel giddy

and the mouth fill with saliva, but the yogi goes on until s/he can hear the innermost, the most subtle…sound…. The yogi visualizes a variety of forms, such as dots of light, flames, geometrical shapes, that in the final state of illumination dissolve into an inner radiance of intensely bright, pure light.[2]

This begins to explain how it feels to pass Reiki attunements.

It is the Hui Yin position, with tongue placed at the roof of the palate, that causes the ascent of Ki up the central Hara Line. Heavenly Ki enters the Master's body from the Crown, and Earthly Ki from the feet chakras. When the Hui Yin position is closed at the Root center, Earthly Ki is drawn upward into the Hara or Tan Tien chakra. The upward-moving channel (Governing Vessel, up the back) is closed at the tongue and palate, so the energy cannot complete its passage out of the body to exit through the Crown. Heavenly Ki moving downward (Conception Vessel, down the front) is likewise stopped at the Hara, and cannot move past the closed Hui Yin to exit through the feet. With nowhere else to go, the intensified Ki energy exits the body through the hands, propelling the symbols into the receiver's aura.

The effect is of moving Ki from the Master's internal dual channels (up and down, Conception Vessel and Governing Vessel) into the single channel of the Hara Line. It is equivalent to changing the normal alternating current of household electricity into a direct current flow—changing A.C. to D.C. The Reiki Master holds this flow in her body, where it feels like the moving figure eight of the Egyptian infinity symbol. The energy is hot and alive, the lightning bolt of the Raku held within. The Reiki II Ki Exercises are designed to train the Master's body to handle this much Ki, but in learning to pass attunements she still must adapt to it. The more energy she can channel, the more powerful the effect of her attunements on others.

For me, the Reiki guides make themselves the most felt while attunements are being passed. They stand behind me and direct the whole process, and I assume they also do this for every Reiki Master. When I pass attunements, I feel their presence strongly and constantly. Sometimes I can see them. If in tracing the symbols, I draw a line out of place, they redraw it and tell me to keep going. If I make a mistake, they say, "we fix," and then they do so. I can psychically watch the energy forms of the symbols shift. When I teach Reiki, and as I write this book, I feel them channeling the teaching through me. Every contact with Reiki becomes a ritual of great beauty. However often I repeat it, it remains miraculous and new.

Suzanne Wagner's channeling tape claims that all the versions of the Hon-Sha-Ze-Sho-Nen we have in the West are incorrect. When asked how to find the correct symbol, the Reiki guides in the session said it didn't matter. The correct symbol is in a library in Tibet or India. When asked what to do, the answer was to "pick one—we fix." During attunements the symbols move too fast to define, but something happens to what is drawn. The symbols change into something else, slightly but definitely different. They are not static or two-dimensional as they are on paper, but three-dimensional and moving. The symbols develop depth, color, movement, breadth. The Reiki guides take what we have and "fix them" so they work. They want Reiki returned to people on Earth enough to do this for us.

Anyone with the desire to pass Reiki on to others is given all the help she needs to do so. I have taught women who could not do the Hui Yin position—one had lost her rectum and rectal muscles to cancer surgery, another had been incested as a child and her vaginal and rectal muscles were severely damaged. Both used what they had and learned to pass attunements easily. The woman who had been incested described the learning as her life's greatest healing. One woman in my classes was on a breathing respirator and could not do the breath control required for the attunement process. The Reiki guides taught her how to pass them anyway, in a manner she could use. A woman who had a heart condition, and also couldn't hold the physical positions long enough, passed attunements effectively, too. With the intent to teach Reiki, every help is given. Do your best with what you have.

One of my Reiki III's is a woman in a wheelchair, with no mobility from her neck down. She uses Reiki II healing methods, and is a powerful distance and psychic healer. Her Reiki I and II teacher refused to give her Reiki III, saying she had no way to use it. The woman joined one of my classes, and I welcomed her. I suspected she could pass attunements in the same way as a distance healing. After giving her the Third Degree initiation, I suggested this and she experimented. She passed the attune-

ment immediately to another woman in the class this way, and the receiver felt her energy strongly enough to see the symbols as she sent them. She called me on the phone one night, crying so hard I couldn't understand her. When she calmed down enough to talk, she told me she had just passed attunements and made her first Reiki I.

Once a Reiki III has become thoroughly familiar with the attunement process, something changes in her Hui Yin position. Since the energy required to pass attunements is not a physical level force, it becomes possible to hold the position on a nonphysical level. With enough practice, the teacher learns to hold Hui Yin on the Hara level and in her Root chakra. For myself, this did not happen by intent, it just happened; I had been teaching for about a year. I found myself passing extremely powerful attunements, while realizing that the Hui Yin position wasn't locked in as required. I should not have been able to pass them at all this way. When it continued, I asked my guides about it, and they explained what was happening. This is something that can occur by intent as well, but learning the control first in the physical body is essential. When I have students with disabilities, however, I ask them to try this, and it usually works for them immediately.

I have also experimented with sending the Reiki attunements astrally, in a psychic distance healing. The woman I tried it on was with me on this level strongly enough to see and touch. I asked her if she wanted it, and felt her sit down in front of me. I then did the attunement as if she were physically present, though she was probably three thousand miles away. The result was truly incredible. I visually watched the symbols enter her Crown and move through her aura, and all her aura colors turned a beautiful violet. She was surrounded by metallic gold energy that seemed to radiate far enough out from her to fill and brighten the room. Her colors were like this for the next several nights when I astrally connected with her. When I am finally able to give her Reiki on the physical level, she will be quite familiar with the energy.

The initiation method that follows passes each Reiki degree in one attunement. It is also the same attunement for all three Reiki degrees. I do not know who developed this method; it has been handed down orally. I have made some minor changes of my own. It is not the Traditional attunement process. In choosing a method, it became clear that I needed a system that could be done very rapidly, as I would be teaching many people at a time. Traditional Reiki classes are very small, with only a few people receiving the attunements at once. The attunement process is highly complicated. Traditional classes also span a weekend each for Reiki I and II, and a week or more for Reiki III. My classes condense the teaching into four or five hours for each degree—I expect the students to do most of their learning at home, and provide handout material to help them. These demands require a fast and simple way to pass attunements.

The same attunement makes a Reiki I, II or III healer. Part of the reason this can happen is intent, and part is the receiver's own capacity to hold Ki. When passing the attunement for Reiki I, it is aura-opening energy that occurs, as no other auric expansion has yet begun. The student receiving the First Degree does not open fully at the moment of the attunement. As her energy bodies expand and adjust to increased Ki, she becomes able to handle more energy, and so she opens further. Full opening of the energy for a Reiki I takes three to four weeks. It has been described to me as a cycle of three or four days at each chakra.

When the attunement is passed as Reiki II, the same thing occurs. The First Degree healer reaches a level of opened Hara Line energy that the Second Degree attunement starts from. It is said that the energy level is mathematically squared with Reiki II. Again, the student goes through a period of adjustment as she grows in Ki channeling capacity. With Reiki III, the energy starts from what the receiver has and then expands it again, to many times the Reiki II level. It is the same process as in Reiki I and II, with increased expansion because the receiver can handle a yet higher level of energy.

These periods of adjustment are the cause of the detoxification reactions that some healers experience after receiving the Reiki attunements. If there are energy blockages in her chakras, Hara Line, or ability to channel Ki, they are healed by the attunement energy. Their release causes the reactions. If the blockages are moved from the etheric body level, the reactions are physical—diarrhea, a running nose, a desire to fast for a few days, or a headache. This is most frequent with Reiki I. If the blockages move from the emotional or mental levels, the detoxification is also on these levels. Here is where emotional-mental

growth occurs along with many life changes. This is the Reiki II detox that can take several months.

Spiritual body changes happen with the Third Degree. Most of these do not manifest as detoxification, but as growing self-realization and a sense of oneness with the Universe. Most students' reaction to the Reiki III attunement is sheer joy. The clearing has already been done. Sometimes the new Reiki III needs additional sleep for a few days, as her energy level and vibrational bodies rearrange to fit the expansion.

Traditionally, with most modern Reiki teachers, the Dai-Ko-Myo is placed into the hands only with the Reiki III attunement. With all three degrees, it is drawn at the Crown but in Reiki I and II it is not put into the palms. When I pass attunements, I always use the Dai-Ko-Myo in the hands, even for Reiki I. Traditionally, also the other Reiki symbols are placed into the Crown chakra, but in Reiki II they are put into only one hand. The student is asked, "Which is your healing hand?" This results in an energy imbalance that I'm told is quite uncomfortable. I place all four symbols in both hands always, for all three degrees. I had no idea that other teachers did it differently until students told me how good it felt to have them placed in both. Frequently students trained Traditionally for Reiki I or II have taken their further degrees with me.

I was taught that when Hawayo Takata passed attunements, she did not use breath control, the Hui Yin position or the Raku. The four Reiki I attunements were not given in a specific order, as long as all four were given by the end of the teaching. She used the Cho-Ku-Rei counterclockwise at the Crown, Throat, Third Eye and Heart for all degrees, and all four symbols were always placed into the Crown. The symbols were visualized and blown into place. In Reiki I, no symbols were placed in the palms at all. For Reiki II, she blew the Sei-He-Ki, Hon-Sha-Ze-Sho-Nen and the Cho-Ku-Rei into the opened palm of one hand, asking the receiver first to designate her "healing hand." For Reiki III, she placed the Dai-Ko-Myo over the Crown, and the Hon-Sha-Ze-Sho-Nen and Cho-Ku-Rei down the spine. All four symbols were placed in both palms for Reiki III only. Though not placed in the palms, the symbols were visualized over the closed hands, and this was also done for all three degrees.

When starting to pass attunements, it is best to begin by doing them with only one person, rather than a full class. It takes time and experience to develop the muscle and breath control required, sometimes several months, so start slow. Do not schedule your first teaching class until you have learned to pass the attunements properly, and can handle several attunements in one session. Keep the first classes small—under five people is a good number—increasing the class as you grow stronger. An optimal number of students for me after several years' teaching is around twenty. I have done as many as seventy-five attunements in a day—and have been sorry afterward. There is a heavy energy drain in doing so much that is not felt until later. During the initiations themselves there is only a tremendous high. You will not know at the time that you have done too much, so listen to yourself carefully before you take on too much.

I like to give an attunement to anyone who is dying, seriously ill, or going through a life crisis. If the person is able to use the Reiki I for self-healing, so much the better, but the attunement is a major healing in itself. It does not matter that such people will not become healers and use the energy for others, though some day they may. What matters is the healing and life benefit that an attunement brings when it is sorely needed. I have done this with infants and also with pets. It is amazing with a baby to feel her hands heat up. I did an attunement on my dog, Kali, who had been abused before she came to me and was angry and rebellious. She was delighted with the process and noticeably started healing. Her behavior began to change for the better as well.

Often students who have taken my classes return just to repeat attunements. This is unnecessary; the attunements are for life, but it feels wonderful and I don't discourage it. It is also perfectly fine for new Reiki III's to practice at passing attunements, and I urge it. Nothing in Reiki, and certainly not the attunement process, can ever cause harm. When I teach the Third Degree to a group, I ask them to get together and practice on each other or on family or friends. There is no danger of energy overload from multiple attunements on one person—each only opens to the extent her Hara Line can handle. It is an incredible joy to realize that someone you have attuned has opened to the energy, especially the first few times it happens. One of my students has passed so many attunements practicing on her cat that I'm expecting reports of Spooky starting to fly! The attunements provide healing for everyone, human or animal, and there is no harm in repeating them.

When beginning to pass Reiki attunements, start with Reiki I. When you have held several classes and feel fully comfortable with the attunement process and the First Degree, move up to Reiki II. Go further only when you feel that you can handle any event in the First Degree. Teaching Reiki becomes the Reiki Master's classroom, but again start at the beginning and work up to advanced degrees. The best way to ready oneself for teaching Reiki is to do as much healing work as possible, both direct and distance, and to practice passing the attunements. By knowing Reiki thoroughly, you learn enough to teach it to others. There is more information on how to teach Reiki in the next chapter.

Most students ask me, "How do you know that someone has opened when you've passed the attunement?" This question terrified me at the beginning. I had very little training and minimal information for Reiki III, and had to learn it as I went. At the beginning I had no idea whether students were opening, and I very much doubted my ability. When I taught my first classes I was scared to death, wondering if I could do it. I knew I made mistakes in drawing the lines of the symbols, and when I did I heard a voice beside me saying, "Keep going, we fix." I was so scared and worried about my own performance that I didn't watch the students. Look at their faces after the attunement, and you'll know.

One simple way, especially helpful for new Masters, is to ask. After passing the attunements to everyone in the group, ask them what they saw or felt. If someone would rather not speak, don't insist. Once one or two speak up, others usually follow. Tell them to look for gentle sensations, instead of big dramas, and when they realize something *did* happen, they may want to join the discussion. With a few descriptions, you will know that they opened to the energy. There is an amazing variety to what people experience, particularly in Reiki I. Next ask, "Is there anyone who didn't feel anything?"

Once in a while, maybe one in twenty-five or thirty students, someone says she felt nothing. First, ask to feel her hands—if they are hot, she has definitely opened to the energy, whether she realizes it or not. Ask her what she saw or felt in the attunement—some students expect drastic happenings, instead of the quiet and subtle sensations that occur. Most of the problems resolve with this. If the woman's hands are cold and she has truly felt nothing in the attunement, ask her if she has any ambivalence toward the energy or toward healing. Students who were raised with fundamentalist upbringings, though they may have rejected them, may have difficulty or fear about psychic healing.

If that is the case, ask her if she wants the energy to open, and assure her it's her choice. Tell her, if she wants it, to do a healing with someone. We do this next in the class after the attunements are passed. Ask her to see what happens then. Also tell her that if she chooses to have the energy, to do some meditating now or later and to ask for it. If she decides against receiving Reiki, the symbols will remain in her aura for a few weeks, then dissipate if she does not accept them in that time. If she decides at some later time to have the energy, she has only to meditate and ask for it, and she will open to it.

I have never had a student completely reject the energy, though a few were ambivalent at first. They chose to take the class after all. Everyone but one of my tough cases opened by the end of the Reiki I class, and the one person who didn't open chose the energy later and opened to it that night. For an inexperienced Reiki Master, this is probably the hardest situation to understand and resolve. Because I learned what to do the hard way, I try to provide solutions and tell my students what they might expect. Remember that free will is paramount—if someone refuses Reiki, it is her right to do so. This is only an issue in Reiki I. I have never seen it happen in the Second or Third Degrees.

I had one First Degree student so terrified of the attunement itself that I thought she might not even receive it. I told her that was also her choice. She watched others in the group first, then sat down in the chair for her attunement. I asked her, "Are you sure?" and she said, "Yes," with tears pouring down her face. I passed the attunement and watched her light up like a candle in a radiant smile. She took her Reiki II the next day as well, and told me she felt Reiki was a coming home to herself. She said she knew it would change her life. Today she is a teaching Master.

Before describing the attunement process, some discussion on initiation is required here. The word "attunement" also means "initiation," and that word in the Sanskrit translates to mean "empowerment."[3] Reiki empowers everyone who receives it, and also the teacher who gives it. A Reiki teacher is called a "Master," but the term is not meant to carry any connotations of power-over or hierarchy. A Master is simply a teacher. If honor is bestowed with the title, it is an honoring of Reiki itself. By receiving the attunement and teaching from a Master the student receives the Reiki Third Degree. The student, however, by her own commitment and her own hard work can make herself a Master. No teacher can make her a master—the student can become a master only by successfully passing the Reiki initiations herself and by teaching Reiki I.

In India and Tibet, a Vajrayana guru (Tantric Buddhist Master/Teacher) is honored for being part of a line of adepts whose lineage stretches all the way back to Gautama Siddhartha, the Buddha. A guru in India takes the responsibility seriously, with no ego and no violation of the student-teacher trust. A Reiki Master today also has a lineage, going back through Hawayo Takata, Jesus and the Sakyamuni Buddha, and before them to Shiva and the stars.

Traditional students and Masters of Reiki also trace their line of teaching. The student identifies her status in Reiki by her teacher, and her teacher's teacher, tracing it back to Takata. The student was trained by Master A, who was trained by Master B, who was trained by Master C—all the way back to Mrs. Takata, who was trained by Chujiro Hayashi, who was trained by Mikao Usui. This is called the student's lineage. Nontraditional Reiki places less emphasis on lineages than Traditional Reiki. The point of nontraditional Reiki training is that the student or Master received it; it doesn't matter from whom. A Master of any lineage has her primary responsibility to Reiki and her students and this is what is important.

In Tantric Buddhism, there are many levels of initiation. The word in Sanskrit is "abhiseka," and in Tibetan "wong." In India it is called receiving "Shaktipat." The initiation process is a sacrament, and I suspect the Buddhist or Reiki attunements to be the origin of today's Christian sacraments, and perhaps of every rite of passage ritual. In receiving abhiseka—an attunement, empowerment or initiation—sacred power enters the body and remains there. In Vajrayana Tantric Buddhism, an initiation always precedes the beginning of a new level of teaching. The four levels of Buddhist empowerment strikingly reflect the three degrees of Reiki.

The first three Buddhist initiations remove karmic obstructions, and the fourth heals consciousness. All of the four types offer the following expansions of Ki: 1) opening energy blockages, 2) increasing power, 3) giving access to new instruction, and 4) allowing the student to do specific processes or rituals.[4] These four benefits also come with the Reiki attunements, each succeeding degree rising to a more complex level. The four initiations are as follows:

1. The Vase Empowerment cleanses the psychic channels and physical body level of karmic obstructions. It allows the student to do visualization of specific deities. Other benefits are kept secret.
2. The Mystical Empowerment opens the flow of Ki, and the power of speech—it gives mantras their effectiveness. Again, there are other hidden results.
3. The Divine Knowledge Empowerment cleanses the mental body and permits the practice of Hathayoga type exercises, plus other things.
4. The Absolute Empowerment leads to recognition of true spiritual essence, and direct experience of once-symbolic understanding. This empowerment allows the study of Atiyoga and "has profound mystical results."[5]

I equate the first Buddhist empowerment to the Reiki I attunement—it opens the Hara channels, and cleanses on the physical body level. The Mystical and Divine Empowerments are Reiki II—symbols can be equated with the power of speech, as bijas are the written symbol forms of sounds. The emotional and mental bodies receive the energy and cleansing, and the Hathayoga type exercises are the Ki Exercises. The Absolute Empowerment is the Reiki Third Degree. It goes directly to spiritual essence, the soul body, and bestows understanding of the process. "Profound mystical results" is a good description of what occurs after receiving Reiki III. The student who becomes a Reiki Master experiences profound changes in her life.

Like everything else in Reiki, the process of passing the attunements is extremely simple. It involves a series of physical body movements that when done in sequence have life-changing spiritual effects. The Master/Teacher need not concern herself with what happens in the process. All she needs to do is perform the sequence. Some very complex things happen in the Reiki initiation, but the Master doesn't even need to know what they are.

She just does the attunement. The Reiki guides and Reiki energy itself will take care of all that follows.

To pass the attunement for any of the degrees, the Master must be able to hold the Hui Yin position, with her tongue tip touching the roof of her mouth throughout the process. The teacher's breath is held at all times when she is not blowing out. While blowing, the tongue stays in place—blow around it. After blowing, take another deep breath and hold it again. Blowing transmits Ki, and the first definition of Ki is "vital breath." When doing several attunements at once, it is permitted to breathe and to let go of the Hui Yin between students. It may, however, be easier to take the Hui Yin before starting, and to hold it locked until all the attunements are done. Remember to reopen it after finishing, and to ground yourself thoroughly. Reconnect with the Earth and run the Microcosmic Orbit to recirculate Ki and reestablish the body's normal energy flow.

The student receiving the attunement sits on a straight-backed chair, feet flat on the floor. She may take her shoes off if she wishes. Some Reiki Masters' energy is strong enough to burst watches during the attunement process—if you are one of these Masters, have your students take theirs off, and take off yours. I inadvertently started the fad of receivers holding crystals in their opened hands when they receive the initiation. A crystal charged this way remains highly charged and seldom needs clearing. If someone does this, just be careful not to drop it, and do the attunement over the stone. Have the students hold their hands with palms together at chest height, and tell them you will manipulate their hands. If the Master has to hunt for hands during the attunement, it becomes very hard to hold the Hui Yin position and the breath at the same time.

Attunements may be done singly or in a group. Begin doing attunements one at a time, and don't proceed to work in rows until you have had more experience and have developed strength. Put two to five students in straight chairs in a row. Five is comfortable for me. Four is too short and stops the energy flow. With six I begin to hyperventilate, and seven is impossible. See what works for you. Remember that you will be tired at the end of this—the tremendous high of the energy passes in about an hour. Conserve your strength as needed. With experience, by using this assembly-line method, you can pass

To Pass Attunements

Hold the Hui Yin position with your tongue at the roof of the palate at all times. Hold your breath unless you are blowing, then take another deep breath and hold it. The Reiki Master stands to pass attunements; the students are seated in straight-backed chairs with hands held palms together at chest height.

1. From the Back:

Open the Crown. This can be a visualization or hand movement.

Trace the Dai-Ko-Myo over the Crown.

Reach forward over the shoulders to take the student's hands, and blow into the Crown.
    Take a deep breath and hold it.

Trace the other symbols over the Crown: Cho-Ku-Rei, Sei-He-Ki, Hon-Sha-Ze-Sho-Nen.

Take the hands and blow into the Crown. Take another deep breath and hold it.

2. Come to the Front:

Open the student's hands like a book.

Trace the Cho-Ku-Rei over both palms.

Tap three times.

Trace the Sei-He-Ki over both palms.

Tap three times.

Trace the Hon-Sha-Ze-Sho-Nen over both palms.

Tap three times.

Trace the Dai-Ko-Myo over both palms.

Tap three times.

Fold the hands together, and hold them in one of your hands.

Blow from Root to Heart. Take a deep breath and hold it.

3. Go To Back:

Close the aura, with the symbols inside it. (Do not close the Crown chakra.)

Trace the Raku down the back of the spine.

Release Hui Yin, release the breath.

many attunements quickly with less waiting for the chairs to be refilled after each group.

I allow my students to watch the passage of attunements, as long as they are willing to remain quiet. This is never done in Traditional Reiki. Play soft music during the passage if you wish, but the room should be primarily silent. This is the one time in the class when there can be no interruptions. A room where attunements are often done becomes charged with the energy and continues to feel good after. The room's temperature will rise considerably while the attunements are going on. In one air-conditioned space where I did twenty-six attunements, the beginning temperature of seventy-two degrees rose to over ninety. Afterwards, people in the store at the front of the building remarked that they knew when I was doing the attunements because the room in front also heated up. So will the Master. Wear loose clothes or a jacket you can take off. Go to the toilet before starting—it is impossible to hold Hui Yin with a full bladder.

While the attunements are going on, Reiki I students who are waiting will need something to do. After each group is initiated, it is extremely important for each student to put her hands down on someone else for several minutes. A back or shoulder is fine. This brings the Reiki energy through the attunement receiver's Hara Line. It also prevents headaches and spaciness from occurring later. I always know the people who didn't touch someone after their attunements by their complaints afterwards—I tell them in advance and have no sympathy for those who refuse to listen. Once they have done this, have them begin a self-healing.

The process for passing attunements is outlined above. Begin behind the student's chair. Center yourself and invite in the Reiki guides. Take a few deep breaths, and establish the Hui Yin position with your tongue on the roof of your mouth. Take another deep breath and hold it. Opening the Crown is primarily a visualization. I make a two-handed motion over the receiver's head of opening and spreading apart, my hands a few inches above the receiver's head. You will feel the aura expand, and may see it. The symbols are drawn with the whole hand, palm down toward the receiver's Crown. It happens too quickly to visualize a color, but it is proper to visualize the symbols in violet going into the Crown. Begin with the Dai-Ko-Myo.

To take the student's hands, bend forward to reach them. They are held together at chest height, in prayer position. Insist that the hands be held high; hunting for them makes it very difficult to hold Hui Yin and your breath. Blow around the tongue, which stays in place, then take another deep breath. Draw the other three symbols, Cho-Ku-Rei, Sei-He-Ki, and Hon-Sha-Ze-Sho-Nen. Visualize the symbols going into the Crown. Blow again and take another breath.

Move to the front of the seated student. Bring her closed hands forward and open them like a book just above her lap. Over the paired hands trace the Cho-Ku-Rei, then lightly tap or slap your two palms upon the student's palms three times. The visualization here is of driving each of the symbols into the hands. Trace the Sei-He-Ki, and tap three times again. Then do the same with the Hon-Sha-Ze-Sho-Nen—draw the symbol, then tap it in. The Dai-Ko-Myo is last, and again tap it in after drawing it.

Bend forward to take the hands, close them again, and hold them aside in one of your hands. Bend further forward, and blow, moving the breath from the Root center to the Heart. Men become very startled by this, and may jump. Some students jump the first time the hands are tapped—do it gently. After blowing, take another deep breath and hold it.

Move to the back of the chairs again. There is some question as to whether the breath need be held any longer, but the Hui Yin is still required. I generally hold both breath and Hui Yin, and the tongue position. Make a motion of closing the aura, with the symbols visualized inside it. This can be a physical gesture of bringing the two hands together, or visualized. Do not close the Crown chakra, ever. It will be wide open at this point and the closed aura covers and protects it. Draw the Raku down the person's spine, from head to ground. You will feel a shift in your own energy and the student's with the Raku. Release the breath and the Hui Yin position.

The attunement is finished. It took about three minutes to do. Learn to draw the symbols quickly so the breath and Hui Yin can be held for less time. With practice and experience, and if you are a clear visualizer, the symbols can be visualized instead of drawn. Send them in violet from the Third Eye. When doing a row of students, move down the back of the row for all of them, then move down the front for all of them, then finish them all from the back. With a large group, this is much faster than doing the attunements one at a time. When I do Reiki III attunements, however, I like to do them individually—the process means too much to each student to do it in a group.

Insist that the room be kept very quiet. The attunement process requires a great deal of concentration, and the Master needs the silence. The Reiki attunement is also a peak event for the receiver, and she deserves to have it happen uninterrupted. I have rarely, if ever, had a problem with classes not cooperating in this. Students can leave the room if they are too restless to wait. In Reiki I only, it is essential that after receiving the attunement, the students put their hands down on someone for a while.

For some time before beginning the attunement process, the Master feels her aura "lighting up." This happens for me with every teaching class and has also happened on an occasion when I didn't plan to pass attunements. I was at a friend's house and someone there asked about Reiki. I had not expected to, but I ended up passing an attunement. My friend said my aura was lit up for at least twenty minutes before I did it. It was a spur of the moment thing; I didn't decide to do it that far in advance. The Reiki guides, however, knew I was going to pass an attunement and readied my aura to do so. If, while teaching, this becomes uncomfortable—the energy can get demanding and sometimes you just aren't ready to start—ask the guides to calm it down. Tell them, "I'm not ready yet, please wait." Sometimes they get anxious or impatient. They have waited a long time to bring Reiki back to the world.

If during passing the attunement you make a mistake, check in with the guides. Mine tell me not to start over. "We fix," they say. Do the process to the best of your ability. Learn it well and practice it, but if you make a mistake or forget something, it is not a disaster. If you forget whole symbols, you may need to go back and draw them, but maybe not—ask the guides. With the positive intent to teach Reiki and some knowledge of the process, every help is given.

Between students, or rows of students, take some deep breaths. Hyperventilating isn't fun. At the end of the attunements, ask the guides for grounding. Use an obsidian or hematite gemstone, or run some Microcosmic Orbits, or go and hug a tree. Touch your thumb to your little finger on both hands— this grounds the flow of energy, though abruptly. Some flower essences work well. Dinner after the class also helps, and receiving a group healing from your new Reiki I's. Whatever works. It may take some hours to come down; expect to feel tired when you do.

There is a way to pass attunements without the Hui Yin position, using the above process and a crystal grid. This was given to Laurel Steinhice and me in her channeling, and it works. To do this, you need at least eight large generator quartz crystals longer than six inches. They must be thoroughly cleared before starting. Only one attunement at a time can be done with this method. The student sits in a straight-backed chair. Two crystals are placed directly behind the chair; one is facing the student's feet. All the crystals point toward the receiver. Around the chair and Master is a circle or grid of at least five more large clear quartz crystals, again all pointing toward the student. There can be many more crystals in the grid, but use an odd number.

The Master begins at the back of the chair, with her bare feet on top of the two close-in crystals. When she moves to the front, the third close-in crystal is between her two feet. Do the attunement process. I find that it requires some very powerful crystals to have the power of the previous method. Crystals used in a Reiki grid develop and maintain a powerful charge, and the grid can also be placed around and under the massage table in healing sessions.

Another way of holding the Hui Yin position, developed by my student Anastasia Marie, is to place a small crystal egg inside the vagina and another one under the tongue. This not only holds the Hui Yin position but magnifies it, and attunements done in this method are extremely powerful. Anatomically, this method only works for women; men will need to experiment. When using crystals for Reiki grids always use the finest quality clear quartz and make sure the stones are fully cleared.

The Reiki attunement can be made into a beautiful ritual, or done, as I do it, swiftly and in a matter-of-fact way. Because I teach large groups in a variety of places and often have time limits for the classes, I leave the rituals to others. In Traditional Reiki, attunements are done one at a time rather than in groups. The receiver is taken to a room away from the class, where the process is done in a lovely and stylized way. However it is handled, an attunement is a very sacred process.

To ritualize it—as I am sure it was ritualized in Tantric Buddhism—creates a sacred atmosphere of great beauty that appeals to all the senses. Begin with the door closed to interruptions in a softly lit room. Remove the telephone or shut the ringer. Light candles, placing them out of the way, where they won't be tipped over as the Master and students move around. Light incense, making sure first that no one is allergic to it. Sweetgrass, amber or rose are especially nice for the purpose. Play quiet background music geared to altered states like that of Enya, Kitaro, or Kay Gardner. I sometimes use a harp tape by Gail Baudino. If the Master/Teacher and students are Wiccan, make an altar with the candles on it, flowers, incense, objects for the four directions, and Goddess images. Or make a nonreligious meditation altar. Remember that Reiki is sacred, but is not a religion.

Begin the attunement process with a meditation. Do a whole body relaxation sequence first, then gear the meditation to opening the chakras or opening the students to receiving the Reiki energy. Take them into a past life where they once used Reiki, connect them to their spirit guides, or simply direct Ki energy through all their chakras by visualizing the colors in sequence. Take the group to a planet where everyone has Reiki and experience daily life there; then take them to a future Earth where everyone is a healer, and see how the Earth is healed. The possibilities for doing a meditation of this type are almost endless. Focus, however, on opening and receiving and perhaps on deserving the energy.

When the students are deeply into the altered state, begin passing the attunements. The Master may place a drop of almond, rose, lavender or peppermint flavoring under her tongue. Use pure essential oils but make sure the fragrance is safe to put in your mouth. It burns a bit, reminding the teacher to keep her tongue on the roof of her mouth, and also carries its fragrance when she blows the symbols into the receivers' auras. Do the attunements. End the ritual with another meditation, and a grounding or blessing at the finish. The Vajrayana Buddhists who developed Reiki use ritual, symbolism and mysticism in their practices. These can be translated into any system of beliefs.

This describes the nontraditional Reiki attunement method. I have tried to teach the process as clearly and simply as possible, and to address the most frequent problems and questions a new Reiki III might have.

Probably the only way to learn to pass attunements is to practice it first, and then go out and do it. Experience comes only with use, and expertise only with experience. Once the new Reiki III has learned to pass attunements, she is ready to begin teaching. In the act of teaching Reiki, she becomes a Master. The next chapter discusses how to teach each of the Reiki degrees.

1 Ajit Mookerjee, *Kundalini: The Arousal of the Inner Energy*, p. 71.
2 *Ibid.*
3 John Blofeld, *The Tantric Mysticism of Tibet*, p. 139.
4 *Ibid.*, p. 144.
5 *Ibid.*, pp. 143–144.

At this point, a student who has received her Reiki I, II and III quickly—as in one of my weekend intensives—may be overwhelmed. Before she starts teaching (or panicking), it is necessary to talk about sorting out the process and the energy. If the student began with Reiki I on Friday and received Reiki III on Sunday, she is not yet ready to teach. First, she needs to learn Reiki for herself before she can pass it on to others. I expect it to take several weeks after Reiki III for a student to be ready to pass an attunement, even in practice. This varies with individuals; it may take several months. A student who has had time with Reiki I and II before taking the Third Degree may be ready much sooner. There is no right or wrong here, only what each person needs.

If you have received all three degrees quickly, the first thing to do is to learn Reiki I. Do hands-on healings for yourself daily, and as many direct sessions with others as possible. I recommend that my students do self-healing daily for at least the first month after receiving Reiki I, and three full-body sessions with others per week. For the time being, forget about Reiki II and III. When you are completely comfortable with Reiki I, and beginning to be experienced with direct healing, move up to Reiki II. Again, the time frame varies with the individual. Move forward only when you feel ready to do so.

At that point, begin doing distance healing in a nightly meditation. Learn how to do distance healing first, then start adding the Reiki symbols to both direct and distance sessions. Keep the symbol drawings in front of you for as long as necessary. Memorize the symbols carefully, taking as long as is needed to learn each one. When I was learning them, I hung them over my dining room table and studied them while eating. First send the symbols whole in absentee healing, then visualize drawing them. Last, learn to draw them on paper without the handouts. Every line must be in sequence.

Next, begin working with the Ki Exercises, half an hour at a time. Spend at least a few weeks experimenting with the Microcosmic Orbit and the First Ki Exercise. These are major practices in themselves. Begin exercising the Hui Yin position and extending the length of time you can hold it. It may take a few weeks until you can hold it long enough to pass an attunement. Learn to feel the sensations of Ki moving through your body, and the changes in sensations with the different exercises.

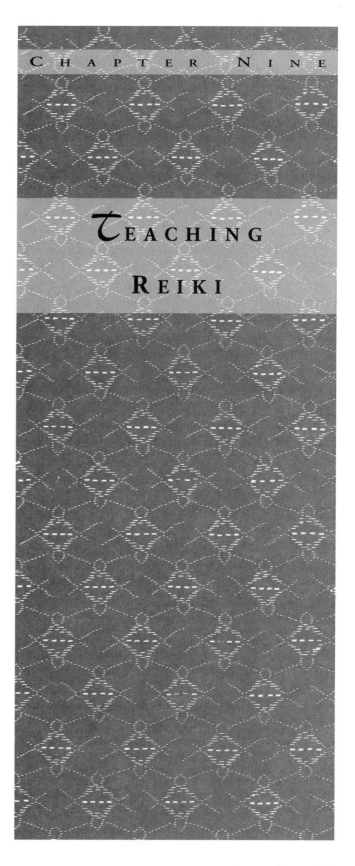

CHAPTER NINE

TEACHING

REIKI

Only when thoroughly comfortable with the above is it time to add Reiki III. Begin with the Third Degree symbols, first choosing which Dai-Ko-Myo appeals to you. Trying them both in distance healing is a good way to test them. Ignore any non-Reiki symbols, they are unimportant for now. Leave personal symbols for later, too. Add the Dai-Ko-Myo into direct and distance healing work and stay at that level for a while. When you are thoroughly familiar with direct healing, distance healing, the five Reiki symbols, and the Ki Exercises, it is time to begin working with the Reiki III teaching energy.

Do this by learning the attunement process and practicing it at every opportunity. If you learned Reiki with a group, it is good to practice together and to do healings for each other. Reiki Shares are wonderful for healing, and may be easily extended to practicing attunements. When giving each other attunements repeatedly, however, don't expect the high energy charge that came from receiving them the first time. You will probably still feel the energy flow, especially if working with the Ki Exercises has made you sensitive to it. You may start seeing the symbols as they are passed.

When you feel comfortable with doing Reiki at all three levels, and with passing attunements, you are ready to start teaching. Begin with one person, usually a family member, and give her Reiki I. Do a few other people singly, and maybe a small group of under five, before considering advertising a class. Information on what to teach in each of the three degrees is discussed in this chapter. When you have increased your capacity for attunements enough to handle some larger groups, and grown comfortable with teaching Reiki I, try Reiki II. Again, begin with one individual or a very small group of friends before advertising a formal class. Learn the energy of teaching each degree before moving to the next level.

I recommend teaching several classes of Reiki I before beginning Reiki II, and teaching at least several Reiki II classes before teaching Reiki III. The process of the teaching trains the teacher/Master. Working in the healing methods of each degree teaches the Master, too. Begin teaching Reiki III individually, rather than in classes, and give your students the opportunity to observe your First and Second Degree classes if they wish to do so. It takes some experience of teaching Reiki I and II to ready you for teaching the Third Degree. There is no need to rush it. Wait until you feel sure of each degree.

Every new Reiki III develops her own teaching methods. Traditionally, this is discouraged, and each degree of Reiki is rigidly defined. No psychic skills are taught in Traditional Reiki classes, and little or no explanation of how and why the system works. Spirit guides and Reiki guides are not mentioned, nor are past lives and healing this-life past traumas. There are no alternative symbols, and no Stillpoint. The Traditional attunement process, though far more complex than the one taught in this book, does not involve the Ki Exercises or using the Hui Yin position.

Anything outside of the strict Traditional outline is defined as "not Reiki" and severely frowned upon. When I received my Reiki I in a full class for the second time, I was appalled when the instructor/Master refused to talk about emotional releases. "That's not Reiki," he said, angry that I brought it up. But of course it is, and Reiki healers need to know about it and know what to do when it happens. The nontraditional Reiki Master has many more choices and more information to learn and work with. I try to be very clear in my teaching about what is Traditional Reiki and what is not.

My students do not always teach as I do, and this is fine. If they are passing successful attunements and teaching hand positions, distance healing, and the symbols, they are teaching Reiki. Sometimes when my students take things too far from the Reiki system, I do not approve of their action. One woman teaches Reiki by having her students design their own symbols, rather than using the Reiki symbols. She offers a Third Degree only to therapists and professionals, but at least she doesn't call her system Reiki, which makes me feel a little better. Once a student is trained and on her own, she develops her own way of teaching. It is not my right to intervene because the student has free will. Most of my Reiki III's teach Reiki in ways that I can be proud of, but few of them teach exactly as I do.

The first thing to learn in teaching Reiki is how to take care of your own needs. Being a Reiki Master is extremely demanding, no one knows how much so until they have tried it. You will probably do frequent healing work as well, and may also be holding a day job. Teaching out of your home or at conferences or festivals may mean that conditions are not always under your control. First become aware of how many attunements you can pass in a day and how much you can teach without becoming exhausted. Too much too often can result in serious depletion. Decide what is comfortable and remain within your limits. Pick the number of students that you know you can handle, and don't go over that number.

I taught Reiki at Womongathering, a women's festival in the Poconos, last year. I had Reiki I on the festival schedule, but fifty women showed up for the class. Even though two of my students were helping me, that is a large number. Adding to the problem, people started asking me for Reiki II and III. I hate to refuse anyone the teaching, especially my Reiki I's and II's from last year's festival who have nowhere else to get advanced degrees. The Reiki I class was Saturday, and on Sunday after lunch I agreed to meet those who wanted Reiki II outdoors under a particularly beautiful tree.

After the Reiki II class, I went on to Reiki III for twenty-some-odd women. These were not festival scheduled workshops, and I had another scheduled workshop that evening. By the time that last class was over at nine o'clock, I was severely sick. I had passed too many attunements (almost a hundred in twenty-four hours), gotten too much sun, and was exhausted. The karmic release that happens with each attunement passes through the Reiki Master's aura, and there is a limit to how much Ki can be channeled by one person in one day. Perhaps it was a lesson for me, since I had done it to myself. I was sick and exhausted for most of the next three months. I try to teach my students to take care of themselves, and need to remind myself to do it also.

When you are teaching, set class size limits and stick with them. This limit varies from person to person, and with different levels of experience. Avoid teaching classes or individual sessions too often—probably not more often than once a week is wise. When I teach a three-day Reiki intensive I give myself at least a month before doing it again, and two months is more ideal. Get enough rest and after you have been teaching often or with large groups, allow yourself more time to sleep if you need it. If you are teaching in the afternoon, give yourself the morning off, and sleep late or stay quiet until the class. Make sure to eat well before teaching and to have a full meal afterward—eating helps to ground you. Healing sessions require less strict limits, as Reiki energizes both healer and receiver. Learn to know what your limits are in healing, too.

Each Master has different needs. Learn what conditions you need, and follow them as much as possible. The teaching always remains interesting and new no matter how often you repeat the same classes. Taking care of yourself helps you teach more often and enjoy it more. Teaching Reiki is a lifelong commitment and blessing. There is no need to rush the process or to get exhausted by it.

Wear comfortable clothing. You will heat up tremendously during the attunements and for a while after, then you will need to cover up again. Jackets or overblouses that can be taken off and put back on are useful. Wear loose clothing. Anything that constricts your hand and arm movements becomes annoying while passing the attunements. Loose bracelets get in the way. I have a workshop outfit with a tight-sleeved blouse, and I've ripped it several times. Wear clothing that is easily washed—you will sweat. Take a jacket for later, even though it seems warm. After the class, when the heightened Ki changes, you may feel colder than those around you. You will probably not be up to partying hard the evening after the class.

Select a teaching space for comfort, too. A living room is where I prefer to teach. I like my classes informal. In Reiki I when everyone is lying down on the floor for healings, a soft rug feels great. If the classroom has a bare floor, have the students bring pillows and blankets. Put this information on the class flyer. A classroom with rows of chairs is never comfortable for teaching, but if no other arrangement is available, move the chairs into a circle. When doing healings, move the chairs against the wall or out of the room completely, and do the healings on blankets on the floor or a sturdy table.

At festivals and conferences, conditions may not be optimal. I taught once in a cafeteria—we put our blankets up on the tables and used them for massage tables. If teaching outdoors, try to find a place that is out of the sun. Soft spring grass is lovely to do healing on. Bring along the sunscreen and water bottles. In any class, keep a glass of water, Gatorade or fruit juice beside you—talking as much as the teaching requires makes you dry. Do schedule breaks during the class. Both teacher and students need them.

Five straight chairs (or however many you decide to use in a row) are needed for passing the attunements. A long bench like a picnic bench can also be used. Holding the Hui Yin position is very difficult if your receivers are seated on the floor or ground, and you may not be able to hold the position and the energy. If there are no chairs in the space, ask your students to bring them from another room or workshop site. When agreeing to do the workshop, specify this need from the start. A bathroom should be nearby—it is extremely difficult to hold the Hui Yin position with a full bladder. The students' hands should also be clean before doing healings—remember they are placing them over their own and others' eyes.

I welcome children in my Reiki I classes as long as they are old enough not to be disruptive. When teaching a child Reiki, her mother or someone close to the child also needs the training, in order to understand what the child is doing and to help. I am increasingly surprised at how much young children can learn and how fast they learn it. One of my first young Reiki I's was Callie, the granddaughter of my friend Carolyn. Callie, her mother and Carolyn all got their Reiki I together. Since she was six and a half years old, I didn't know what to expect. By the end of the evening, however, Callie was teaching me how to teach Reiki I. Her comments about "socks and not mittens" for the hand position in Reiki, and "It goes up and then it comes down, and then you can move" are now part of my Reiki I teaching.

Children learn the Reiki positions, but spend very little time at each of them. Callie informed me that she knew exactly when to move, and it was more like thirty seconds than five minutes at each place. Children's energy runs so clear that Reiki moves through them quickly. When I later trained Kayla, who came to Reiki Shares when she was four, I observed the same thing. Kayla liked to walk into a room where a healing session was happening, put her hands on someone for a few moments, and then leave. She walked in and out from table to table, doing her healing on several people at each Share. She was always completely accurate in the positions and people she picked, and knew just where she was needed without talking about it. She participated at the center of each healing.

Kayla got her Reiki I attunement at three and a half. She came to my classes with her daddy who couldn't find a babysitter. The little girl was quiet and unintrusive, and when it was time for attunements I offered her one. Her dad said okay, and she liked the idea so she sat on his lap to receive it. She went to sleep after, and I didn't give her much thought. I didn't expect any healing from her at three and a half. A few months later, her dad called me on the phone. "You won't believe what Kayla did," he said. It seems that he had a headache and went to bed, telling the child to play quietly. Instead, she climbed into bed with him, put her hands on his forehead and said, "I'll fix it for you, Daddy." And she did. Later she joined the Reiki Shares.

My youngest Reiki II was eight. Again, it was unplanned. Molly came to my workshops with her mother, and at eight did fine with Reiki I. When her mother came for Reiki II the next day, Molly came along. I told her she could come, but to bring some things to keep her busy if she got bored. I told her she didn't have to stay any longer than she wanted to, she could go outside. Molly stayed with the class and got her Reiki II attunement. When I began to teach the Ki Exercises, she left, returning again at the end of the class with several sheets of perfectly drawn Reiki symbols. "You copied your handouts," I said. "No," said Molly, "I know them now." She became a competent distance healer at eight, and also joined the Reiki Shares—mostly to babysit for Kayla.

One young girl came to Reiki I and II, and I thought she was about fifteen. When she wanted to take Reiki III with her mother, her mother said no. She told me that Addy was only eleven. "When you can hold your muscles I'll teach you myself," said her mom. Addy will be a wonderful Reiki Master, probably when she is very young. The Third Degree is not for children, however; it requires teaching and a great deal of responsibility. It always delights me when children come to the Reiki I classes, and I encourage it. Some of my students teach Reiki I classes just for kids. Keep the numbers small if you do this.

My youngest Reiki I so far is six months old. His family is in crisis and I gave them all attunements to help them. I had no thought of a baby becoming a healer because the attunements were given to be healing. Bradley was too small to place the symbols in his hands, and he wiggled too much, so I put them down the front of his little body. I was amazed to feel his hands heat up immediately after the attunement. The infant got passed around a bit for all the grown-ups to feel this for themselves. He did an unusual amount of crying afterwards and may have been going through a cleansing. A month later, his mother says his hands are still hot.

I accept virtually anyone into Reiki I who wants to be there. The energy can never be used for harm, and the attunement heals everyone who receives it. If someone wants to come to the class and can't afford it, I always arrange for scholarships. There was only one time that I refused someone, and I think it was Reiki II that she was not supposed to have. Generally I assume that if someone comes to a class she is supposed to be there. On this occasion, a woman came to Reiki I so late that she missed the attunements and at least the first half of the teaching. Ordinarily, I would just give the attunement and set her to do a healing, letting others in the class show her the positions. Something this time kept me from doing this.

The woman wanted the Reiki I attunement so she could be accepted for the next day's Reiki II. I told her that she was too late, and would have to do it another time. After, the women in the class and I participated in a healing with her. We learned why she wasn't supposed to have Reiki II. In the healing we uncovered a past life where she had ritually sacrificed others. This lifetime had direct relation to the issues she was working on. She was not consciously aware of this past, but three healers saw it psychically and we talked about it later. We were all directed not to speak of it in the session. The woman was working off some very heavy karma with a blocked awareness. Reiki II would likely have opened the memories before she was ready for them, and may have been too much for her to handle at that time.

I have never refused anyone else for Reiki II training. If you know a prospective student to be manipulative of others, however, or deliberately misusing psychic energy, she may not be ready for Reiki II. The symbols cannot be misused and will not do harm to anyone no matter what intent they are sent with. Reiki is designed for healing, not for harming. The karma of misusing Reiki would be quite serious, however, and it may be best not to put someone who might try it in karma's way. When there is any doubt in a situation like this, follow your gut feelings and make contact with your guides or Reiki guides. Be very careful not to allow personal ego or a snap judgment into the decision. Sometimes you may be surprised at the results of guidance—as I've been.

I have refused only one person for Reiki III in a workshop out of town. Two women from the group came and said that if Beth (not her name) took the class they would refuse to be there. I knew one of the women well

enough to know that something serious was going on. They said that Beth had cheated at least half of the women in the workshop group at one time or another, and that she advertises teaching Reiki when she had only gotten her Reiki I and II with me that very day. I knew that there were personal feelings between Beth and one of the women who came to me and didn't know what to do. I wasn't sure if this was a personality conflict or if indeed Beth was a bad egg.

I had received no psychic impressions of this woman at all, which was unusual in itself, and therefore asked someone in the group to point her out to me. I still was getting no impressions to go on. I hid in the bathroom with my pendulum to talk to my guides. Sometimes on workshop trips it's the only private place. I was told to refuse her, and since I had never refused anyone before, I was quite concerned. I went to the woman and told her that I was making no judgment about her since I didn't know her, but that some women in the group did not want her in the class and I had to honor their decision. Beth started crying and I felt awful.

A longtime friend and student of mine was there for the weekend, and I asked her what information she got psychically about this woman. I didn't tell her why. My friend who had not previously seen or known her, said, "She has a slimy brown aura and something's wrong." I felt a little better with my decision. Later, I told the two women organizing the weekend what I had done, telling them that I'd be responsible. Both said they had thought of saying something to me about her since they too did not want to share Reiki III with her. They confirmed all the bad things the other women had told me. The next morning I did a ritual with the group and the woman completely disrupted it. I had all the confirmation necessary.

On another occasion, I disliked a woman who came to Reiki I and II sessions. She was quarrelsome and abrasive through both classes. She was actually a nuisance, very negative—she accepted nothing without arguing about it. I strongly hoped she would not come for Reiki III, but when I asked the guides about telling her not to, I wasn't given the go ahead to do that. Sunday and Reiki III came and she was in the class. I asked my guides again and was told to teach her. Afterwards, I wanted more information as to why I was supposed to give this person the Third Degree. She was definitely not Reiki Master material. The guides' response was that she would never use the energy or try to teach it and could do no wrong with it, whereas the Reiki energy would heal her.

As a rule, I accept anyone who comes to me for teaching, unless I am given strong reasons not to. When teaching a group, I don't feel a woman's lack of money to be reason for refusal. I feel that whoever comes to participate in a class was meant to be there, and that Reiki itself or the guides weed the wrong people out. If someone is not ready to go past Reiki I, she either knows that or has to work the next day. If she is not meant to be in the Reiki III class, she may even get a flat tire or be called away for an emergency errand. Most people know how much Reiki energy they are ready to take, and they abide by that decision. I feel that someone not ready for a degree but who nevertheless insists on taking it will not use it until she is able.

By teaching the Third Degree in open classes I have little say as to who comes. If I feel strongly that someone shouldn't be there I say so, but that has happened only the one time. I am sure that several of my not-ready or not-qualified students were there only to be part of a New Age class. They will not teach Reiki, and maybe won't even do the work required to learn the healing techniques. I feel that this is their choice and that they will not hurt Reiki in any way. They cannot use the energy for harm, and perhaps it may heal them or someone else through them one day. I have had students who I felt were not ready take the class, and return again the next time I'm in town to repeat it. The second time they were ready, and the changes in them emotionally were evident. I leave the final say to the Reiki guides. Ultimately, if there is something I need to know they tell me.

Another issue in teaching Reiki is scholarships. Should you teach someone who can't afford to pay? How many scholarships should there be? Will people who don't pay for Reiki use it and appreciate it? In Traditional Reiki there are no scholarships, and no sliding scale. I do not know of any Traditional Reiki Master accepting barter. The Traditional stance on scholarships is that unless people pay for Reiki and pay dearly they won't use it or respect it. My policy is that there must be scholarships with every class, and while some people (paying or not) don't use the energy, there seem to be as many (paying as not-paying) people who reject it.

If you are teaching six people, adding a seventh makes little extra work, just one more attunement. If someone wants the teaching enough to ask for a scholarship, I generally give it. She can join the class or the next class coming up. If she offers barter, I accept it. When I travel to teach, I usually have no idea who has paid and who hasn't, and I really don't care. At festivals I give the teaching without charge—all the way up to and including Reiki III. I have many teaching Reiki III's who received their training in this way, and they certainly appreciate it. What I ask in return from scholarship students is that they use the healing and/or teaching to help others. If they are willing to do that and most of them are, they have paid me in full.

Sometimes there are people with exceptional healing ability who need training in how to use their gifts. Reiki gives the framework to these people, and provides the basis for any other healing skill. I have trained several psychic healers in Reiki as a way of enhancing their abilities and teaching them how to use them. I have three "psychic daughters" this way. All of them were poor. Two were college students when I met them. They had no way to pay for Reiki classes, and I offered them without charge. These were women who needed Reiki, and all of them are teaching and healing today. I was such a healer when I received my first Reiki attunement, though I was not as young. I also had no money to pay for the degrees, but I certainly use and appreciate Reiki in every way.

Even when someone does not use what she has learned, Reiki gives her healing and something that she needed at the time. The attunements are a lifelong healing. I have no regrets for anyone I've ever trained. I feel that there was a reason for the teaching every time. Money is not an issue in this. Healing needs to be universal, and it is priceless. What the student does with the teaching afterwards is her own choice. If she makes use of it, she gains immeasurably. If she doesn't, it has still done good, having given her something that was needed. Reiki changes the life of everyone that receives it. It is rare for a person not to appreciate or use it.

Traditional Reiki I classes take a full weekend, and involve four attunements. When I took Reiki I, Friday night was a lecture on the history of Reiki and the Master gave one attunement. Saturday involved self-healing, with practice on the positions all day long, and two more attunements. All day Sunday was spent healing others and for the last initiation. The process was miserably slow in a room with a hard floor and no chairs. I teach Reiki I in three to five hours, with the single attunement method.

The Traditional Reiki II also involves a weekend, mostly of drilling the symbols, and an attunement. The students are required to memorize the symbols in the class. They are not permitted to take home drawings or to copy them in any way, and at the end of the weekend, the class ritually burns the handouts they've been given. I teach Reiki II in about two to three hours, sending handouts home so the students can learn the symbols at their own speed. Nontraditional Reiki requires one attunement for each degree.

The Traditional Reiki III takes a week of teaching, and a year or more apprenticeship; there is only one attunement. During the apprenticeship, the student may teach only with her Master present, and when she does so the Master is paid the class fees. I teach Reiki III in about five hours, and ask my students to work together to learn the attunement process and teaching methods. When in the same city, students are always welcome to observe my classes, and though I can't pay them I don't charge them for it, either. No one has ever needed me to supervise her class. I welcome student Reiki III's (or teaching ones) to help me pass attunements at festivals, and am grateful for their help. I provide my students support by phone when they ask for it and offer any other help I can.

I do not offer certificates or diplomas routinely, except in Reiki III. If someone wants it in the other degrees, however, I provide it. Sometimes at workshop weekends, the presenters make certificates for all the degrees available, and I sign them. I have a bit of disdain for credentials—the paper doesn't make a Reiki Master, her healing and teaching ability does. Likewise for Reiki I and II, it's the healing she does that makes the healer. Some Traditional teachers accept my certification, and some do not. As more of my students become teaching Masters, all three degree classes will become available anywhere. In the meantime I offer them while I am travelling and at festivals as frequently as I can. I ask my Reiki III's to seriously consider teaching, and many of them are doing so.

In Traditional circles, the certification and lineage have become status symbols. Healing isn't paramount, the diploma is. I once went to a Traditional Reiki Share. Several people there were quite wealthy; all were Reiki I's and a few II's. The Reiki II's had clearly more status than

the Reiki I healers and acted the part. They did healings for each other as a social event, but when I mentioned AIDS work, they all moved far away from me and left me sitting alone on the couch. A certificate doesn't make a healer; a healer is someone who actually does healing.

Nevertheless, in this status-conscious world certificates have meaning for many people. I am always glad to give them if someone wants them. Sometimes they help people to come for Reiki healing sessions who otherwise would not appreciate or understand the teaching. A certificate means authority for some people, and is what they are taught to trust. Traditional Reiki Masters ask to see a Reiki I certificate before accepting a student for Reiki II, but a certificate is no assurance that the person has learned the material.

Most nontraditional teachers offer some sort of certification for the Reiki degrees, and I have no problem with this. A suggestion, for those who use them, is not to buy diplomas individually from office supply stores where they cost about a dollar each, but to have them made up on a computer. With the form made this way, they can be xeroxed on nice paper far more cheaply. This can be done at most print shops and copy centers, if you don't have the capability on your own computer. The form costs about thirty dollars to make up, but saves money in the long run if you teach frequently.

The following material lists specifically what is to be taught in a Reiki I, Reiki II and Reiki III class. Each degree requires an attunement, and the teacher needs a series of handouts for each student in each degree. (Copy centers get rich on Reiki Masters.) My students have permission to copy any of my handout sheets for their classes, as long as they identify the source of the material (see Appendix). As new Masters gain experience, they usually develop handout material of their own. The following is just an outline; this book itself is the teaching guide. The best way to know what to teach in each degree is to remember what you learned when you took it, and what worked best for you.

REIKI I

I like to begin by going around the room, asking everyone's name and what previous experience they have had with healing. Keep it brief; you may need to stop someone who wants to tell her autobiography. This gives the Master some idea of the level of the group. For someone who has never had experience with healing or energy work at all, Reiki is a good place to start. For someone who uses other methods, massage for example, Reiki becomes an addition to their work. Next, I introduce myself and give a brief introduction of why I am teaching Reiki rather than some other method. I tell the group that by the end of the afternoon they will be competent healers and will no longer need a Reiki I teacher.

Next, give a short definition of what Reiki is and does, and tell the Reiki history. This takes about twenty minutes. Describe the three degrees. Someone will want to know what an attunement is—define it as best you can. I usually tell them that it has to be experienced, that it cannot be adequately defined. Everyone who has had experience with Reiki healing has stories to tell. Tell a few of your own and the class may have some to add. If someone in the group has already had a Reiki healing or Reiki I, ask her to talk about it. If she has Reiki degrees, ask her how Reiki has changed her life. Talk about the Reiki principles—you may wish to have them on a handout.

Pass out sheets picturing the Reiki I hand positions for self-healing. Show the positions, asking the students to feel the energy in their hands now, and to compare it after the attunement. Describe the energy cycle, and how long the hands remain at each position once they have had their Reiki I attunement. This is a good place for a break. During it set up the chairs for the attunements, and before or after the break describe what comes next. Do not allow the group to scatter too far during the break, set a time limit, and bring them back when you are ready. Breaks can stretch for the afternoon if you don't set limits.

After the break, pass the attunements. Tell the students that you need their silence, and that you will work in groups of five (or however many you use). Show them how to hold their hands, and tell them that as one group is finished and gets up the next five are to fill the chairs quickly. Passing attunements for a group of twenty-five people takes at least forty-five minutes, even if you work rapidly. Keep it moving and keep the chairs filled. At the end of each group, let them know that you are finished and they can move.

As each group is finished and leaves the chairs, tell them to put their hands down on someone else in the class, and to keep them there for several minutes. They will know when the energy has moved through them; it

begins flowing out their hands and their palms start to heat. They can put their hands on someone's shoulders or back, or wherever the person receiving the energy wants it. Once this is finished, the students begin a self-healing. This will keep them busy while you do the attunements for all the rest.

When everyone has received her attunement, ask who wants to talk about what she has experienced. Don't spend a long time at this but get a few responses. Ask if there is anyone in the group who felt nothing. If someone indicates this first feel her hands; if they are hot, no more is needed. If she needs more help, wait until the others begin healing to talk with her privately. Occasionally someone has a strong reaction to the attunement and it worries her. She may feel extremely spacey and unbalanced, may feel a release of unpleasant emotions or energy, or she may feel uncomfortably hot. Get such people doing healing on someone else immediately. This is the best way to balance their energy. I also use flower essences to help here—the Bach/Traditional Rescue Remedy or Clematis, or Perelandra's Grus an Aachen Rose or Oregold Rose Essence. The sensations pass in a few minutes, particularly once the student starts bringing the energy through her hands.

At this point, pass out sheets that show the hand positions for direct healing for others. Set up a massage table, if one is available, or work on the floor at the front of the group to demonstrate the hands-on positions. There is always someone who wants to be a model for this—make sure the model sees the positions on other people after. Don't take the time to do a full healing; just go over the positions briefly. Use the time when your hands are down to talk about such things as how long to hold the hands in place, the energy cycle, emotional releases, etc. Talk about the Reiki I ethic—that healing is to be done only with permission.

Once you have shown the positions on front and back, and everyone has understood them and has no more questions, show a group healing. I always want to wait until later for this, but then I forget to do it when the group breaks into pairs. Show it now. Using a new model, bring several people to the front of the group to demonstrate it. Talk about Reiki Shares. Someone interested may want to pass around a sign-up sheet for starting them; encourage this. If the class is in your home town, you may become the organizer for these.

Have the class break into pairs to do healing with each other. Each student gives and receives a session. If there is too little time or too many students, do this as group healings, but the one-on-one sessions are important and should be used as often as possible. Tell the class that if anyone is still having uncomfortable sensations with the energy, doing healing is the cure. If this happens after the class, as it may for the next few weeks, doing healing is the way to resolve it. Tell them that the sensations are harmless, discuss what they might expect, and mention detoxification. The paired healings take almost half of the class time and are extremely important. They bring the attunement energy through the students, teach the positions kinesthetically, and make the healing system real to them. It is these sessions after the attunements that make them Reiki I's.

Be available for questions, but from this point the teaching is pretty much done. If everyone is paired off, join the pairs in giving and receiving a healing. Doing so helps the Master to come down from the attunement energy, and it feels great. Too many healers have no one to do healing for them, and they need it as much as everyone else does. If there is time at the end of the class, do a few more group healings. From this point your class doesn't need you anymore—they're on their own. It's a miracle every time. Allow about five hours for Reiki I, plus possibly a lunch break. I usually prefer to make it a long evening or afternoon, as meal breaks take so much time.

The handouts for Reiki I include hand positions for self-healing and for healing others. They may optionally include the Reiki principles, and information on emotional sources of dis-ease. The ethic for Reiki I is to do healing only with permission. This is a bare-bones Reiki I class outline; add what other information you feel is needed.

REIKI II

Reiki II takes less time to teach than the other degrees, but requires more handouts and more work by the students at home. I again prefer an informal setting, but a classroom is feasible. Place the chairs in a circle, or if it is comfortable have everyone who can do so sit on the floor. Some chairs should be available for those who can't sit comfortably on the floor. Go around the room for names again, and ask if anyone has questions about Reiki I. When I do weekend intensives, this establishes a

continuity to the class work and clears up anything you may have missed the day before. If you have forgotten anything in Reiki I, this is the place to add it.

Even if the students have been using the First Degree for some time, they may have questions to ask.

Next describe what is different in Reiki II—that it works with distance healing, adds the symbols, etc. Ask who in the class has done distance healing work before. I am always surprised that usually less than half have done so. Go around the room again, asking those who do distance healing to describe how they do it. There will be a variety of methods. People who think they haven't done it before may be surprised to realize that they do it often. Then give your own method of doing absentee work, or give a step-by-step simple distance process.

Teach the four specifically Reiki ways of doing distance healing. These are 1) imagining the person shrunk small and held in your hands, 2) imagining being with them to do a direct session, 3) using your knee and leg as a focus, and 4) using a teddy bear or other surrogate. Tell them that the Reiki symbols are added to whatever method of distance healing the student uses, and explain how they are visualized and sent.

Talk about the ethics for Reiki II, which begins with how to obtain permission if someone has not given it on the physical level. This is important. I emphasize ethics in Reiki II, as it is the first conscious use of a highly expanded energy. When talking about non-healing uses and manifesting, I emphasize ethics again. It is not ethical to manipulate anyone in any way. When manifesting, put yourself in the picture, but others only by permission. Bringing abundance into one's life is very ethical—some people may not know that—but taking abundance from someone else so you can have it is not.

Next, explain the symbols, using handouts that picture all three and how to draw them. The handout may include some further information on using the symbols. Trace the symbols in the air with your hand to show how they are drawn, and you may wish the class to practice this. Stop for questions frequently. Then discuss non-healing uses for the symbols—blessing and clearing over food, clearing houses and entities, protection, past-life work. Invite discussion here. Whereas the material in Reiki I was hands-on and kinesthetic—it had to be felt rather than talked about—Reiki II is intellectual. In the Second Degree, worlds are created from the Void by the mind.

Offer a break at this point and then pass the attunements. There are none of the opening difficulties that can occur in Reiki I, and no need to put their hands down on someone. The students may be spacey, more so than with the First Degree, but this is usually the only immediate reaction. Warn them about spaciness later, and about the six-month period of emotional healing and life change that follows Reiki II. When they leave, they need to be careful driving.

I once taught Reiki I and II together, and as the group left, I warned them that they might be very spacey. Everyone said they felt fine. About half an hour later, one of the group called and asked if she could come back to the house where the workshop was and spend the evening with us. I was staying there with the women who had organized the weekend. We agreed and we all went out to dinner and spent the evening talking. At one point I asked the woman why she had come back. She turned bright red and seemed upset, so I told her she didn't have to tell me. She decided to and said, "You were right about being spacey. I couldn't find my way home."

Finish Reiki II by handing out the information on the Ki Exercises and talking a bit about why they are important. Tell the group that if they are not going on for Reiki III, they can send the symbols in healing whole without memorizing how to draw them. They can also ignore the Exercises if they are not going further. Completing the process gives them so much, however, that they may wish to do it all. I encourage my Reiki II's to do the work—to memorize the symbols and practice the Ki Exercises. I also urge them to take Reiki III if they are committed healers and interested in teaching Reiki. With the nontraditional simple methods and low fees, Reiki III can be available to anyone who would benefit from it and use it.

The handouts for this degree include the three symbols and how to draw them, some information on how to use the symbols, and an explanation of the Ki Exercises. The ethics for Reiki II are non-manipulation, and receiving permission for distance healing.

REIKI III

The program for Reiki III sounds simple, but teaching it takes a longer time than Reiki I or II—at least five hours with a lively group. The outline involves teaching two additional symbols, the attunement process, the material on Buddhism (see the next chapter) and information on how to teach each of the three degrees. There is also an attunement. Teaching Reiki III is the most exciting of the three degrees. The students are advanced healers and the cream of the crop, and there are fewer of them. In the course of Reiki I and II you have begun to know them individually. Those students not ready for Reiki III, or not able to make the commitment, are no longer present.

You will already know these students' names, but if not go around the room once more. Ask if there are any questions about Reiki so far, or anything left undone from Reiki II. If any of these students have not had Reiki II in the nontraditional format, the Ki Exercises and a discussion of the Hui Yin position begins the class. Have handouts available for those who need them. Tell the class that whatever Reiki II symbols they are already using are fine to continue with, even if they are different from what you otherwise use. There might be some discussion of the differences in symbols.

Now present the Reiki III symbols, spending time with the Dai-Ko-Myo and Raku and their uses in healing and out of it. Give handouts containing both Traditional and nontraditional versions of the Dai-Ko-Myo, telling students your preference and the advantages of each, and telling them they have a choice. A discussion of non-Reiki symbols is optional. Talk about the information of the next chapter. This is advanced material on the origin of the symbols which brings the whole Reiki system into fascinating perspective. I save it for Reiki III to keep the symbols as simple as possible while students are learning them.

The attunement process is next. Explain and demonstrate it. Placing a single chair in the center of the room, pass the Third Degree attunement for each student, while the others watch the process and follow it with the handout sheet. Unless the group is very large, I prefer to pass the Reiki III attunement individually. Everyone has a strong reaction to this very powerful energy. Some sit there giggling as I did after it, some break into tears, some people go out of body completely for a few minutes, and more than one person starts to channel. The Third Degree attunement energy is total joy. You may wish to do some explaining between attunements, or save the commentary for the beginning or end.

Once the attunements are passed and the demonstration on doing them and questions are finished, ask if anyone in the group wants to try doing an attunement right then. They may look at the handout sheets for the symbols and outline. Some brave students may want to do this, but usually I find that they are too overwhelmed by this time. Don't push them. They can practice later, and they will. In one class I had a woman, who though she did well at everything all weekend, was convinced that she would never have the ability to pass attunements or to teach. I told her I would prove otherwise for her, and coached her through the process of passing an attunement on me right then. I held the symbol sheets and outline for her, and told her what to do step by step. She was thrilled and delighted at the energy she felt, and it raised her self-confidence tremendously.

It takes most students at least a couple of months after the Reiki weekend to be ready to pass attunements or to teach. For most people, holding the Hui Yin position long enough takes a few weeks of exercises. It takes time to memorize the symbols and to learn the process. Students who have started with Reiki I and gone to Reiki III in a weekend need much more time; they must learn all three degrees. After the Reiki weekend, most students are overwhelmed with the information and the energy, and it takes some time to integrate and assimilate it. They may need several days of increased sleep while their Hara Lines expand to the energy. There are exceptions to this, however.

One student had Reiki I and II Traditionally, and brought me to her city to teach a weekend. She would get her own Reiki III on Sunday, but I sent her the Hui Yin material before I got there. When I arrived, she was so eager that I gave her Reiki III on Friday afternoon. Friday night when I taught Reiki I, I teased her about being ready to help me. She placed the handout pages on a chair beside her and proceeded to pass two attunements successfully. Then she broke down and cried, saying she could go no further. She taught her first Reiki I class within a month, and I'm sure she did it well. She had waited ten years for her Reiki III and was not willing to wait any longer.

After the attunements, talk about what information to cover in teaching each of the three degrees. The material of this chapter discusses this. Most of the discussion and questions come in the attunement section. I often go overtime, with everyone ready to leave and hungry for dinner. It might be helpful to make a handout with an outline of the class work of each degree. Things that are important to talk about include how to know that people have opened to the attunement, what to do if they haven't, and how to help people with strong reactions to them. When teaching Reiki I insist that people put their hands down on someone after receiving the initiation. Students always want to know whom to allow into a class or to refuse entrance for advanced degree classes.

Hopefully the day is over when the requirement for healing and healer's training is wealth. Healing needs to be available to everyone, and healer's training needs to be accessible to anyone with talent or the desire to do it. There is nothing wrong with charging for healing sessions or for teaching; a healer has the right to make a living. Reiki provides abundance and every type of riches for its practitioners and teachers. When prices are kept reasonable and there are scholarships available, abundance will come. In the United States today, we have a medical system that leaves uninsured and poor people out in the cold. It is wrong in medicine, and especially wrong in a healing system that comes out of the Buddhist philosophy of compassion for all living things. What you send out comes back to you manyfold.

Often Reiki III students discuss the problem of money. They want to know what to charge, when to have scholarships, whether the healing/teaching will be appreciated without payment, whether they can make a living ethically from Reiki? I feel that the above paragraph states my position, but again there is free will. Class discussion on this issue will be lively as it is an important topic. Since all of the area's Reiki teachers are probably together in the room, it is an important discussion. Agreement among the students now may have implications for years to come. Allow the discussion to go on as long as it seems to be getting somewhere, but realize that each student must make her own choices and come to terms with the problem in her own way.

A number of Reiki Masters from other modern and Traditional methods have taken my training. One couple wanted to teach Reiki at an AIDS center but felt their attunement method was impossible for large groups. They joined my classes for the three-day period, observing me teach each degree, and receiving my method of attunements. They liked the feeling of the modern attunements and their simplicity, and used my methods when they began teaching. Before long they switched to the nontraditional methods completely. I have often had Traditionally trained people come to my workshops with the purpose of checking me out or of complaining to or about me. They leave with a different idea. One woman told me she had expected to find "a witch teaching Reiki" and instead found "a Reiki Master who is also a witch." We both considered this a compliment. The nontraditional methods are tried and true, and very powerful.

I like to talk a bit about the possibility of becoming self-important when one becomes a Master, and I remind students to be humble. Reiki has an intelligence and sacred quality beyond anything of human design, and as teachers our responsibility and dedication are to Reiki and to those we teach. I talk about the need for us to make more Reiki III's, both to encourage the group to go out and teach, and to ask them to train teachers. There is a temptation for some new Reiki Masters to hold on to the secrets and the miracles. Remember the world we live in, and how much need there is to heal it. With more teaching Reiki III's, Reiki can become universal on Earth again, and everyone who receives it will benefit.

The handouts for a Reiki III class include the Ki Exercises for those who have not seen them before, the Third Degree symbols and how to draw them, and a sheet of instructions on passing attunements. Optional additional handouts might include an outline of the next chapter's Buddhist information, and an outline of what to teach in each degree. The ethic for Reiki III involves charging reasonable fees and allowing scholarships. I also consider a committment to teach as part of the Third Degree ethic.

This is a brief outline of a Reiki III Master's class. I can't begin to describe how wonderful it feels to teach it. I have trained several hundred Reiki III's, and a large percentage are teaching. So far they are bringing Reiki at reasonable prices to people in the United States, Canada, Germany and Mexico. There is need for many more teachers and healers everywhere, and I ask my Reiki IIIs to teach. I can give a woman the potential by passing the attunement and the teaching information, but she must make herself a Master by her own efforts.

The above material outlines what to do in each Reiki class for the three degrees. Each teacher develops her own methods—those given here offer only a starting point

and guidelines. The last chapter of this book discusses Reiki and Buddhism. These are the keys to the entire Reiki system, and discovering them has been the most exciting piece of the entire Reiki puzzle for me. I have placed it last because it puts the whole system of Reiki in perspective.

In my quest to understand the meaning and origins of the Reiki system, I had the good fortune a few years ago to talk with a Mahayana Buddhist nun. She was quite familiar with the Reiki symbols in her Buddhist practice, though not with Reiki healing, and her information gave me a whole new perspective to the subject. When I researched this book and added the insights emerging from additional reading on Buddhism, I received answers to some questions on the Reiki process. Mikao Usui spoke of a simple formula from which Reiki and the symbols were derived. In the information I received from Buddhist philosophy, I think I have found that 2500-year-old formula. Much of the expanded information I have on the Reiki symbols comes from this research and the formula that is presented below.

From my reading in Mahayana and Vajrayana Buddhism, I see striking resemblances to the root philosophies of virtually all religions. Buddhism does not worship a God or Goddess, but accepts the deities of whatever culture it finds itself in. It is a universal philosophy of Be-ing, rather than a system of worshipping a prime mover. Tantric mysticism that arose from Mahayana Buddhism displays the essence of every world metaphysical system, including Wicca. It was brought to the West as Theosophy by Madame Helena Blavatsky. The original teachings of the historical Jesus are found in Buddhism as well, including his healing ability, parables, philosophy, attitude, and miracles.

Gautama Siddhartha, the Sakyamuni Buddha, was born in 620 BCE in India on the Nepal border. He died in 543 BCE. Like the teachings of Jesus, the words of the Buddha were not recorded in his lifetime; the first records originated several hundred years later. This is a long time. In the Christian Bible, only a few lines are directly indicated to have been Jesus' own words and teachings; more of the words of Gautama Siddhartha remain.

The Buddha sought a way to free all people from suffering, pain and reincarnation. He accepted both men and women in his teachings and people of all castes and classes—both as unusual in traditional Hindu society as they were when Jesus did the same thing six centuries later in the Middle Eastern patriarchy. The Buddha's Enlightenment did not depend on a patriarchal god or even a teacher, but on understanding gained from within. When he found his answers, he did not enter the state of bliss/Nirvana offered him, but returned to help others

CHAPTER TEN

Reiki and the Path to Enlightenment

find the way. Enlightenment is "a direct, dynamic spiritual experience brought about…through the faculty of intuition…. or more simply, 'seeing clearly'."[1] It results in liberation and freedom, the "light" of information and understanding.

The Sermon at Benares is the Buddha's equivalent of Jesus' Sermon on the Mount. In it, the gist of Buddhist teaching is given. There are "Four Noble Truths" that are contained in this document. The first is, "Existence is unhappiness." The second is, "Unhappiness is caused by selfish craving." Truth number three is, "Selfish craving can be destroyed." The Eightfold Path is the fourth truth, by which this can happen. The Path's steps are: 1) right understanding, 2) right purpose or aspiration, 3) right speech, 4) right conduct, 5) right vocation, 6) right effort, 7) right alertness, and 8) right concentration.[2]

Existence is unhappiness just as a condition of being alive. There is sickness, old age, and death plus the grief of watching loved ones suffer. Pain and suffering cause unhappiness, and these are the central problems of existence. They are the problems that the compassionate Buddha sought to solve. In his Enlightenment, Gautama Siddhartha was shown that suffering is caused by attachment to the process of living and to other people. The cravings of life can never be fully satisfied. This attachment results in frustration and negative action that generate karma. Life creates karma which makes the necessity for further lifetimes, as karma is both made and cleared while in the body.

Attachment and craving can be released and karma healed so that the soul no longer needs to return to be embodied. In Buddhism this is the way to end unhappiness, and the only real means of healing—to end reincarnation. The Eightfold Path, the Buddhist moral code and equivalent of the Ten Commandments, provides the means to accomplish this. In his Enlightenment, the Buddha was shown that this ending of the wheel of incarnation and karma is possible for every person. His teachings are centered on bringing others to Enlightenment, an inner understanding process of karma release, with him.

Effort, alertness and concentration—the means of controlling the mind—are among the skills required to meet the goal, as reality is subject to the mind's creation. When the mind is completely freed of attachment or craving, the person enters Nirvana and no longer needs to be reborn. Understanding the truth of the Mind and the process of existence results in this freedom. Nirvana is described not as extinction, but as "liberation, inward peace and strength, insight into truth, the joy of complete oneness with reality, and love toward all creatures in the universe."[3]

Reality is created by the action of Mind from the Void. The Void is the depths of fathomless peace, purity, perfection, mystery and joy. In Wiccan terms it is Spirit, Ether or Goddess. All Be-ing comes from the Void, and it is the essence of all existence. All Be-ing (everyone) is already in a state of perfection, a part of the Buddha Nature (or Goddess Within). Reality is also the Non-Void, which is all potential, and a vast complex of worlds and shifting universes. Mind emerging from the Void is the first Buddha source, but this source is obscured to most people by the illusion of the senses, the Non-Void. The reality created by this obscuring of Pure Mind is like the reality created in a mirror. People in incarnation do not awaken to their intrinsic purity (the Void) which exists beyond the senses. Their understanding is based upon the Non-Void's illusion. A distorted mind on Earth acts to creates a distorted reality, resulting in suffering.

"Mind, which manifests itself as wisdom, is intrinsically Void; yet everything proceeds from it and is therefore mind's creation."[4] Everything real is created from the perfection of the Void. Yet, because of distortion and illusion, we perceive the world as imperfect and remain attached to delusion. Wisdom=energy=creation is the Void, and participates in Nirvana. Human perception of reality is Non-Void, based upon potential, and participates in the Mind's creation of suffering in the world. Enlightenment is understanding the joy of the Void, one's perfect Buddha Nature, and leaving the attachments and delusions of the Non-Void and the senses. Once true reality is perceived, attachments and cravings no longer have meaning, and Nirvana is attained. This understanding is Enlightenment, which leads to the release of the soul from karma and incarnation. It happens by the freeing of the Mind from delusion.

The foundation of Buddhist teaching lies in the Divine Abodes, the qualities of loving-kindness, compassion, sympathetic joy and equanimity.[5] The Buddha expressed these virtues when he refused Nirvana to save others from suffering. After the beginnings of Theravada

Buddhism in the earliest centuries after the Buddha's death (Parinirvana, ascension), Mahayana Buddhism developed in northern India by the first and second centuries. This branch of Buddhism is still central today and bases its teachings on the above foundations. A primary tenet of Mahayana Buddhism is the surety that everyone can gain Enlightenment, including those who cannot devote their lives to the religious life. Another contribution of the Mahayana is the concept of the Bodhisattva.

A Bodhisattva is someone who has achieved Enlightenment, but delays his or her entry into Nirvana until everyone achieves Enlightenment with her. She stays in the world to help all Be-ings. Kwan Yin is probably the best-known example of a Bodhisattva. She is known as Kannon in Japan, and her near equivalent in Tibet is Tara. Jesus probably fit the Bodhisattva description, as did his mother Mary. Most of the Bodhisattvas are male. A Bodhisattva has the virtues of a Buddha and will become a Buddha when she leaves the Earth at last. Gautama Siddhartha was not the only Buddha, but the first to find the Path. The Bodhisattva is the Mahayana ideal person.

Vajrayana or Tantric Buddhism developed in Tibet from the Mahayana sect. It is the mystic and esoteric outgrowth of Buddhism, affirming loyalty to a teacher or guru, and containing colorful ritual, initiations, mandalas and mantras, peaceful and wrathful deities, visualization to control the mind, advanced meditation practices, and a rich and varied symbolism. Because of the harsh climate and isolation of Tibet, Vajrayana Buddhism developed into a far different religion than that which was practiced in India, but its basis is nevertheless in the Mahayana *Sutras* and philosophies. Tantrists worship the Buddha as symbolized in sacred statues and artwork, but in meditation they seek the Buddha and the Bodhisattvas within their own minds.[6] They work to understand the many realities and the perfection of the Void.

The Reiki formula is from the Mahayana *Sutras* and the Vajrayana mystical interpretation. The five Reiki symbols are the five levels of mind that lead to Enlightenment. They are familiar to Buddhists as the Path to Enlightenment itself. They are also the five elements, five colors and five forms represented everywhere in Tantric art. The five elements are earth, water, fire, wind (air) and Void (Spirit). The five colors are yellow, white, red, black and blue, and the five forms are the

The Stupa and the Five Elements[7]

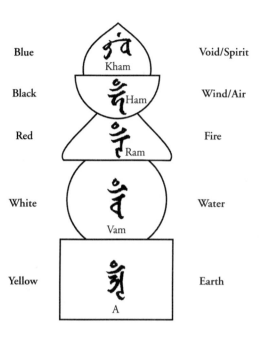

Blue		Void/Spirit
Black		Wind/Air
Red		Fire
White		Water
Yellow		Earth

The Five Forms

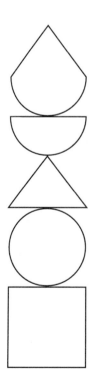

The Stupa and the Body

Void/Spirit/Goddess
Blue
The Absolute
The ninth Consciousness
Enlightenment
The Raku

Wind
Black
Nirvana
The five senses
Spiritual Body
Dai-Ko-Myo

Fire
Red
Enlightenment
Mind
Mental Body
Hon-Sha-Ze-Sho-Nen

Water
White
Practice
The "passionate mind"
Emotional Body
Sei-He-Ki

Earth
Yellow
The initial Awakening
The "store" Consciousness
Physical/Etheric
Cho-Ku-Rei

square, circle, triangle, half-circle and cintamani (composite) of the Stupa. They may be compared to the five points of the pentacle in Wicca, with the Void as Spirit or Ether. The five elements are also associated with the chakras.

Together the five Reiki symbols are the non-duality of mind and object and the emptiness from ego that achieves Buddhist Nirvana. Once attained, the formula and process of Reiki releases the soul from the wheel of incarnation. The symbol system's original use was not for healing, but spiritual— Enlightenment for the purpose of helping others, the Bodhisattva Path. The Reiki symbols are wisdom-energy-creation, the undistorted perfection of the Void, and they culminate in liberation.

It is important to note here that the *Sutras* and the Vajrayana texts were written in Sanskrit (the earlier

Theravada texts were in Pali). The Buddha did not speak Sanskrit, which is a scholar's language like Latin in the West, but the Bihari dialect from his birth district. India is a country of many languages. Buddhism travelled from India to Tibet, across Southeast Asia, then to China, Korea and Japan. Along the way it was changed by many interpretations in several different languages and cultures over many centuries. The Reiki teaching travelled this way as well for over 2500 years, transcending a variety of languages and cultures to reach the West. Its translation into English by modern Western society represents yet another major change.

Through all of these changes, translations, and reinterpretations, both Buddhism and Reiki have survived. Buddhism is the religion of between a third and a fifth of the world's people today, and is alive in a variety of cultures. It is a tribute to the Buddhist Reiki healing system that it remains as vital for Western users as it did in its countries and languages of origin. The Reiki of India was probably different from the Reiki of Tibet because the cultures and customs were different. The Reiki that Jesus brought from India was probably different from the Reiki of today. Likewise, the Reiki of Japan must have differed from that of Tibet and India.

And Reiki is different in the West from the tradition that Mikao Usui revived, but it is still vital and alive. That the healing system is evolving today in Western culture is no surprise to someone knowledgeable in Buddhism. Like Buddhism itself, Reiki fits whatever culture and century it finds itself in, and adapts to different languages and societies. This is another of the Reiki miracles.

Psychic phenomena are not encouraged in Buddhist practice, but they happen along the way. Meditation designed for learning control of the mind also opens the inner senses. The exercises for moving Ki clear the Hara Line and the chakras. Healing is not as discouraged by Buddhists as some other psychic skills, but healing is still considered a distraction from the Enlightenment Path. The Buddhist nun I talked with felt that my interest in healing was misplaced, when I could do more good for the world by attaining Enlightenment for others' sake and going on the Bodhisattva Path. When Mikao Usui tried to find information on the Buddha's method of healing, he was probably given a similar response. It is not that healing is considered unimportant, but that it requires many years of training toward Enlightenment

before the skills manifest. And even then, healing is secondary to achieving the Path.

Spirituality supersedes all worldly concerns in Buddhism. When Mikao Usui found the beggars he had healed returning to the slums, he realized what the Buddhists had told him all along—that without addressing the process of the mind and spirit, the body cannot be permanently healed. Buddhists feel that the only healing is achieved by gaining freedom from the wheel of incarnation. As long as reincarnation in the body is required, there is dissatisfaction, illness and suffering. Karma can only be healed while in the body, creating an ever-turning cycle of hopelessness. By entering the Path to Enlightenment, attachment is released, karma is healed, the mind is freed from its continual re-creation of delusion, and reincarnation ends. This path to end reincarnation is the symbol formula of Reiki.

In the five symbols are the five stages to this process or Path. The Cho-Ku-Rei is the beginning stage and represents the physical/etheric double level. The Sei-He-Ki is the transformation of emotion and ego (the emotional body), and the Hon-Sha-Ze-Sho-Nen is the creation of true reality by the understanding of Pure Mind on the mental body level. The Dai-Ko-Myo is the attainment of the Bodhisattva Path and represents the spiritual body. The Raku is Enlightenment itself, transcendence and Nirvana, the beyond-the-body Transpersonal level. Each of the symbols has representation in one of the vibrational bodies, and each of the symbols primarily affects one of the four bodies and is used for healing at that vibrational level. The formula is the major path of study of Mahayana and Vajrayana Buddhism, where it is openly discussed and far from secret. The symbols' healing uses were considered incidental to their spiritual value.

The Reiki symbols are Sanskrit-derived Japanese forms, at least 2500 years old. They are designed psychically as pictures and sounds (mantras), and also are letters spelling out a meaning. The nun recognized the symbols and felt that the variations were cultural. One set looked more to her like an attempt to transfer the Sanskrit into Japanese. She identified them clearly, knew their names and the concepts each invoked. They are the Path to Enlightenment symbolized, a formula in this context as they are a formula in Reiki healing. Discussion of each symbol follows, with an interpretation that is my best attempt at understanding their complexities.

THE CHO-KU-REI

The Cho-Ku-Rei is the first step and the first experience on the Path, the generation stage. The student is given a mandala to meditate upon. Her goal is to focus in an altered state upon the circular picture until she perceives no difference between the world of her meditation and the physical Earth. Detachment from the Earthplane and entrance into the egoless state of the Void is the goal of the exercise. The student begins to learn meditation, to detach from daily life if only for a moment, by concentration on the image. The mandala is then drawn into the student's heart. By transferring reality to the mandala, the person detaches from the Non-Void of the world, and enters the perfection of the Void. Some meditators begin

The Mandala

with a simple object, like a bowl of water, while other mandalas are more complex. The student learns to focus her attention beyond herself and into the picture.

The mandala form in Tantric art represents the All-One and the All-Many. It symbolizes the Enlightenment process, as the One is the Buddha and the Many refers to All People. Ultimate reality is the union of matter and energy, and of the first five elements (earth, water, fire, air and the Void/Ether) with the sixth element, consciousness. A mandala represents the non-duality (union) of the ultimate reality of the universe, and the word itself

means "to have attained perfect and unsurpassable illumination."[8] "Manda" is essence, and "la" is completion.

Visually, these are not simply abstract patterns, but picture within them deities, Buddhas, and Bodhisattvas. Their use in meditation trains the mind in complex visualization practices. In Vajrayana Buddhism, this is done to gain mind control, skill in creating mental images, to contact Goddesses and other psychic forces (also mind-created), and to achieve altered consciousness states. The mandala is described as a great circle of peaceful and wrathful deities.[9]

As she becomes more skilled, the deities in the mandala help the student to overcome obstacles on her path. They are recognized as having life and also as being mind-created constructs. By identifying with the deity, the student realizes the emptiness (Void) of all things. Student and mandala are one, student and deity are one, and both partake of the Void. The deity and mandala are drawn into the heart, and the student becomes the deity. In alchemical terms, "the worship, worshipper, and the worshipped are the same."[10]

John Blofeld, in *The Tantric Mysticism of Tibet*, presents a Cho-Ku-Rei stage meditation on Tara, the Tibetan Bodhisattva/Goddess:

> Tara's heart reveals the syllable *Dham* surrounded by her special mantra from which light-rays shine in all directions. The adept draws these rays 'like nectar or rain' through the crown of his head and down into the heart, whereupon his body becomes "pure as a crystal vessel...."

> Tara gazes at him with great joy and, gradually diminishing to the size of a thumb, enters his body through the crown of the head and comes to rest upon a solar-disc atop a lunar-disc and lotus in his heart. Now the adept's own body begins to diminish in size, getting smaller and smaller until it is coextensive with the diminutive figure of Tara. "Tara...and adept are truly one with no distinction whatever".[11]

Meditation on the Cho-Ku-Rei itself has similar results, taking the person into the labyrinth, detaching her from the Earthplane world. In current metaphysical terms, it teaches her to go out of body by going within. Learning to meditate and enter altered states, to let go of the mundane world, and to experience the peace of the Void and emptiness of the ego is the beginning process of every spirituality discipline. In any deep meditative state, the ego is withdrawn and the Buddha Nature or Goddess Within comes forward. At first the beginner can focus only briefly, but with practice her concentration grows. In time, she trains her mind to create worlds. In Reiki, the Cho-Ku-Rei is the "light switch" that turns the healing energy on and increases its power. As the generation stage, it is the physical body healing level, the beginning of healing and the use of Reiki energy. It is the doorway to Reiki and healing.

THE SEI-HE-KI

Transforming the emotions is an alchemical process and the second stage on the Buddhist Path to Enlightenment. Earth and the person incarnated upon it are considered to be impure ground. They are represented by the color yellow. The fire of wisdom purifies, raising the Earthly level and the student to a new awareness (gold). This is a transmutation reminiscent of the European Renaissance alchemist. In that culture, the alchemist wanted to turn lead into gold, but what was changed in the process was the consciousness of the alchemist herself. Alchemy was a combination of magick and the beginnings of science. So too with the above. In Buddhism, wisdom equals energy equals creation.

This is a nonconceptual (subconscious) state of Be-ing changed to realization and awareness. The person who has lived in a distorted world suddenly perceives the truth of the Void. She goes through the distortion of the mirror and beyond it. By realization of the emptiness of the self, she reaches Enlightenment. Impure ground is purified by wisdom from yellow to golden light. Few people achieve this stage of development—it is the Buddha status. The Buddha is the union of the One and the Many, and exists as the true nature of all Be-ings.

The nonexistence of self is a central concept of Buddhist teaching. The ego is seen as an artificial construct obscuring the Buddha Nature, an illusive housing for actions on the Earthplane. It is impermanent, as life is impermanent, and filled with misconceptions, delusions and flaws. What one gives up by emptying oneself of ego are the things that prevent spiritual progress. Resistance, blockages, delusions and pain, negative habits, and emotions such as envy, hatred, greediness, and anger are the ego to be emptied. Emptiness is the central quality of the Void, a place of total peace, inner calm, and joy. In the great emptiness, only wisdom can enter.[12]

From the *Sutra of the Essence of Perfect Wisdom (The Prajna Paramita Hrdaya Sutra)*:

> Emptiness does not differ from form,
> form does not differ from emptiness;
> whatever is form, that is emptiness,
> whatever is emptiness, that is form.[13]

The ultimate reality of the universe and the ego is the Void.

Once the negative emotions are released, the Divine Abodes are cultivated, replacing negative emotions with positive ones. When the ego is released, there is oneness with all things, another central Buddhist concept. The Divine Abodes are loving-kindness, compassion, sympathetic joy, and equanimity. A major premise of Mahayana Buddhism is that all people can attain Enlightenment. In Reiki, the Sei-He-Ki is the symbol for healing the emotions, and transforming negative feelings to positive ones. It provides a way for everyone to do this. It is also the alchemical/magickal processes of purification, cleansing and protection. Emotion creates attachment creates karma.

THE HON-SHA-ZE-SHO-NEN

I have written more about the Hon-Sha-Ze-Sho-Nen than any of the other symbols. The information that follows led me to use the symbol for past-life work and for releasing this-life traumas, and to discover how powerful these uses can be. I was not taught these possibilities in Reiki II and wonder how much they are known today to most Reiki practitioners. They would have been intrinsic for healing in the Buddhist culture and world view. Mental healing is healing all Be-ing in Buddhism, as all reality is created by mind consciousness. All karma is created and may be released by the mind.

Mind in Buddhism is ultimate reality, and mind, thought and consciousness are interchangeable terms. The literal translation of Hon-Sha-Ze-Sho-Nen is "no past, no present, no future." By nonexistence of the self (emptiness of the ego) all limitation is transcended. Enlightenment is going beyond the mind to the Buddha Nature (Goddess Within) in all of us. When the mind is aware of true reality (the Void), there is openness. The result is freedom from time, space, delusion and limitation. The dissolution of limitation means understanding all things. Freedom from the delusion of the Non-Void is freedom from karma, as karma is the action of the mind.

All human limitation is mind-created. Because we perceive reality as in a mirror, this truth is obscured. When we know this truth, however, all the things that hold us back from Enlightenment and keep us tied to the delusion of the Earthplane are released. This realization is an understanding of how the world works. In distance healing, Reiki energy can be sent thousands of miles. It can be sent to repeat at a particular time, or even sent into the past or future. Linear time is a delusion that can be transcended. Once we know that time is a fake, we can live accordingly. Mind is the senses coming in contact with their objects. Reality is what we make it. There is a Wiccan saying that "Magick is the art of changing consciousness at will." There are no limitations, there is only will.

The central concept here is the awareness of the mind. This awareness releases the limitation of karma and the need to return again and again in body to resolve karma on the Earthplane. One of the things happening to most people in these Earth change times is resolution of past lifetimes and karma. In healing after healing these issues arise, to the point that for almost every negative happening in this lifetime a karmic pattern may be discovered. The Hon-Sha-Ze-Sho-Nen helps to complete the karma and release it, and the process is created in the conscious mind. By directing the images of the present to heal the past, karma is released. It is permanently released, and with each piece that is lifted, another need to resolve it by reincarnating is released.

The symbol is an entrance into the Akashic Records, the life book of each soul's incarnations. With consciousness of mind, it can be used to rewrite the book. Use its power wisely. Every Buddhist exercise and practice is designed to train the mind—meditation, visualization, contact with deities, focusing on the body and the movement of Ki. The training to control the conscious mind will also change reality. In Reiki the symbol heals the past, present and future, transcends time, heals karma, and allows for distance psychic healing. It has tremendous implications for our end-of-an-age generation. Another definition for this energy is "Open the book of life and now read." The symbol heals the mental body.

THE DAI-KO-MYO

The Dai-Ko-Myo is the Bodhisattva Path. This is "the one with the Mahayana heart of giving," the person who desires Enlightenment for others' sake and will achieve it. She realizes that great unification is the basis for understanding all things. When she becomes enlightened, she is *freed from incarnation and all suffering*. Yet the Bodhisattva refuses to accept the bliss of Nirvana as long as anyone remains behind in pain, ego and delusion. She returns/reincarnates to help others also achieve the Enlightenment Path. The word "Bodhisattva" itself means an "Enlightenment Be-ing," and in the Tibetan language translates to "heroic being." The Mahayana or Vajrayana adept dedicates herself to working hard to achieve Enlightenment, but vows not to enter Nirvana until everyone can enter with her. She condemns her soul to endless incarnations doing good in the world, while waiting for that day.

One of the foundations of Buddhism is respect for the oneness of all life, and compassion for the suffering of everyone. Animals are included, and many Buddhists are vegetarians. This compassion is the beginning of Bodhisattva-hood, and there are other virtues to develop. They are giving, morality, patience, zeal, meditation, and wisdom.[14] Some of the world's best-loved figures are Bodhisattvas, respected and worshiped by as many non-Buddhists as Buddhists. The foremost of these are the Chinese Goddess/Bodhisattva Kwan Yin, the Tibetan Tara, and the Christian Mary and Jesus. The full name of Kwan Yin is Kuan Shih Yin, She-Who-Hearkens-to-the-Cries-of-the-World.

Enlightenment requires the perfect union of wisdom and compassion. Direct understanding of the nonexistence of the self is a part of wisdom, and compassion is the foremost way to release fully the delusion of selfhood. The self is a concept of separateness, while nonexistence of the self is oneness. The urge to compassion and Enlightenment is called Bodhi. From this source comes the liberation energy of wisdom and compassion. The flow of Bodhi energy becomes embodied in celestial forms—Buddhas who have entered Nirvana after Enlightenment, and Bodhisattvas who attain Enlightenment but remain on Earth.[15]

Early Buddhism recorded few female Bodhisattvas, stating that a woman would have to be reborn in a male body before she could reach Enlightenment. Even Kwan Yin and Tara both derive from a male Bodhisattva, Avelokitesvara, who was changed to female in China, Japan and Tibet. The Buddha's wife, Yasodhara, may

SUMMARY: TIBETAN BUDDHIST DEFINITION OF THE FIVE REIKI SYMBOLS

The five reiki symbols are the five levels of mind. Together they are the non-duality of mind and object and the emptiness from ego that achieves the highest level of the end of the Path of Enlightenment (Buddhist nirvana). Once achieved, this releases the Be-ing from the wheel of incarnation.

The symbols' original use was not for healing (worldly) but Enlightenment to help others—five levels of wisdom that culminate in Enlightenment.

Cho-Ku-Rei - Beginning or entrance, generation stage. Placing the mandala into the heart. Meditation until there is no difference between the meditation and the world. Emptiness—nonattachment from the Earthplane. The first step, the first experience. (Reiki definition, the light switch.)

Sei-He-Ki - Earth (and the person in incarnation) are considered impure ground. Impure ground (yellow) is purified by wisdom to gold—purification, transmutation, alchemical change from dross to gold. This is Enlightenment which few achieve (Buddha status), by realization of the emptiness of the self. Purification by the fire of wisdom to gold/purity. (Reiki definition, emotional healing, purification, cleansing protection.)

Hon-Sha-Ze-Sho-Nen - No past, no present, no future. Freedom from delusion and karma (karma defined as the action of the mind). The mind creates time, space, limitation and delusion. Enlightenment is going beyond the mind to the Buddha Nature (Goddess within) in all of us. When the mind is aware, there is openness and release: freedom from time, space, delusion, limitation. Dissolution of limitation means understanding all things. (Reiki definition, healing past/present/future, healing karma, distance healing).

Dai-Ko-Myo - "The one with the Mahayana heart of giving" or "Temple of the great beaming light." The person who has the desire for Enlightenment for others' sake and will achieve it. She realizes that great unification is the basis for understanding all things. (Oneness, You are Goddess.) When she becomes enlightened, she is *freed from incarnation and suffering*. In Buddhism, this is the only real healing. (Reiki definition, healing the soul.)

Raku - Completion, achievement of lower nirvana, emptiness of self of existence. The appearance of an image of the Buddha (or Goddess) within the self. Freedom, Enlightenment, total peace. Release from the illusion of the material world, release from the body and incarnation, total healing. In Buddhism, this symbol is used in the direction from feet to crown to take one out of body; in Reiki it is used from crown to feet for grounding and to draw the energy from the universe *into* the body (opposite intent and meaning—Reiki is worldly use for the symbols, Enlightenment is the spiritual and Buddhist use. Buddhist thought makes the body and healing irrelevant). (Reiki definition, the lightning bolt, completion, grounding.)

Attunement = Initiation = Empowerment

have been the prototype of Kwan Yin. Likewise in the West, Jesus takes the forefront over Mary, but it is to Mary that people in need apply. This misogyny, typical worldwide, is giving way in modern times. A great many women are Buddhists, and have taken the Bodhisattva Vow to forego Nirvana until everyone can enter together. The qualities of Buddhism are far more feminine than masculine, involving compassion, oneness and respectful conduct. In today's Buddhism, they also include activism to change the world. Tibetan Buddhism particularly accepts the feminine, with the Bodhisattva Goddess Tara. In the Vajrayana, oneness can only be achieved through the female.

The Dai-Ko-Myo is soul level healing, and it is freedom from the need to reincarnate that heals the soul. Buddhist doctrine, focused on transcending the body, accepts no other healing than that which occurs from the spiritual body level. The Dai-Ko-Myo flies from heart to heart in Reiki, and it is in the heart that Tara or Kwan Yin reside. The symbol spirals in and out from the center of the Void, and form and non-form are one. The Dai-Ko-Myo level is the oneness of all life. The healer is on the Bodhisattva Path, whether she has chosen the Buddhist Path to Enlightenment or not. She works to change suffering to freedom for herself and for all. In Wicca, the concept is "You are Goddess." Reiki is a tool and a virtue of Bodhi, the urge to wisdom, compassion and Enlightenment that are central to the healed soul. If the soul is in pain, there can be no physical, mental or emotional healing.

THE RAKU

The Raku is much more than a grounding mechanism at the end of the attunement process, though it also has that use. It is the point of the entire system, and Enlightenment itself. The Raku is completion, the achievement of lower Nirvana. It is attainment of the emptiness of the self of existence. When the Buddha attained Enlightenment, he returned to the Earthplane to teach others what he had learned. When he completed his teaching and finally left, or died, he entered a state of Parinirvana or ascension. From this state, beyond Nirvana, there is no return from the Void, no reincarnation in the body. The Sakyamuni Buddha will not return, but he left behind instruction on how others may attain the same state and follow him. Others may attain

Enlightenment and become Buddhas themselves. This is to be interpreted as a longed-for rest and the blessed achievement of total peace.

Enlightenment, as symbolized by the Raku, is release from the illusion of the material world. In meditation an image of the deity appears, whatever deity is meaningful to the adept. The experienced meditator has achieved absolute concentration, freeing her mind from distraction and all selfish craving. There is oneness between worshiper and the worshiped, union or non-duality of mind. Freedom from craving means freedom from reincarnation and illusion, and the meditator/adept enters Nirvana. She is free, and filled with truth and joy. E. A. Burtt, in *The Teachings of the Compassionate Buddha*, defines Nirvana as "liberation, inward peace and strength, insight into truth, the joy of complete oneness with reality, and love toward all creatures in the universe."[16]

The mind is the senses coming in contact with their objects. The causes are the senses, the conditions are the objects. But the causes and conditions are really one. The object creates an appearance—how one person sees it may be different from how someone else does. Perception differs, so when two people see a tree, one may love its fall colors and the other sees only leaves to clean up. We project our images on reality, and what we create is based on belief and conditioning. The non-duality of mind is the resolution of opposites—the knowledge and understanding that the two, though they seem contradictions, are one.

With completion or Enlightenment, belief and conditioning give way to Nirvana and the Void. Illusion is stripped away and what is real (mind, the Void, and the Buddha Nature) remain. The object and mind are one, and the illusion of the material world is released. The seeds of Enlightenment are imprints of consciousness. With awareness, the blissful state of lower Nirvana is attained. It is the union of the Many and the One. The Raku symbolizes the Absolute and the Ninth Consciousness. It is also Ether, Spirit, and the Void. The self gives way to the All, and liberation is the result.

The Raku is also the lightning bolt, the Vajra of Vajrayana Buddhism. "Vajra" means adamantine (diamond) and "Yana" is vehicle. The word in Tibetan is "Dorje." Diamond is a "a substance so hard that nothing in the universe can dent or cut it. Irresistible, invincible, shining and clear."[17] It is unbreakable and nothing can withstand it. When an adept has come so close to Enlightenment that nothing can take her from the Path, she has attained a Vajra-body and become a Vajra-Being. The Vajra-Being, a Vajrasattva, is the purest form of the Buddha principle, and the name for the Buddha-form in the center or east side of mandalas. The Vajra is diamond hard and sharp wisdom that leads to Buddhahood by cutting through illusion. Those who wield the Vajra, the Vajra-Dharas, are the Bodhisattvas and Buddhas.

The Vajra [20]

The Vajra as a ritual tool symbolizes the skill, compassion and wisdom that lead to Buddhahood and Enlightenment. It is ultimate reality, the Path and Enlightenment itself. The Vajra is the resolution of opposites, the non-duality of mind and object, and the union between the Buddha World and the World of Be-ings. It is a scepter composed of two five-pronged ends; the two ends are the oneness of opposites, and the five prongs repeat the fives that appear throughout Buddhist symbolism. They are the five levels of Mind on the Path to Enlightenment, the five elements, five colors, five bodies, five Buddhas, and five Reiki symbols. They also represent the five energy-wisdoms of the mandala.[18] The Vajrayana teachings state that by the adept's mystical exercises, rituals and meditations, she attains her Vajra/diamond nature, her Buddha Nature. She gains a diamond body

(Vajra-body) and becomes a diamond/Vajrasattva enlightened Be-ing.

In Reiki, the Raku or Vajra is drawn from head to feet, from the Universe into the body. It grounds the consciousness level Enlightenment energy of Reiki into the body of the healer. In Buddhism, it is used in the opposite direction, from feet to Crown, taking the person out of body and into the Universe/Void. Reiki is the worldly use for the five symbols and the five steps on the Path to Enlightenment. Buddhist thought makes healing irrelevant, as the only healing is Enlightenment itself. Reiki brings Enlightenment into the body, instead of taking consciousness out of body to achieve it. Sandy Boucher, in *Turning the Wheel*, defines Enlightenment as "seeing clearly."[19] It is also the light of knowledge, information and Ki, the life force energy of the Raku and Reiki healing.

In passing attunements, I have had students ask to experience the Raku in the feet-to-universe direction. It is a quick trip out of body and they describe it as the trip of their lives. The Raku is used only in passing attunements for completion and grounding; it is not used for healing work. It is the lightning bolt of Vajrayana Buddhism, the Tantric mystical sect of the Mahayana, and the insight, revelation and electricity of Enlightenment.

This symbol sequence is the center of Buddhism, and also the center of the Reiki healing system. Yet I have never heard discussion of it by any other Reiki teacher. My conversation with the Buddhist nun and my subsequent reading have been an exciting revelation. The nun's insights into Reiki (from someone who did not have Reiki or want it) brought the whole healing process into clear perspective. As a Buddhist at the time of his Reiki opening, Mikao Usui would have been wholly familiar with the formula and the Path to Enlightenment. If Jesus was a Reiki Master trained in India or Tibet—as seems to be the case—he would also have understood Reiki in terms of the Enlightenment process. The historical Jesus may have been more involved with Buddhism and the Bodhisattva Path than Christians today realize. Where did the transmission of this information stop? It is also a major part of the Reiki story.

From the information above, the uses of each symbol for healing become more clear. The symbols have more purpose than is usually taught, and more power for healing and change. Reiki is at least 2500 years old and may be older; it is a product of the rich mysticism of the Vajrayana Buddhist tradition. It may have been an earlier product of the isolated Tibetans. In channeling, we were told that Reiki was brought to Earth with the first people to incarnate in bodies. Shiva brought the healing energy and wants to be remembered for it. Reiki may be older than even the Mahayana Buddhists, with its origin in the stars.

1 Sandy Boucher, *Turning the Wheel: American Women Creating the New Buddhism* (Boston, MA, Beacon Press, 1993), pp. 15–16.

2 E. A. Burtt, *The Teachings of the Compassionate Buddha* (New York, NY, Mentor Books, 1955), p. 28.

3 *Ibid.,* p. 29.

4 John Blofeld, *The Tantric Mysticism of Tibet*, p. 112.

5 Sandy Boucher, *Turning the Wheel,* p. 17.

6 *Ibid.,* pp. 18–20, and John Blofeld, *The Tantric Mysticism of Tibet,* p. 91.

7 Pierre Rambach, *The Secret Message of Tantric Buddhism* (New York, NY, Rizzoli International Publications, 1979), pp. 56-57, 60.

8 Pierre Rambach, *The Secret Message of Tantric Buddhism,* p. 44.

9 John Blofeld, *The Tantric Mysticism of Tibet,* pp. 84–85.

10 *Ibid.,* p. 85.

11 *Ibid.,* p. 216.

12 Edward Conze, *Buddhism: Its Essence and Development* (San Francisco, CA, Harper and Row Publishers, 1975), p. 101.

13 Pierre Rambach, *The Secret Message of Tantric Buddhism,* p. 42.

14 John Blofeld, *The Tantric Mysticism of Tibet,* pp. 135–136.

15 John Blofeld, *Bodhisattva of Compassion: The Mystical Tradition of Kuan Yin* (Boston, MA, Shambala Publications, Inc., 1977), p. 22.

16 E. A. Burtt, *The Teachings of the Compassionate Buddha,* p. 29.

17 John Blofeld, *The Tantric Mysticism of Tibet,* p. 117.

18 John Blofeld, *The Tantric Mysticism of Tibet,* pp.117–118.

19 Sandy Boucher, *Turning the Wheel,* p. 15.

We live in a time of accelerated change, and personal and planetary pain. Time has speeded up with the magnetic shifting of the planet's poles, resulting in chaos at every level of planetary life. Countries are disintegrating, people are homeless and under siege, political situations are volatile. The Earth is in physical crisis as well, with hurricanes, earthquakes, fires, volcanos, droughts, tornadoes, floods, and mudslides threatening existence at every turn. There are new incurable dis-eases and harder to treat recurrences of old ones thought long gone. The majority of people in America will die of cancer, heart dis-ease, or stroke. Our water systems are unsafe, and the air and soil are contaminated and polluted. Rape, shootings, robberies, child abuse, and every other sort of violence are a fact of daily life in new and appalling ways. Children are preyed upon, and are themselves predators.

The old is making way for the new. It is a process of rebirth, but birth is never easy and it often is accompanied by death. We are in a time of death, and in a time when new life is beginning. The leaders of nations are helpless as are medical authorities to ease the change and pain that no one is exempt from. Misogyny, homophobia, religious intolerance, every sort of discrimination, and racism are reactions to this pain and helplessness—futile attempts to find someone (anyone) to blame for it. The life being born now is fragile, and its survival is still unsure.

But a new birth is clearly happening. There is an increased awareness of the need for change, the need to clean up the Earth and our acts upon it. Though governments are fossils and big business blocks many changes, a slow but sure progress is under way. Political systems are dying in one form to resurrect as something new. Child abuse, woman battering, incest and rape are finally recognized and hopefully will be prevented for the generations to come. In times of disaster, people pitch in and help each other. They can no longer wait for bureaucracies to lumber into inept action. Governments are being forced to take care of people as best they can, instead of making wars.

A new awareness is slowly being born. Authority is shifting from "out there" in government and medicine to power from within. This is most clearly represented by the empowerment of women. We live in a time when power is being wrested from the few and given back to the many. The clearest voices for change in the world are the voices

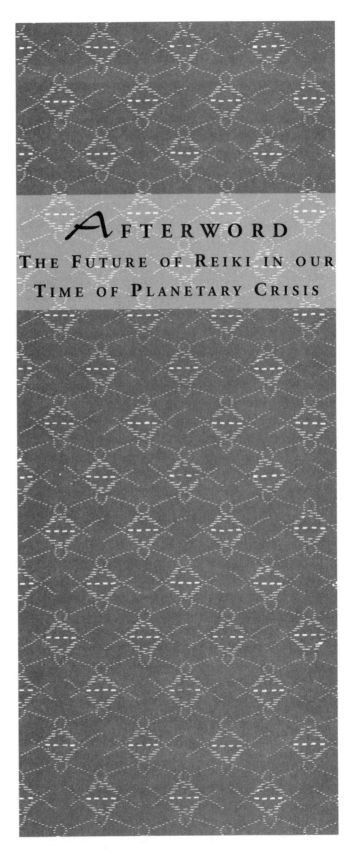

Afterword
The Future of Reiki in our Time of Planetary Crisis

of women, women are saying "no" to abuse and violence, and "yes" to compassion and peaceful change. Women are refusing to accept the rape of their own bodies, their children and the Earth, and they are insisting on equality, common sense, sustenance and healing.

Along with the freeing of women is the freeing of human development. The metaphysical New Age movement is offering awareness and inner growth to many people. This may start as the more mainstream Human Potential movement and may grow to radical divergences from standard religions, like Wicca, Spiritualism or modern Buddhism. It is a return to old ways of perception and thought, to values missing from the breakdown of modern life. It is a return to who we really are, psychics, healers, and people that participate in conscious Be-ing and the examined way of life.

More and more people are also rejecting mechanized medicine for the older inner ways. Medicine's over-technology, its lack of compassion, its treatment of the body as a dead machine, and its cruelty and aloofness turn people away in increasing numbers. Its excessively high fees and control by big business, insurance and drug companies take it out of reach of a growing majority of people. And standard medicine has few answers for today's dis-eases and ills. There is a resurgence of the methods taken from women and the common people by the Inquisition in the thirteenth to seventeenth centuries, and a resurgence of other noninvasive methods of the present and past. Herbs, homeopathy, massage, midwifery, acupuncture, flower essences and psychic healing are among the techniques being rediscovered. They are effective tools and often succeed where the medical system fails.

Reiki is one such method, a major and important one. No tools or products are required, only the healer's hands, and it can be used as a part of every other method of healing. It is a method available at short notice, and everyone including children can learn to use it. Simple and profound, Reiki teaches a basic treatment useful for any dis-ease—emotional, mental, physical or spiritual. It is easily taught. It is part of women's empowerment in an age of powerlessness and fear. Reiki is a return to the ancient past and a birthing of the unknown future.

Coming from a culture where compassion and oneness are paramount, Reiki brings peaceful values back to planet Earth. It is gentle and noninvasive, it never causes

pain or does harm. In a world of suffering, Reiki is a refuge of well-being. It comforts, calms and soothes, relieves pain, speeds physical healing, stops bleeding, and releases emotional trauma from the present and past. It cannot be misused, or twisted into evil, or taken away from the healer—the Reiki guides knew what sort of world would need it and have seen to its protection. And Reiki's growth in the West is in its infancy.

In this time of change and violence on Earth, Reiki is a part of planetary healing. It belongs to everyone and to Earth herself. It is the greatest single potential for good that can be given to the people of this planet. In the Earth's beginning cultures, Reiki was universal. It was wired into our genetic systems, our DNA, and was never meant to be lost. The more people who can be taught this method of healing, the easier the coming years of Earth change will be, the less the human suffering, and the safer the new births. Now is the time to begin bringing Reiki back to all.

This is a call to action, for women and aware men, for healers, peace-workers, and light/information workers. This is a call to action—to bring Reiki back to people and make it universal as it was meant to be. Heal the people of this planet, heal the animals, heal the Earth, heal human awareness. Do Reiki and teach Reiki to manifest peace, healing, wellness and positive change. The techniques are in print now for the first time, there is no more secrecy or exclusiveness. Now is the time. I ask all Reiki healers to make a commitment to using this healing in every way they can. I ask all Reiki III's to make a commitment to learning the system fully and to teaching it. I ask that there be reasonable prices or no prices, so Reiki can be returned to all.

Now is the time to heal the Earth and her people and animals. Now is the time. There can be no more excuses and no more delays. Every day brings more suffering, more pain, more world crises. There is no more time. Remember the qualities of kindness, compassion and oneness that are the basis of Reiki and all healing. Recognize the need for the healing of all people in this time of planetary pain and change. Now is the time to bring Reiki back to all.

APPENDIX

Workshop handouts for Reiki I, II, and III follow for teachers to use in their classes if they wish. Most teachers prefer to make their own. Please use the material freely but credit this source.

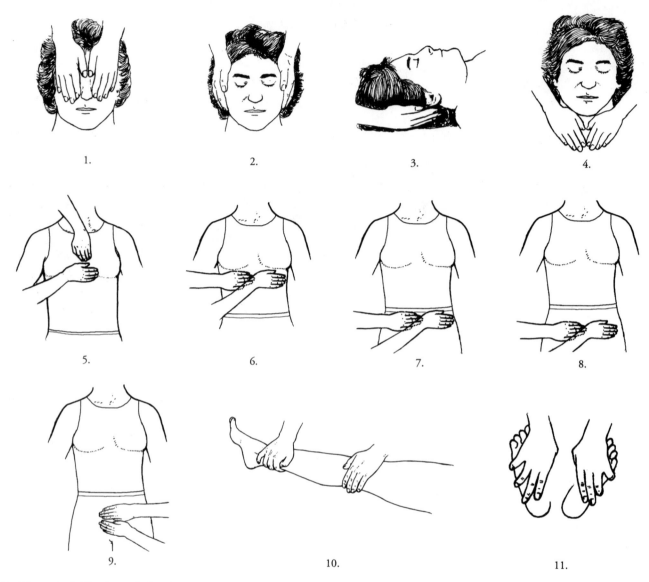

1.   2.   3.   4.

5.   6.   7.   8.

9.   10.   11.

Positions 1-4, Healer is behind; positions 5-9 move to the side; and positions 10 and 11 you will need to move further down. For the feet you may move below or not. Repeat same positions on the back.

1. Diane Stein, *All Women Are Healers* (Freedom, CA, The Crossing Press, 1990), pp. 45-46.

The Reiki Principles
Just for today do not worry.
Just for today do not anger.
Honor your parents, teachers and elders.
Respect the oneness of all life.
Show gratitude.
Make your living honestly.

Reiki II
The Second Degree Symbols

1. **Cho-Ku-Rei** (Cho-Koo-Ray)—Increase Power, the Light Switch. Reverse to decrease power (as over a tumor). Use for all healings. Focus power in one spot, by calling in the energy of the Goddess/Universe. Visualize the figure and/or say the name aloud or in your mind three times. Beginners meditate on the symbol to learn its depths.

2. **Sei-He-Ki** (Say-Hay-Key)—Emotional and Mental Healing, also Protection, Purification, Clearing/Cleansing, Releasing Attachments. "The Earth and Sky come together; as above, so below."

3. **Hon-Sha-Ze-Sho-Nen** (Hon-Sha-Zee-Show-Nen)—No past, no present, no future; distance healing, an entrance into the Akashic Records. "Open the Book of Life and now read," or "The Goddess in me salutes the Goddess in you." Heals past, present and future, karmic healing. Always use when doing distance healing.

These symbols must be memorized and you must be able to draw them precisely. The lighter lines with arrows (next page) show you how to draw them. You may use them in direct healing by visualizing them as you do the body positions; you may use them once at the beginning of the healing, and/or at any time you feel they are needed. You may repeat the Cho-Ku-Rei a number of times, if you wish. Follow your guidance. The symbols are sacred and contain great power, use them with respect.

Hand Movements

Trace the symbols with your whole hand, as if smearing paint on a canvas. Visualize them in violet or allow them to change color. For distance healing, visualize the symbols rather than drawing them. *Send them whole* and they will transmit whole. To increase the power of the symbols, press the tip of your tongue against the groove in the palate of your mouth while using them. For direct healing, you may trace the symbols with your tongue, draw them with your hand, or visualize them.

The symbols may be used for manifesting (Cho-Ku-Rei in particular). Visualize with clarity, be careful what you ask for, and make very sure not to violate anyone's free will. Make the affirmation, "I ask for this or its equivalent or better, according to free will, harming none, and for the good of all." The symbols can also be used doubled.

The Reiki II Symbols

Cho-Ku-Rei
Increase Power

Sei-He-Ki
Emotional Healing

Hon-Sha-Ze-Sho-Nen
Distance Healing

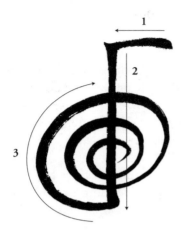

Cho-Ku-Rei
"The Light Switch"
Increase Power (clockwise)

Sei-He-Kei
Emotional Healing, Purification, Protection, Clearing

Hon

Sha

Ze

Sho

Nen

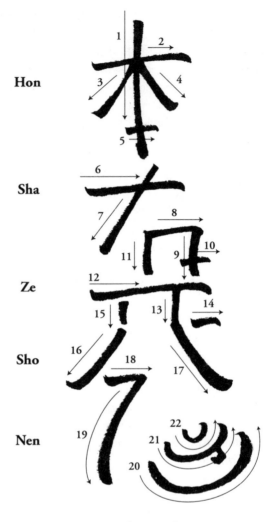

Hon-Sha-Ze-Sho-Nen
"The Pagoda"
Distance healing, the Akashic Records, Past-present-future

Manifesting Grid

1. Visualize your wish with you in it.
2. Place the earth behind it (and you).
3. Bring a golden grid over the picture, diagonal or spiral, running from sky to earth.
4. Draw the Cho-Ku-Rei over the whole picture.
5. Hold the image for as long as you can, then let go.
6. **Be careful what you ask for, you might get it!**

Reiki II
Alternate Reiki II Symbols and how to draw them
Usui Traditional Reiki

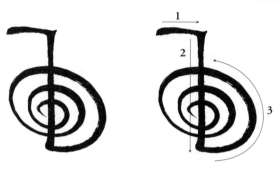

Cho-Ku-Rei
"Put the power here" or "God is here" (counterclockwise).

Sei-He-Ki
"Key to the universe" or "Man and God becoming one."

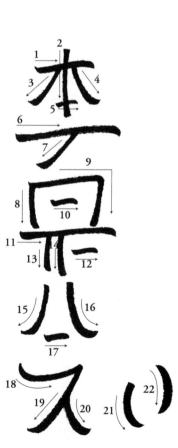

Hon-Sha-Ze-Sho-Nen
"The Buddha in me reaches out to the Buddha in you to promote enlightenment and peace."

Reiki II

Power Exercises

The nontraditional form of teaching involves using the body as an energy channel to pass the attunements. Usui Traditional Reiki does not use this method, or the power exercises given here. The advantage of these exercises is that with them you need to pass the attunement only once to transmit the Reiki degree, rather than up to four times for each degree. The following exercises teach you the method for holding the energy and transmitting it through your body to pass Reiki attunements. If you are not interested in completing the Reiki III, you do not need to know or use these. The exercises prepare you for receiving the Reiki III degree, with the information and ability to pass the Reiki attunements on to others. Anyone familiar with advanced yoga or Ch'i Kung will find the following exercises familiar.

You are a channel for healing and for the sacred energies of Reiki. Keep your body pure—never attempt to do healing or pass attunements when you are angry, ill or under the influence of harmful substances (drugs). Many believe that a smoker cannot be a clear channel for this energy; if you wish to quit smoking, the Reiki itself is a great help in clearing your body of the drug. The Sei-He-Ki is the symbol to focus upon for aiding you in breaking an unwanted habit/addiction.

Preparation

When I first learned these exercises I had very mixed feelings about teaching women to increase/decrease breast size or control their body cycles. So many women have told me that these exercises are important for them, even lifesaving, that I have revised my assessment. The Stage One exercises are to teach you to channel Ki energy; they are not required for passing attunements or doing Reiki healing. Stage Two is required for passing the Reiki attunements and the Reiki III. Do not use or visualize the Reiki symbols while doing these exercises.

Stage One for Women

Sit with legs open, so that you can press the heel of one foot against your vagina and clitoris. Use a firm, steady pressure. If you cannot bend your body to do this, use a tennis ball or larger crystal to create the pressure. You may experience sexual stimulation or orgasm.

Rub your hands together, creating friction and heat in them; raise the energy in your hands.

Place your hands on your breasts, feeling the heat from your hands, but not stimulating the nipples.

Move your breasts slowly up and out in upward circular motions. Do the rotation no less than 36 times and no more than 360 times twice daily. You may start with 36 and gradually increase the rotations. It is positive to be skyclad when doing them.

This form of rotation (up and out) is called Dispersion. Using the rotation in this way only will decrease or eliminate (disperse) breast lumps, and it will also reduce breast size. It may decrease or eliminate unwanted menopause symptoms as well.

Rotation in the opposite direction (up and in) is called Inversion. Doing the exercise in this direction may increase breast size, but it may also increase breast lump size if any are present. If you have breast lumps or fibrocystic breasts, do Dispersion movements only.

You may use half of each of these movements, half Dispersion and half Inversion. Breasts will then remain the same.

Reiki II

Stage Two for Women

This is the Hui Yin (Hon Yin) position required for passing the Reiki attunements.

From a sitting position, contract the vaginal muscles and anus, as if to close them. If you have ever done Kegel Exercises, this will be familiar. Next further contract the anal muscles, as if you were trying to draw your rectum up into your body. You will know you have it if it feels like air is entering your vagina and rectum. Hold as long as possible and comfortable; relax and repeat several times.

This will be hard to do at first for many women. As you practice it and develop muscle control you will be able to do it more easily and hold it for longer periods each time. Eventually you will be able to hold this position and go about your day—you must be able to hold the Hui Yin position for as long as two or three minutes with your breath held, and longer without holding your breath to pass an attunement. Initially try doing this with your breath held. When you are holding the position correctly, you will feel a charge of energy travel through the Microcosmic Orbit/Hara Line.

While holding the Hui Yin contraction at your perineum, place your tongue on the roof of your mouth, in the groove behind the teeth on the hard palate. Holding your tongue in this way connects the Governing and Conception Vessel meridians, creating a closed energy circuit. Hold the positions in the perineum and tongue and feel energy travel through you. Take a deep breath and hold for as long as you can; practice this. You must be able to hold this (standing up!) for as long as three or four minutes with breath held and both positions closed. The purpose here is to close the channels, diverting energy through the Hara Line, then transmitting it through your body to release in your breath and hands. This is what passes the Reiki attunements and makes a Reiki Master. You may sense the moving figure 8 of the Egyptian Infinity symbol.

Notes

The focus of these exercises is spiritual awareness and connection of the spiritual and physical through the controlled transmission of energy. Energy is diverted from running through the body and out to being placed where you wish it—into your hands and breath for the passing of the Reiki attunements.

During the process, you may experience sexual arousal or orgasm, or become multi-orgasmic. After a while, the orgasms will cease when you do the exercises.

Some women experience what Ch'i Kung calls "Turning Back the Blood." This means that the menses will lessen or even cease for women who do the Stage One exercises. This means that the woman's estrogen levels have also decreased. Use the exercises in moderation; stopping the menses is not necessarily positive. Try a lower number of breast rotations, under 100 twice a day. If menses cease, there can be no conception until they begin again, and they will not begin again while the high number of breast rotations continues. The theory here is that the energy used to ready an egg for conception is diverted upwards to the crown instead. The woman's female power is thus channeled for spiritual growth, bringing high energy into her physical body. When the rotations decrease, the menses return.

There are no known ill effects from either of the exercises. They are empowering, and may produce great healing for women who have breast lumps, or who need to experience mind/body control of their processes. For menopausal women, the exercises lessen or stop the symptoms of menopause. They stop the biological clock. Creativity and mental awareness are also enhanced.

Do the exercises twice a day, upon awakening and before going to bed. The Stage Two are the required exercises for the Reiki III.

Reiki II

For Men

These are the Reiki Power Exercises designed for male physiology. They have four objectives:

1. To strengthen the physical tissues of the sexual organs.
2. To elevate spiritual awareness and the mind/body/soul connection. The prostate connects hormonally to the adrenals, and then to the other glands moving up the kundalini/spinal channel and the Hara Line. The resulting increase in circulation from the abdomen becomes an energy rush that transports the nutrients and spiritual energy of semen through the rest of the body, and particularly to and through the crown. When the energy connection is complete, you will feel a chill or tingling move through the spine to the head, similar to orgasm. If you feel this in the crown but not in the middle of the back, your sensitivity will increase with practice. If the energy sensations do not develop in time, there may be blocks that need to be released first. Try the Microcosmic Orbit
3. Self-determination is the third objective. If one of the chakras or energy points is blocked, energy movement will stop at that point. Direct healing to the blocked area, do emotional work to release the energy stoppage, and the block will open. When that gland/chakra is again open, the flow will move upward. If the energy moves all the way to the crown during the exercises, there is no impeding block. Make sure to ground it in the Hara.
4. Growing inner peace is the fourth objective. Over time, creativity and mental processes are heightened, and you will experience a growing tranquility and spiritual opening and peace.

Stage One for Men

Do this exercise sitting, standing or lying down, preferably skyclad. Rub your palms together rapidly, raising heat and energy in your hands.

Next, cup the testicles with your right hand so that the palm completely covers them. Do not squeeze, use only slight pressure, and the heat in your palm.

Next, place the palm of your left hand at the Hara, an inch below your navel. Using slight pressure, and feeling a growing warmth from your hand, rotate your left hand clockwise in a circle 81 times.

Reverse hands, first rubbing your palms together to raise the energy and heat again. Place your left hand to cup the testicles and your right hand over the Hara. Do the circular motion counterclockwise this time, 81 times. Concentrate upon the physical motions while doing this, and feel the increasing warmth.

A unity of body, mind and spirit is the result of this exercise.

Caution: Do not visualize Reiki symbols, or use your mind to build upon this energy. Visualizing the Raku here could be dangerous, an overstimulation of Ki forces. If you overdo, use grounding methods—hug a tree, lie on the ground, center and balance seated, send roots into the heart of the Earth; visualize the fire energy being banked, returning to the Earth chakra down the front of the body.

REIKI II © DIANE STEIN

Reiki II
Stage Two for Men

This is the Hui Yin (Hon Yin) position that transmits the Reiki attunements. It is similar to the Stage Two for women, with the exception that only the anal muscles are contracted.

Tighten the anus muscles, drawing the muscles up and in. When you have the position correctly, it feels as if you are drawing air into your body through the rectum. Tighten and hold as long as it is comfortable to do so. Relax and repeat several times, as much as you can without discomfort.

You will feel a tingling electrical sensation move through the Hara/Kundalini pathway. This is a natural reaction that comes and goes quickly; do not try to use your mind to force it in any way. This is not meant to be consciously controlled.

Place your tongue in the groove between the two ridges of the hard palate on the roof of the mouth. Hold the Hui Yin position, the tongue in groove position, and hold your breath for as long as you can. Then release and try again. You will need to hold this position for three to four minutes, standing up, to pass the Reiki attunements.

Do these exercises twice a day, in the morning upon waking and at night before going to bed. As you learn to hold the positions for longer and longer periods (Stage Two) and do the rotations (Stage One), you will start to experience natural highs and feelings of total well-being. As for women, it is the Stage Two exercises that are required to pass the attunements, but the Stage One is important for men in releasing energy blocks, for increasing spiritual awareness, and for a sense of body/mind connection and well-being. They also aid sexual performance and reduce prostate problems.

I particularly salute the men who are developing spiritually in this era of the changing Earth. Your awareness began with a healing of yourself that is a part of the healing of all men and of the planet.

Reiki III Symbols and how to draw them

Dai-Ko-Myo

Healing the soul, passing attunements
(to be used in all healings from here on).
Draw from center of spiral.

Raku

The lightning bolt, banking the fire
(for passing attunements only).

Traditional Third Degree Symbols: Alternate Dai-Ko-Myo Forms

Symbol for Reiki mastership; man-woman-universe=whole energy

REIKI III   © DIANE STEIN

To Pass Attunements

Hold the Hui Yin position with your tongue at the roof of the palate at all times. Hold your breath unless you are blowing, then take another deep breath and hold it. The Reiki Master stands to pass attunements; the students are seated in straight-backed chairs with hands held palms together at chest height.

1. From the Back:

Open the Crown. This can be a visualization or hand movement.

Trace the Dai-Ko-Myo over the Crown.

Reach forward over the shoulders to take the student's hands, and blow into the Crown. Take a deep breath and hold it.

Trace the other symbols over the Crown: Cho-Ku-Rei, Sei-He-Ki, Hon-Sha-Ze-Sho-Nen.

Take the hands and blow into the Crown. Take another deep breath and hold it.

2. Come to the Front:

Open the student's hands like a book.

Trace the Cho-Ku-Rei over both palms.

Tap three times.

Trace the Sei-He-Ki over both palms.

Tap three times.

Trace the Hon-Sha-Ze-Sho-Nen over both palms.

Tap three times.

Trace the Dai-Ko-Myo over both palms.

Tap three times.

Fold the hands together, and hold them in one of your hands.

Blow from Root to Heart. Take a deep breath and hold it.

3. Go To Back:

Close the aura, with the symbols inside it. (Do not close the Crown chakra.)

Trace the Raku down the back of the spine.

Release Hui Yin, release the breath.

Summary: Tibetan Buddhist Definition of the Five Reiki Symbols

The five reiki symbols are the five levels of mind. Together they are the non-duality of mind and object and the emptiness from ego that achieves the highest level of the end of the Path of Enlightenment (Buddhist nirvana). Once achieved, this releases the Be-ing from the wheel of incarnation.

The symbols' original use was not for healing (worldly) but Enlightenment to help others—five levels of wisdom that culminate in Enlightenment.

Cho-Ku-Rei - Beginning or entrance, generation stage. Placing the mandala into the heart. Meditation until there is no difference between the meditation and the world. Emptiness—nonattachment from the Earthplane. The first step, the first experience. (Reiki definition, the light switch.)

Sei-He-Ki - Earth (and the person in incarnation) are considered impure ground. Impure ground (yellow) is purified by wisdom to gold—purification, transmutation, alchemical change from dross to gold. This is Enlightenment which few achieve (Buddha status), by realization of the emptiness of the self. Purification by the fire of wisdom to gold/purity. (Reiki definition, emotional healing, purification, cleansing protection.)

Hon-Sha-Ze-Sho-Nen - No past, no present, no future. Freedom from delusion and karma (karma defined as the action of the mind). The mind creates time, space, limitation and delusion. Enlightenment is going beyond the mind to the Buddha Nature (Goddess within) in all of us. When the mind is aware, there is openness and release: freedom from time, space, delusion, limitation. Dissolution of limitation means understanding all things. (Reiki definition, healing past/present/future, healing karma, distance healing).

Dai-Ko-Myo - "The one with the Mahayana heart of giving" or "Temple of the great beaming light." The person who has the desire for Enlightenment for others' sake and will achieve it. She realizes that great unification is the basis for understanding all things. (Oneness, You are Goddess.) When she becomes enlightened, she is *freed from incarnation and suffering.* In Buddhism, this is the only real healing. (Reiki definition, healing the soul.)

Raku - Completion, achievement of lower nirvana, emptiness of self of existence. The appearance of an image of the Buddha (or Goddess) within the self. Freedom, Enlightenment, total peace. Release from the illusion of the material world, release from the body and incarnation, total healing. In Buddhism, this symbol is used in the direction from feet to crown to take one out of body; in Reiki it is used from crown to feet for grounding and to draw the energy from the universe *into* the body (opposite intent and meaning—Reiki is worldly use for the symbols, Enlightenment is the spiritual and Buddhist use. Buddhist thought makes the body and healing irrelevant). (Reiki definition, the lightning bolt, completion, grounding.)

Attunement = Initiation = Empowerment

BIBLIOGRAPHY

Larry Arnold and Sandi Nevius. *The Reiki Handbook.* Harrisburg, PA, PSI Press, 1982.

Bodo Baginski and Shalila Sharamon. *Reiki: Universal Life Energy.* Mendocino, CA, LifeRhythm Press, 1988.

Alice Bailey. *The Rays and the Initiations, Volume V.* New York, NY, Lucius Publishing Company, 1972.

Raoul Birnbaum. *The Healing Buddha.* Boulder, CO, Shambala Publications, Inc., 1979.

John Blofeld. *Bodhisattva of Compassion: The Mystical Tradition of Kuan Yin.* Boston, MA, Shambala Publications, Inc., 1977.

John Blofeld. *The Tantric Mysticism of Tibet: A Practical Guide to the Theory, Purpose and Techniques of Tantric Mysticism.* New York, NY, Arkana Books, 1970.

Sandy Boucher. *Turning the Wheel: American Women Creating the New Buddhism.* Boston, MA, Beacon Press, 1993.

Barbara Ann Brennan. *Light Emerging: The Journey of Personal Healing.* New York, NY, Bantam Books, 1993.

Fran Brown. *Living Reiki: Takata's Teachings.* Mendocino, CA, LifeRhythm Press, 1992.

Rosalyn L. Bruyere and Jeanne Farrens, Ed. *Wheels of Light: A Study of the Chakras, Vol. I.* Sierra Madre, CA, Bon Productions, 1989.

E. A. Burtt. *The Teachings of the Compassionate Buddha.* New York, NY, Mentor Books, 1955.

Earlyne Chaney and William L. Messick. *Kundalini and the Third Eye.* Upland, CA, Astara, Inc., 1980.

Dr. Stephen T. Chang. *The Tao of Sexology: The Book of Infinite Wisdom.* San Francisco, CA, Tao Publishing, 1986.

Mantak and Maneewan Chia. *Awaken Healing Light of the Tao.* Huntington, NY, Healing Tao Books, 1993.

Mantak Chia. *Awakening Healing Energy Through the Tao.* Santa Fe, NM, Aurora Press, 1983.

A. J. Mackenzie Clay. *The Challenge to Teach Reiki.* Byron Bay, NSW, Australia, New Dimensions, 1992.

A. J. Mackenzie Clay. *One Step Forward for Reiki.* Byron Bay, NSW, Australia, New Dimensions, 1992.

Mary Coddington. *In Search of the Healing Energy.* New York, NY, Destiny Books, 1978.

Edward Conze. *Buddhism: Its Essence and Development.* San Francisco, CA, Harper and Row Publishers, 1975.

John Diamond, MD. *Your Body Doesn't Lie.* New York, NY, Warner Books, 1979.

Sherwood H. K. Finley, II. "Secrets of Reiki: Healing With Energy in an Ancient Tradition." In *Body, Mind and Spirit,* March–April, 1992, pp. 41–43.

Laeh Maggie Garfield and Jack Grant. *Companions in Spirit.* Berkeley, CA, Celestial Arts Press, 1984.

Helen J. Haberly. *Reiki: Hawayo Takata's Story.* Olney, MD, Archedigm Publications, 1990.

Louise L. Hay. *Heal Your Body: The Mental Causes for Physical Illness and the Metaphysical Way to Overcome Them.* Santa Monica, CA, Hay House, 1982.

Louise L. Hay. *You Can Heal Your Life.* Santa Monica, CA, Hay House, 1984.

Frank Homan. *Kofutu Touch Healing.* Philadelphia, PA, Sunlight Publishing, 1986.

Holger Kersten. *Jesus Lived in India: His Unknown Life Before and After the Crucifixion.* Dorset, England, Element Books, Ltd., 1991.

Barbara Marciniak and Tera Thomas, Ed. *Bringers of the Dawn: Teachings From the Pleiadians.* Sante Fe, NM, Bear and Company Publishing, 1992.

Paul David Mitchell. *Reiki: The Usui System of Natural Healing.* Coeur d'Alene, Idaho, The Reiki Alliance, 1985. Booklet.

Ajit Mookerjee. *Kundalini: The Arousal of the Inner Energy.* Rochester, VT, Destiny Books, 1991.

Duane Packer and Sanaya Roman. *Awakening Your Light Body.* Oakland, CA, LuminEssence Productions, Inc., 1989. Audio Tape Series, Six Volumes.

Pierre Rambach. *The Secret Message of Tantric Buddhism.* New York, NY, Rizzoli International Publications, 1979.

William L. Rand. "A Meeting With Phyllis Furumoto." In *Reiki News,* Spring, 1992, pp. 1–2.

William L. Rand. *Reiki: The Healing Touch, First and Second Degree Manual.* Southfield, MI, Vision Publications, 1991.

Starhawk. *The Spiral Dance: A Rebirth of the Ancient Religion of the Great Goddess.* San Francisco, CA, Harper and Row Publishers, 1979.

Alice Steadman. *Who's the Matter With Me?* Washington, DC, ESPress, Inc., 1966.

Diane Stein. *The Natural Remedy Book for Dogs and Cats.* Freedom, CA, The Crossing Press, 1994.

Diane Stein. *Natural Healing for Dogs and Cats.* Freedom, CA The Crossing Press, 1993.

Diane Stein. *Dreaming the Past, Dreaming the Future: A Herstory of the Earth.* Freedom, CA, The Crossing Press, 1991.

Diane Stein. *All Women Are Healers: A Comprehensive Guide to Natural Healing.* Freedom, CA, The Crossing Press, 1990.

Hawayo Takata. *The History of Reiki as Told by Mrs. Takata.* Southfield, MI, The Center for Reiki Training, 1979. Audio Tape and Transcript.

Amy Wallace and Bill Henkin. *The Psychic Healing Book.* Berkeley, CA, The Wingbow Press, 1978.

Marion Weinstein. *Positive Magic: Occult Self-Help.* Custer, WA, Phoenix Publishing Co., 1981.